D0336202

COVENTRY LIBRARIES

**Please return this book on or before
the last date stamped below.**

PS130553 Disk 4

~~WITHDRAWN
FOR SALE~~

0 7 APR 2009

1 3 MAY 2009

10/7/09

NS

06 JAN '16

23-4-16

To renew this book take it to any of
the City Libraries before
the date due for return

Coventry City Council

Beg, Steal or Borrow

Spencer Honniball

CASSELL ILLUSTRATED

A CASSELL BOOK

An Hachette Livre UK Company

First published in the UK 2008 by
Cassell Illustrated, a division of
Octopus Publishing Group Ltd.
2–4 Heron Quays,
London E14 4JP

Text copyright © 2008 Spencer Honnibal
Design and layout copyright © 2008 Octopus
Publishing Group Ltd.

Distributed in the U.S. and Canada by Octopus
Books USA:
c/o Hachette Book Group USA
237 Park Avenue
New York NY 10017

The moral right of the author of this Work has been
asserted in accordance with the Copyright, Designs
and Patents Act of 1988.

All rights reserved. No part of this publication may
be reproduced, stored in a retrieval system or
transmitted in any form or by any means, electronic,
mechanical, photocopying, recording, or otherwise,
without the prior permission of the publisher.

A CIP catalogue record for this book is available from
the British Library.

ISBN-13: 978-1-84403-660-8

10 9 8 7 6 5 4 3 2 1

Commissioning Editor: Laura Price
Production: Caroline Alberti
Publisher: Mathew Clayton

Printed in Italy

Contents

Contents

Coventry City Council	
CEN	
3 8002 01721 502 3	
Askews	Jan-2009
784.0922	£14.99

Introduction

Babyshambles. Raw, personal and approachable. Unpredictable and intense. Creating blazing anthems, they – like their legion fans – are as comfortable in a skanky old back room of a pub as they are on the big stage.

The band and, most dramatically, frontman Peter Doherty, are embedded in the public consciousness as a consequence of the tabloid feeding frenzy that follows Peter wherever he goes. In their early days, however, the band made only tentative steps towards widespread public recognition. Predominantly embraced by fans of ex-Libertine, Peter – whose staggered, messy exit from the band he formed with Carl Barât was played out under the scrutiny of the public eye – the birth of Babyshambles was overshadowed by the The Libertines' split and the widely reported attempts by Peter to overcome his crack and heroin addiction.

Despite the gross, tabloid-generated caricature of Peter, the band's reputation as credible artists gathers pace, their music reaching a wider and more appreciative audience not solely on the back of the circus their frontman has inadvertently created.

A couple of albums in and Babyshambles has grown to become one of the music industry's most unpolished pearls. Surviving the kind of knocks that might have seen lesser bands call it a day, while producing some of the freshest, most exciting music around, the learning curve hasn't been realised without a great many growing pains. Indeed, they have made it through deep personal loss, betrayal, incarceration, severe addiction, numerous no-shows and annihilation in certain sections of an ever-observant media.

Initially a vehicle of creativity and freedom of expression that delivered Peter from what he grew to regard as the increasingly dispiriting, commercially-driven grind of life with The Libertines, Babyshambles have blossomed into a band in their own right.

And now, some five years after the band's earliest, inauspicious shows, it could well be the right time to pose the question: are they standing on the frontier of greatness, or destined for the gutter?

I

The Babyshambles Sessions

In 2001, the music scene in Britain was crying out for something fresh and exciting. With the fanfare that greeted Oasis' arrival on the wane, and bands such as Coldplay and Travis offering a more melodic sound, the country looked across the pond for inspiration.

The subtle emergence of The Strokes and The White Stripes on our shores gave bored kids something to believe in again, and when the home-grown Libertines – deemed an extension of The Strokes' reinvigorated, ballsy and guitar-driven sound – broke through they were embraced by legions of fans desperate for something new and exciting.

Having established themselves as one of the country's most controversial and inspiring bands, and hailed as anti-establishment heroes, The Libertines – fronted by Peter Doherty and Carl Barât and featuring bassist John Hassall and Gary Powell on drums – gained a reputation for chaotic performances characterised by stage invasions, with Carl and Peter often encouraging fans to join them during shows, quite literally smashing the barrier between entertainers and the entertained.

Début album *Up The Bracket*, released in October 2002, while not a massive mainstream success, was warmly received by reviewers desperate for the kind of anarchic spirit that had been missing for years.

The Libertines, rather than aspiring to the cliquey, false environment inhabited by many artists, promoted a community-based, inclusive alternative; a party atmosphere with a folk mentality. A shift in emphasis from a music industry-led to fan-led scene arose out of this interaction between band and audience. Music had a sense of importance again. Kids felt that they belonged to something again.

The internet became a vital instrument through which Peter and Carl communicated with their fans – to revolutionary effect. Gigs would routinely be posted on the web at less than an hour's notice, frequently held in Peter and Carl's flat or round friends' and fans' houses – 'living room tours', as they became known – on the tube, buses and practically anywhere else with enough room for a handful of instruments.

A U.S. tour and a performance on the *Late Show with David Letterman* in May 2003 demonstrated that the band were capable of cutting it in the notoriously hard-to-crack American market but, as The Libertines grew in notoriety, so did tensions within.

Despite earning critical acclaim and a larger fanbase, Peter felt increasingly that his artistic aspirations were being compromised, the commitments that come with heightened popularity stifling the spontaneity of spirit that so inspires him – to the point where he considered the four-piece "as manufactured as the fucking Sex Pistols… and the Spice Girls."

Carl, in contrast, looked upon the band's more formalised activities as a necessary evil; a medium through which the band could spread their message: "The reason we justified that at the time, to each other, was because we were getting out to a bigger audience, and through that we were touching hearts and minds in Wigan – people who were having their beans and watching the telly, and going: 'Fucking hell, I understand this…' You've got to reach these people, otherwise what use is the message?...

"I loved, as Pete did, the short, sharp hard hits and the little riots and little clubs, and I wanted to do that on a bigger scale… as it is, it has permeated and, you know, there's a lot of little movements because of it, but I felt that we weren't ready to explode; I mean: implode – either way. We could be bigger than that…

"It wouldn't be true to say that I wanted the quiet life, as if I'd happily play bass in U2 for the rest of my life, d'you know what I mean? I'm not fucking like that at all; I've got fire in my belly."

Peter's drug intake was another bone of contention, but while, by his own admission, his ingestion was mushrooming, he didn't consider it to be hugely detrimental to his creative output. His bandmates, however, thought differently, and by the spring of 2003, tensions had escalated to the point where The Libertines' European tour had to be shelved after Peter decided against returning to a tour bus heading for its first stop, Hamburg, electing instead to get off at King's Cross to escape the suffocating confines of what he had grown to regard as a "hyped-up", regimented group: "I freaked out a bit in King's Cross. I went to go and score; I just wanted to go for a little walk and I wanted my mate to come with me – get off that fucking bus for a bit. In the end they left without me…

"They were just locked into this conveyor belt – nothing else seemed to matter, apart from doing what the record company wanted… It wasn't like I didn't want to be on stage and play gigs, because I did, but I wasn't gonna just fall into place as part of the system… I think they were glad to be shot of me in a way, especially the rhythm section… Carl was kind of getting into his head that he *had* to just stay on course – he had to stay on the tour bus with the machine – because that was the only way he was going to survive financially and that."

Carl, however, has a different take on the occasion: "I don't like the conveyor belt. If I did keep on the conveyor belt I could have got rich and 'still be in The Libertines' now, d'you know what I mean?... But if that meant it wasn't me and Pete together, doing our thing, then that would be something that I found disgusting, which is why I decided I had to disband it… I could still be touring with them now, raking it in, selling hoodies. I'm not fucking doing that…

"I feel nothing but love for Peter, and… the last thing I want to do is instigate a bitching, but when he got off at King's Cross it was: 'Let's score and get back on the bus' – that's what it was, I remember that… and I was fucking worried about him. It was just getting silly; because of all his little flights of fantasy, it was becoming inoperable… [It was about] commitment, in keeping a promise. And if that promise is to, like, seventy German kids,… [to] bring something of importance to their lives, you know?"

While in the U.S., and with his dependency on drugs increasing, Peter sought to feed his habit, soon finding himself in the company of the dubious characters who supplied him – much to his bandmates' chagrin – while songs that he and Carl laid down, christened the *Babyshambles Sessions*, were concluded without Carl, who was growing increasingly alarmed at the company his friend was keeping.

Carl Barât — "There was a lot of shady people…they just wanted fame/drugs, and they were hanging around for that. For that, and that alone. And I didn't wanna see my mate getting taken for a ride and getting used, and so, you know… I had to physically kick them out of the room. It was fucking scary at one point: when Pete phoned up and said it was all too much one day, and there were loads of pipe-hitting New Yorkers and little me having to kick them out – that's not good.

"And then he was all grateful, and then the next day they're all back. And it's, like: well, what can I do, apart from extricate myself from the situation and say that I won't have this? I can't just be the fucking maid, so I had to leave that."

By the time the cancelled European tour had been rescheduled that summer, relations within the band had soured to the point where they broke down completely.

Peter started playing solo acoustic gigs to distract himself from his estrangement from The Libertines, and in June 2003 was persuaded to enter rehab for the first time – at The Priory's Farm Place in Surrey – hoodwinked into a meeting with record label Rough Trade, which, he'd been led to believe, wanted to discuss his plans for Babyshambles. But with his heart not in it, he left after six days to concentrate on his new band, using the fabrication that friend Peter Wolfe, affectionately known as Wolfman, was getting married.

Then, on the night that Peter planned to launch Babyshambles, 25th of July 2003, he was arrested for breaking into and stealing from Carl's flat, while The Libertines, who had played a number of dates – including Glastonbury, on the 28th of June – without him, were touring in Japan.

Arriving in what his lawyer at the time, Richard Locke, later described as "a highly emotional and drug-befuddled state", Peter said that he had gone there in search of money to pay his new bandmates, leaving instead with a number of Carl's belongings, having kicked the door in.

Freed on bail until the 11th of August, Peter retook the reins of his fledging Babyshambles outfit, the name of which was spawned from spontaneous demos that had been recorded in New York with The Libertines in May of that year – songs which were to appear on the second and final Libertines album, *The Libertines*, Babyshambles' début album, *Down In Albion*, and their EP, *The Blinding*, released in December 2006.

Peter —

"The original *Babyshambles Sessions* were in New York, the summer I went [there] with The Libertines. It was, like, this conveyor belt promoting this album, the album coming out, and all these new tunes. At the time, they [Rough Trade] thought I was cutting off my nose to spite my face. I said 'I want a studio, I want to record these new songs,' and they were, like: 'No.' I don't know what they'd say now, but they said no.

"So I went and got the local paper in New York, found a studio, got in there, and started knocking out these tunes. Carl popped down, someone from Rough Trade popped down, and they were, like: 'Oh fuck, he has actually got some new tunes.' And then they decided they wanted to pay for it. At the end I had, thirty, forty tunes, and just put them on the net.

"The truth of the matter is I advertised for someone who was a computer expert who could help me put two or three songs on the net, and this bloke didn't quite get the hang of what I was saying, and whacked the lot up, and I said: 'Oh fuck it, leave it up,' and that was the start of the *Babyshambles Sessions*.

"Not long after, I think, I got booted out of the band and tried to carry on calling ourselves The Libertines, but no-one was having it, so we called ourselves Babyshambles.

"And we all got one of them [shows Babyshambles tattoo – spelt Baby Shambles, as the band were then called – which arcs over his left nipple] tattooed. We had three Yorkshiremen: Neil Thunders; Steve Bedlow on vocals; me on guitar; and a guy called Max on drums. We threw ourselves into eternity, … but really and truly it only lasted about three or four gigs. There was a night at The Troubadour. We all started at the same time, but different songs, and I ended up swinging for Steve with the guitar, and then legging it out of the venue. And that was kind of the end of that, really."

Fans Amah-Rose Abrams and Hannah Bayes, who became friends with Peter and Carl the day before they were signed to Rough Trade, were at The Troubadour that night.

Seeing how distressed Peter was, Amah-Rose, who in the summer of 2004 appeared on stage with Peter during a solo gig at the Rhythm Factory, thought it best to find him. Some ten minutes later, having caught up with him, she recalls Peter's fears that he may have jeopardised his new band: "I just knew he was very concerned about the future, what was gonna happen; how things were gonna pan out."

Peter, while inheriting the freedom of creativity and spontaneity that had been compromised by signing to a label, suddenly found himself horribly exposed. For now, there would be no bossing around by any form of authority; but, at the same time, he would be deprived of a foil in Carl, and felt isolated and vulnerable – "removed from his group of friends and from the people he was working with, and was in a completely different situation socially", as Hannah, who went on to design the artwork for *For Lovers, Killamangiro, Fuck Forever* and *Albion*, recalls.

For Carl, the manifestation of Peter's side project signalled a major departure from their shared vision: "It felt like Pete saying: 'Look, I can still do this, with or without you… I still can do this, so fuck you.' But I suppose I thought it would pass. But I guess that's when I knew that our distant trajectories had crossed, that the first fork had come, really."

This early version of Babyshambles was fronted by Steve Bedlow – more commonly known as Scarborough Steve – who had also appeared in earlier versions of The Libertines. A friend of Peter's since before the band formed, he proposed to take lead vocals in Babyshambles in exchange for finding a bassist and drummer who he persuaded to leave the first incarnation of The IV's with him and come to London.

Conceding that the early shows were messy, Steve puts the lack of finesse down to a woeful lack of rehearsal time, Peter's failure to teach him the songs, and "far too much time spent scoring and smoking drugs."

Peter —

"In the end he was, like: 'You known what, you sing them better than me anyway.' And that was that, really. And I'd just got done then, for the burglary, and was just doing little terrorist gigs, literally playing in crack houses around Kilburn – little dives, and a few half-decent clubs; didn't really make any money, but just getting these songs out. There was a mad, mad group of kids following us around then, all getting tattooed – all getting Libertines tattoos and Babyshambles tattoos.

"I was quite creative then, but I wasn't in a good way. My drug use was in overdrive… I was mixing with the wrong people."

Scarborough Steve —

"It's, like, you know, starting a band with someone who's already got, sort of, iconic status, so loads of people come to see you, but the guy with the iconic status hasn't allowed the band to rehearse to its true potential. We were all smoking crack and heroin, rather than rehearsing, but Pete would instigate that and say: 'Right, let's go and score,' or whatever. But we all used to do it. We'd all done it before."

Opposite: Peter during the trip to the "Late Show with David Letterman" — May 8, 2003

Anthony Thornton, *NME* journalist and author of *Bound Together*, which details how The Libertines scaled the giddy heights before their fall from grace, remembers the very first Babyshambles performance.

Antony Thornton —

"The first Babyshambles gig at the Tap 'n' Tin was pretty ropey. Scarborough Steve – who was once a Libertine – was on vocals. No one could really understand – it seemed a little odd that Peter gave up the opportunity to sing. I think it was Peter seeking some security, though; he went backwards to a situation he could feel comfortable in, while he licked his many self-inflicted wounds.

"The place was pretty packed – Dean Fragile had arranged it after becoming close friends with Peter. They went at it with some gusto, but they weren't doing the songs a great service. It was a pretty inauspicious beginning for Babyshambles all in all…

"You'd go and see Babyshambles and two weeks later it would be a completely different line-up, pretty much, apart from Pete. Every one was different. Some were fantastic, some were bloody awful, and you didn't know what you were going to get, which of course is half the fun… I like my rock 'n' roll to be a bit unpredictable, a bit raw; a bit like you don't know what's going to happen, and that was it – definitely."

Ronnie Flynn, a long-standing friend of Peter's who has amassed film footage documenting the band's history, as well as that of The Libertines, was one of the few to see promise in those early shows: "Pete's always had some sort of magic… You could see that something was going to happen sooner or later. Although the early Babyshambles gigs were shambolic, there was a magic; they had the quality of something that you couldn't quite define. You couldn't see where they were going… But it wasn't going to be run-of-the-mill bullshit."

Peter carried on gigging – sometimes with a rotating Babyshambles crew; sometimes on his own with an acoustic guitar – freed from the formalised, sterile routine of life as a rising star in a band becoming increasingly dictated to by the money men. Now, on his own or accompanied by like-minded musicians, he was able to effect his spontaneous, unorthodox style of performance without constraint.

Free to play with whoever he chose, whenever he chose, future guitarist Patrick Walden, then in White Sport, remembers a scenario where "whoever turned up on the day would be involved."

Patrick —

"That I would not call the beginning of the band. I really wouldn't. They got terrible reviews and it was shit, it was awful… I don't think he really left [The Libertines]; I think he got pushed out. And I don't think it was right, because it was his band. And I know it hurt him a lot, because – I'm not saying he didn't want to do Babyshambles – but respect to the fella: instead of moping about, he started another band."

Peter continued to use the internet to advertise his gigs and would play at every opportunity, "putting our strings on our guitars, if we had them, and just getting them down in some back room somewhere or on some fucking roof or in some garden or some bus stop, or even from the back of a van. Sometimes just an acoustic guitar and a harmonica, sometimes just myself, and I'd just play and play and play and play, for an hour, two hours. We'd book hotel rooms and use the pavilion of the hotel and play."

Early reviews were generally unkind – a perverse form of flattery, given that while most new bands would be given a good eighteen months in which to prove themselves, Peter's increasingly messianic status gave cause to believe that he could somehow transform his growing collection of interchanging bandmates into a tight, cohesive unit practically overnight.

The fact that there was such grand expectation underscored the regard with which people held him, but to expect this new outfit to immediately produce anything like the quality of music that The Libertines created, was unrealistic, not to mention unfair.

Antony Thornton — "I'm not sure he realised just how difficult it was going to be, just how concentrated everybody's gaze would be, and everyone had an opinion about it. I mean, everyone. People who'd never seen Babyshambles before had an opinion about them, which is bizarre."

Peter — "A lot of negative things were said… but my salvation was the music, and I don't think we ever let 'em down on that front – we belted out a good tenner's worth of tunes. That's what we were all about – the music… People could say what they liked on the internet, they could type what they liked, they could be spiteful and vitriolic and as hurtful as they liked, but at that time there was no way in the world anyone was gonna come up to my face and say anything to me…

"It was all word-of-mouth, it was all internet, the media didn't wanna know at all. No-one wanted to know, we got slated all over the place. And we knew that people coming to gigs were there because they wanted to hear the tunes and nothing else. You don't fucking trudge from fucking Southend to Whitechapel at two hours' notice because of the media hype; you do it because you think: fucking hell, I love this bloke's music and I wanna hear it, and that's what I was feeling."

But with his impending court case over the break-in at Carl's, the building blocks of his Babyshambles project were in danger of dissolving. Though Peter had been warned of the likelihood of a spell behind bars, it still came as an enormous shock when, at Horseferry Road Magistrates' Court on the 8th of September, he was sentenced to six months' imprisonment.

Peter —   "I wasn't really helped by the pre-sentence probation report. Mind you, I was kind of shot with my own gun, because I was told that if I play-up down the probation office – you know, exaggerate the extent of my drug and alcohol abuse; not that that was technically possible at the time anyway: it would have been hard to pretend that it could get any worse in any way, the way I was living – but nevertheless I really played up at the interviews for the reports, because I was told the more fucked-up you are, the less chance you've got of going to prison.

"But on the actual day, it turned out that the judge presiding over the case, it made things worse for you, in his eyes. He actually commented on the report. He said [effects snooty accent]: 'Mr Doherty, I've seen the report and, quite frankly, you have continued to lead a wilfully dissolute lifestyle.' Whereas if I'd gone into those probation meetings and just told them: 'Yeah, I have been using a bit of drugs, but I've been clean for three weeks, rah rah rah,' they probably wouldn't have sent me down at all…

"I was *absolutely gutted* – there was no way in the world I should have been sent down with no previous for that type of offence. It was a horrible crime as well to be done for, but I had no previous… I think they tried to make a bit of an example of me, as they say."

His lawyer at the time, Richard Locke, had brought to the court's attention "a long acrimonious history" between his client and Carl. He said that Peter "felt he had been victimised by the band" following his ejection, though Peter refuted suggestions of revenge, talking instead of remorse and explaining, in an interview with the *Evening Standard* a day after his 11th of August hearing, that it was more a case of: "Why are you ignoring me? – a cry from the darkness." He also attested to Locke's description of a "drug-befuddled state" when admitting: "I found myself shouting at him and it turned out I was arguing with my reflection. When I realised, I booted the door in. I was engulfed by complete misery and despair."

In the event, the appeal was successful, Peter's sentence was reduced, and on October 8th he left Wandsworth Prison, where he was greeted by Carl, the animosity between them shelved as they embraced warmly among family and friends. Together again, they set off an adventure that culminated in that night's gig at the Tap 'n' Tin in Chatham, Kent – later named *NME*'s Gig Of The Year, Carl remembering: "The optimism in me was just fucking celebrating, and I convinced myself that we were gonna set sail again. That's how I felt – completely."

The boys in the band were back together. They would put past disagreements behind them, wipe the slate clean, and fulfil their huge potential. Except that they wouldn't. Already existing tensions would fester, mutate and become uglier. And with his appetite for creative liberty whetted in the form of Babyshambles, Peter would only last so long back on the conveyor belt.

The only question now was: would he jump, or would he be pushed again?

2

Killamangiro

Back in The Libertines' fold, Peter and Carl failed to build on the euphoria generated at the Tap 'n' Tin, and while more gigs followed in the latter part of 2003 and the first half of 2004, including a UK spring tour, underlying tensions continued to surface.

In October 2003, the band were packed off to new manager Alan McGee's Welsh retreat. The idea had been for the songwriting team to escape the distractions of London, to take their foot off the pedal for a while, bond, and, in a gentler environment, write material for The Libertines' second album, *The Libertines*.

A violent outburst between Peter and Carl, however, saw Carl bash his face against a sink in a fit of anger, nearly losing an eye in the process – an injury that derailed their plans.

A trip to France, with similar intentions, while garnering, perhaps most tellingly, "Can't Stand Me Now", which details the breakdown of their relationship, didn't prove the success that had been hoped for. But while, further down the line, security – nicknamed Tweedledum and Tweedledee – were hired, in part, to prevent the tension between Carl and Peter exploding into brawls, reports that they were constantly at each other's throats were somewhat exaggerated, says Peter: "It wasn't like in a cartoon strip, where they all have a punch-up and you see a big ball of smoke with a fist sticking out and Alan McGee's false teeth flying out – it wasn't like that."

Peter, meanwhile, reaffirmed his aspirations for Babyshambles, which on occasions shared the same billing as his other band. On November 19th 2003, for example, at north London's Duke of Clarence pub, two versions of The Libertines, one of which included former drummer, Paul Dufour, better known by the moniker Mr Razzcocks, followed a Babyshambles performance, as envious onlookers pressed their faces against the glass from outside, keen to savour the highly-charged ambience generated inside this tiny venue.

Carl Barât – "That just felt like a bit of a beano, really… I didn't want to be a child about it – music's music, and if we're all together and all happy, then let's play the music we love and the music that we've created…

"It wasn't really weird. It was weird to see a few old faces… because some people were such staunch side-takers, and then seeing them together… giving awkward smiles and then, like, you know, turning away. It was, like: 'Oh, yeah?!' There was a bit of that, but I knew that was all bollocks anyway – it was about my friendship with Pete."

Anthony Thornton — "It was an extraordinary gig – it felt special – once-in-a-lifetime; two incarnations of The Libertines and Babyshambles. Babyshambles opened – the place was already packed. People outside in the cold, fogging up the window they were staring through.

"Pete and Carl had just returned from an aborted songwriting session in Wales at Alan McGee's where Carl had smashed his face in the corner of the sink after a booze-fuelled row. The gig was special because it offered a tantalising possibility that Pete could pursue both his songwriting partnership with Carl and his more freeform partnerships in Babyshambles. That they could co-exist easily without rancour."

For a while it seemed as if The Libertines and Babyshambles could indeed run concurrently, but as Carl, Gary and John grew increasingly concerned about Peter's drug use and apparently erratic behaviour, the freedom that Babyshambles afforded him made Peter all the more reluctant to return to what he considered the oppressive routine of The Libertines, by now a virtual straitjacket constraining his musical aspirations.

Peter expressed his dissatisfaction in a posting on his Babyshambles website, writing: "The one true horror is that if I was to be true to myself as an artist, as a man, as a Libertine, I would not work with the band as it stands anymore. The release and liberty of the other path, i.e., Babyshambles, Peter Doherty solo or whatever, is immense."

In April, his pursuit of outside interests saw him feature on Wolfman's "For Lovers", which reached No.7 in the UK Singles Chart. In Wolfman, Peter found a kindred spirit with whom he developed a songwriting partnership to supersede the one between he and Carl; "For Lovers" was another stepping stone out of The Libertines.

Peter — ""For Lovers" came about initially due to the Wolfman's exquisite genius and a combination of persistent pressure on Rough Trade and a great production by Jake Fior and video by Douglas Hart. In its original form I first heard the song during the Amwell Village Wolfden era, when days were measured out in spite and rum. Wolfie was a plumber back then and very bad tempered. He refused to be my friend unless I became famous. Anyway, one thing led to another and I ended up changing the second verse.

"New found fame encouraged him to let me sing it – by the time I had left The Libertines for the first time we were set up camp together in Gunter Grove. Bang at it. Recording "For Lovers" involved two takes and bouts of mutual mutilation. Dark days. Very proud of it.'"

Iain Gore, who later worked on Babyshambles' début album, *Down In Albion*, recalls the pride Peter exuded at making a record with his new band, having turned down the opportunity of having a hand in its production.

Iain Gore — "The first time I heard about Babyshambles was when I was working on the second Libertines album… I was in the machine room changing some tapes and Pete came in and was trying to get me to record their first single in Metropolis using all The Libertines gear, the studio, and doing it overnight when everyone had left. But I said we couldn't do it; I think it probably would have all gone wrong and I probably would have ended up being fired. Obviously Pete using all The Libertines gear to record a Shambles single might not have been the best move.

"Then I think about a month later, maybe, he came into the studio, into Metropolis again, and he had the Babyshambles single, the first single, *Babyshambles*, and then went and gave every member of The Libertines people in the room a copy of it. I remember it being quite a poignant moment – he goes: 'Here's my band,' to his current band. I think the main person who he wanted to get a reaction from would have been Carl."

In May 2004, Peter's drug problems intensified and he booked into The Priory for treatment, staying for a week, and returning again, at the end of that month, only to leave early. The day that he left for the second time, June the 7th 2004, he showed up at Carl's first club night, Dirty Pretty Things, at the Infinity Club, Old Burlington Street, Mayfair, in which they, along with the rest of The Libertines, played a short set that turned out to be their last publicly as a unit.

Peter had spoken of his leaving for Thailand the next day, in another bid to overcome his addictions – this time at the jungle-based Wat Tham Krabok monastery, notorious for its harsh heroin and opium detoxification treatment, including induced vomiting, though he left after just three days, explaining to Betty Clarke in an interview in *The Guardian* in July: "To get the most out of that place isn't to approach it like I'm going to recover from a drug. It's to enter on a spiritual journey within yourself to find that precious thing you might call a soul."

The press thought different, alluding to a search for heroin in the opium capital of the world, and, indeed, Peter made for Bangkok, and a copious supply of the cheapest heroin he'd ever set eyes on.

Running up a hefty bill, even by Thai standards, he posted an appeal on the internet for funds sufficient to finance a flight home, a fan soon coming to his rescue. "Fortunately, someone got their mum to pay for the flight with a credit card", Peter explains.

Just hours after landing back on British soil, on the 17th of June, he was arrested for possessing an offensive weapon – a flick knife that had been bought as a birthday gift for Carl.

By now, despite stating their willingness to welcome him back once he'd overcome his drugs problems, his Libertines bandmates had lost patience with Peter, effectively sacking him a second time after he skipped a band meeting.

In a statement released on the 30th of June, the band added that: "Peter's erratic mental state worries us greatly and having him on tour would only compound his problems. We aim to complete all existing tour commitments without him."

Peter — "The idea was, I think, for Rough Trade or McGee, at various stages, that I was just gonna get clean and we were gonna live happily ever after, but for me it was never really about the drugs – it was just not being able to record and release stuff when I wanted to, which I thought was the whole point of signing to Rough Trade."

The Libertines carried on playing, Anthony Rossomando, who had previously appeared with the band – most notably at the Reading and Leeds festivals the year before – taking Peter's place at T In The Park on the 10th of July. There were more public declarations of concern from members of the band, who hoped that their friend would clean up and rejoin them, Gary saying, in an article in *The Guardian*: "The worst thing they [Carl and Peter] did, and are doing, is to ignore the fact that things have gone wrong between them. They've never once tried to sit down and talk to each other."

Without a home of his own, Peter moved between crack houses in Kentish Town, his estrangement from The Libertines exacerbated by their playing the Reading and Glastonbury festivals without him, Anthony Rossomando continuing to fill his rather capacious boots.

Peter — "It got to the point where I was, like, unplugging John, pushing him over, kicking his bass amp over and smashing the drum kit up, pushing Carl's amp over… A lot of them [Libertines fans] didn't really know what I meant – it was kind of half and half with some of the crowd – but that's just the way I felt…

"It wasn't like pantomime for me; it was, like, this song actually meant something to me when I wrote it. This song is actually fucking real and I'm singing it, and I'm feeling fucking awful. I got into this tradition every night where I'm just winding myself up so much all I wanna do is smash up the whole fucking auditorium. I just didn't wanna do it any more. I wanted to sing the odd mellow song and I wanted to work on new stuff and explore new ideas…

"The way they saw it, I was destroying myself wilfully, with drugs and my behaviour, but I felt what was making me do that was the fact that I was in this band that, to them, it was a different kind of show; but to me it was, like, getting up there and telling people how fucked up I am, and I just didn't wanna do it. I didn't wanna do it."

Carl Barât — "I've never liked those drugs, but if Pete could still be the Pete I knew and loved and be on those drugs, then that wouldn't have been a problem, but it's just the people that those drugs involved… You can't be on the same level as someone when every day what they want is the opposite of what they wanted the day before – it drives you insane, man; it's impossible. And I tried for a long time. And my voice and what I wanted wasn't being heard or understood, either."

Future tour manager Sally Anchassi, a friend of Peter's since they became pen pals in their teens, remembers being astonished when learning of his addiction, such had been his opposition to drugs growing up – so much so that Peter would have long conversations with her mother about the people she was mixing with and what she was up to. A fall-out interrupted their friendship when Peter started The Libertines but, when a chance meeting with Carl drew attention to his deepening problems, Sally took it upon herself to re-establish contact, guessing a number of email addresses that she copied the same message to, before sending them off into cyberspace.

A couple of months later, she received a call from Peter, suggesting that they hook up. When they met, their severed ties were fixed and they spent the best part of a week hanging out, during which Peter told Sally of his plans for Babyshambles, asking whether she'd like to help out. Having just left her job, she didn't have much to lose.

Regardless of the criticism aimed at him, Peter considered the citing of his drug use more than a little hypocritical, and that, in failing to address other aspects of their flagging relations, people were led to make incorrect assumptions – namely, that he was a slave to hard drugs, unable to function at all coherently without them, as he sunk further into an abyss crafted by his own hand.

Peter —   "First of all I'll say that heavy drug use, or any drug use, has been detrimental to the creative process. The truth is I was always a little bit fucked up, and it's going to sound really, really strange, but in those early days of using crack, using heroin, I just came out with a lot of songs, and I was revelling in it and there was nothing that could stop me; there was no drug in the world that was gonna stop me.

"It didn't really matter to me that I was using loads of drugs. What it did do was create a huge divide socially: all of a sudden I had a kind of hardcore block of friends and, yeah, we all started to use crack at the same time.

"I didn't hate anyone and I wanted to just play the music, and the whole thing was a lot mellower. And we got really shit reviews, where The Libertines ones got really good reviews, and that's when I realised this whole thing was fucked-up and I've gotta carry on with the Babyshambles… After being blocked out of The Libertines… and having all of that taken away from me, I wanted to create something very secure, very personal, very insular, and no-one would ever be able to take it away from me. Ever." Carl insisted in an interview with theage.com.au, on the 6th of August, that: "Pete's not out of the band, he's just not playing with us because he's not well. And he hasn't acknowledged that fact yet," going on: "To say it's not about drugs is a cop-out, as far as I can see. That's just denial. I mean, he can say that, or he can make the concession that would change everything… But believe you me, we had no choice." He referred to Babyshambles as Peter's "denial band", and claimed that "everyone [around Babyshambles] is more tolerant of his drug use", the "brown", or heroin, scene coming between them. "And slowly I just got further and further away from Pete", Carl said.

Carl Barât — "I guess at the time that's what I wanted it [Babyshambles] to be [Peter's 'denial band']. You know, I understand; part of me kind of even respects Pete for sticking to his guns. That's one thing I've always admired about Pete: if he believes something, and truly believes it, then he does it, and I absolutely respect him for doing that. And sometimes that has its pitfalls, and sometimes it has its triumphs, but all the time it kind of somehow garners respect from me…

"It was a painful time. I think what we achieved has been beautiful in hearts and minds, like we intended to, and, you know, times have moved on… I think what we done was a wonderful thing… I regret hurting every day of my life, but I wouldn't change it, for what we've achieved through it… I've done wonderful things, seen wonderful things… and people have drawn on the spirit. And you can't buy that."

Tony Linkin, who has managed both The Libertines' and Babyshambles' public relations interests, noticed changes in Peter's behaviour as his drugs intake increased.

Tony Linkin — "With any drug, or with drinking or whatever, if you do too much of them your moods change and everything, and you become quite erratic… your mental state changes quite a lot because you haven't slept for four or five days; it's bound to, isn't it, really? So he [Peter] was in a very fragile [state], but also quite manic as well… [Carl] didn't want to do what he had, what he *felt* he had, to do, but… I suppose he, and all of them, were trying to hope that that would be the trigger for Pete to sort himself out."

Ben Bailey, a friend of Peter's since meeting him at a Libertines gig, and who's supported Babyshambles with Thee Unstrung and current band, His Lost Boys, put the split down to "too many drugs, too much fame, too much stuff given to them", coupled with Peter's need to consistently showcase new songs at the drop of a hat. As far as he's concerned, however, blaming drugs for the breakdown is "a little bit wide an assumption."

Ben Bailey — "I never really got Carl's take on it; I suppose, for him, he always wanted to play music, but it always seemed that Peter wanted to do it *now*, like he wanted to play a gig that night and stuff, and he'd be, like: 'C'mon, everyone come and play this gig tonight.' And I think eventually people get sick of being beck-and-called to, don't they, all the time? So I suppose Carl just got pissed off with it in the end…

People say that drugs were a massive thing to do with [the split], but I dunno. Because as long as I've known Peter he was doing drugs, but he was still writing songs and stuff, and he still does write songs, so is it really fair to blame drugs for the break-up of a band?

"All he [Peter] wanted to do was create music, and have the freedom to create it. And I suppose that's what he's been given the freedom to do in Babyshambles."

It was, Tony Linkin believes, the anger at what he considered mistreatment at the hands of his former fellow Libertines that gave Peter the impetus to drive Babyshambles – which he says got really good, really quickly – forward.

The new Babyshambles audiences would typically include a mixture of loyal fans and voyeuristic spectators, drawn to the spectacle of a man with his finger on the self-destruct button. Peter was well aware of this negative element, and it was impossible not to question the motives of some of his followers, despite gratefully acknowledging the unwavering support of a hardcore fanbase who, it seemed, wouldn't desert him however low he sunk.

Peter — "It was almost, in acknowledging that they liked the music, they were kind of contradicting their disapproval of what I was doing. It was all quite contradictory. They were coming and giving me the money to hear me chucking out *Horror Show* and hearing these amazing tunes, and just got off on the whole thing.

"It was magic, though. I was like the Pied Piper, literally. It wasn't all drugs and grime either; it was a really romantic time as well… It was a mad time of freedom. The Arcadia that I'd always searched for really only came into fruition then. Freedom, and this idea that no-one was going to force their opinion on you, and you weren't gonna force anyone to do anything."

While critics derided Peter in their droves, many spurred by numerous reports of behaviour that, for the most part, was far less degenerate in the flesh than on the page, a new type of fan, initially lured in by their own curiosity, but not swayed by a predominantly blinkered perspective of events, took up the baton.

Forward-thinking and with minds of their own, they wanted to know what this Doherty character was all about; they'd listen out for songs on the radio, maybe read a review or two, and buy the records, for no other reason than they liked the music.

Peter — "A lot of the time people's interests are, I dunno, born out of this kind of mythology, you know? But then again, it's their mythology that kind of gets people involved in the first place, and then all of a sudden they'll hear something and think: oh no, that's quite a good tune, and then – bang –you've got 'em, hook line and sinker, and you kind of reel 'em in, because I know that's what happened to me as a kid growing up: at fifteen, sixteen, hearing a snatch of something or even just seeing a bit of a cover of a seven-inch and just being reeled in, and then that's it – once you've found something that which to you is perfect and faultless and true, and touches your soul or makes you dance or makes you sing along, and makes you want to emulate it, then that's it, especially at that age…

"I was basically obsessed with The Smiths at one point, even though I missed them when they were about. Probably for the best part of a year-and-a-half I was, like, obsessed, for the first time really in a way; it just went through my head all the time, every day, living in Smiths songs, living in that three minutes at a time, and getting completely carted away. And that's all I ever wanted to do myself, was just to be able to do that."

Spared another stretch in jail, when on the 1st of September, at Thames Magistrates' Court, Peter was handed a four-month suspended sentence for possession of the flick knife he brought back from Thailand, he had by now steered Babyshambles through their teething problems to establish a stable line-up that saw him take lead vocals, Patrick Walden on guitar, Drew McConnell on bass, and Gemma Clarke on drums.

A revolving door of raw, unrehearsed talent, earlier incarnations of Babyshambles had included drummer Seb Rochford, who would later appear in bands including Acoustic Ladyland, and who featured on their very first single, "Babyshambles"; Neil Thunders; and the Perrett brothers, Jamie and Peter, sons of The Only Ones guitarist Peter Snr, who had himself played with The Libertines.

Wolfman aside, though, Peter had yet to discover another songwriting talent capable of gelling with his own inimitable style; that is, until he met Patrick Walden.

Patrick and Peter became loosely acquainted at Rooz Studios, Old Street, north London, owned by Gemma's father. Patrick worked at Rooz, and Peter used the studio to rehearse.

At the time, Patrick had been playing in a band called White Sport, an electro punk band that featured future Babyshambles drummer Adam Ficek. White Sport was managed by James Mullord, who ran High Society Records, which licensed the first Babyshambles single from Rough Trade, and it was James who told Patrick that Peter was looking for a new bassist.

An audition was arranged, the pair clicked, and they started working together. The first project was the *Babyshambles* single, featuring Patrick on bass, Seb Rochford on drums, and Peter on guitar and vocals, and there was a fluidity between them that really worked.

Babyshambles was nailed in about three takes, and an energised Patrick could see the potential magic in collaborating with Peter – "We had something, definitely, without a doubt. There was a sense of excitement, and everyone there felt it."

Patrick — "To me, Babyshambles started when we put the first single out with Seb. Babyshambles at the beginning was me and Peter, officially – I'm talking about as a band unit releasing records. It was me and Peter…

"There were a few shows to do with the White Sport and Babyshambles in the early days where I'd be playing with both bands in the same night; so I'd be playing bass and guitar in the White Sport, and quickly changing over and doing Babyshambles. It was pretty hectic. It was pretty fun…

"And then [after recording *Babyshambles*] he went back to The Libertines, I didn't hear much from him for a while, and then he got chucked out of The Libertines again. And he'd met Peter Perrett of The Only Ones, that band whose song is always on the Vodafone advert now – *Another Girl, Another Planet*. A punk classic. He got along with their sons, so their sons were playing with him a bit, and I was speaking to James and he goes: 'Yeah, he's playing with them guys now, unfortunately.' So I thought: fuck it, try and push me in there, man. I know Peter.

"So Peter went up to him and said: 'Pat's the best bass player I've ever played with, I wanna play with him.' Great. Fantastic. So we practised a lot, and the line-up at that point was: me; the two Perrett brothers, one of them plays guitar and one of them plays the bass; myself playing guitar; Peter singing; and Gemma playing drums – I got her in, I asked her to join, because I was good friends with some of the guys at the time at Rooz…

"When Pete wasn't around I was, for want of a better word, the conductor of the band; I was looking after the band, getting people there. I'd spend days with Peter learning the songs, and then take it to the band and rehearse it with them."

Peter — "I didn't want it [Babyshambles] to be negative, especially in light of what people expected; they expected us to be shambolic, expected us to be shit. And then when I met Pat, something really special started to happen. We were both so driven, we both had quite a lot to prove, and we didn't want to be thought of as ramshackle and shit. We wrote some fucking blinding tunes together. I felt proud and excited to be in a band again, y'know?"

Adam — "I remember those early days, as Pat was still playing with the White Sport. He was putting a lot of effort into starting the whole Shambles thing – every time I spoke to him he told me about Peter's new band."

The very first Babyshambles gig in the band's second incarnation was staged at Rooz on the 20th of April 2004, a line-up comprising Peter, Patrick, Gemma and the Perrett brothers playing to an audience that only heard about the show a few hours beforehand, via an internet posting. "We charged on the door, about five, ten quid, and there was a queue round the block," says Patrick of the occasion. "And it was absolutely rammed. We had it in one of the rehearsal rooms upstairs and there were about four songs. We played them all twice and did the set again, and it was chaotic, it was great… pretty under-rehearsed, but it was fantastic."

A gig in Telford sticks in his mind as a reminder of how rapidly a fervour built up around the band in those early days: "I think Mullord booked the venue under a

Opposite: Peter and Drew on stage at The Forum, Kentish Town December 13, 2004 in London.

different name, so people were expecting a jazz band or something small, and there were about sixty-five to seventy people. And then word got out that Babyshambles were playing, and this small little pub filled up with hundreds of kids. And hundreds outside couldn't get in.

"It was fucking crazy. There wasn't even a stage: there was us and two monitors... The kids were all around us. It was a fucking riot. As soon as we started playing the place went crazy. It was one of the most amazing gigs we've ever done. There wasn't enough room for my amp – I had to stand on top of my amp... Pete had a fight, someone bit him in the head, and there was a punch-up... if you saw the footage it would put it into context for you. It was one of those one-in-a-lifetime gigs."

When the Perretts' inclusion appeared not to be working out for the best, Patrick stepped in to exert a little more authority in shaping the band: "The songs were getting messy. It wasn't an ego thing, but I did want to be the only guitarist and have control over that aspect of it – to have direction of the band – in the early days. Pete was showing me the songs and I was taking them to the band, and I'd rehearse them up.

"Part of his charm is part of his weakness... it's, like, he got everyone involved not thinking about the best thing musically. I made it pretty clear to him how I felt about it, how I wanted it to be. I wanted it to be a band, and I think he understood that and took that on board."

In addition to recruiting Gemma, Patrick was responsible for bringing Drew on board, in the wake of a request by Peter, prior to departing for Thailand's Wat Tham Krabok monastery, to have a full line-up in place by the time he returned. The following year, he would have a significant role in the recruitment of future drummer, Adam Ficek.

A fertile breeding ground for Babyshambles members, Rooz was where Patrick and Drew had become friends, meeting as co-workers, while Drew and Gemma Clarke had grown close when Gemma's band, The Suffrajets, supported Drew's – Elviss – with whom Drew had become disenchanted.

Drew —   "When I moved my stuff out of the room I'd been in with the old band, she [Gemma] let me put my stuff in her dad's studio. I got to know her dad, got to know her whole family, and ended up working in the reception.

"The first time I met Peter, he stumbled up towards the reception where I was working and said he had a gig with The Libertines in ten minutes, and could he borrow a guitar. And I lent him a guitar. And then the second time I met him I had a room in the studio, and I was in there playing with some guys from another band, and, again, Peter fell through the door, looking half-asleep and pasty, and asked if he could borrow a guitar...

"There was another lad that worked there at the reception who had known Gemma for years as well, called Patrick [Walden]. And we became friends, and I guess I admired his guitar playing and he dug how I played as well. And we realised we were into the same things, like American hardcore post-rock and punk, and pre-grunge stuff like Sonic Youth and Dinosaur Jr, and things like that. We were about to start a band ourselves, and then he came to the studio one day and he was, like: 'Listen to this, man.' And he played me a recording… with Seb Rochford, and Peter was playing guitar and Patrick was playing bass. He went: 'I've been recording with that lad, Peter… '

"Patrick came in one day and said: 'Peter's gone to Thailand, and before he left he asked me to get the best possible band that I could together. The thing is, don't get too excited about it or anything, but the band could maybe do some recording and some gigs with this new thing that Peter's got called Babyshambles.' And I go: 'Okay.'

"So when Peter got back, Patrick played me a couple of songs, so I kind of had an idea of what they were going to be like, and I got a call to come down to HQ, this studio near Brick Lane, and went down there. We were there for about half-an-hour, and then, again, a clanking at the door, and Peter bowls in, stumbling around. Picked up a guitar. I remember he was wearing too many clothes. It wasn't that cold a day, but he was wearing about three coats. He'd just got back from Thailand and he'd just been driving around.

"And he muttered something about the police stopping him and having a flick knife or something. And then he picked up the guitar and started playing "Gang Of Gin". I remember being quite taken with how unselfconscious he'd been – he didn't give a fuck. A lot of people are quite shy and they take a bit of a chat and stuff before they eventually pick up the guitar and go: 'Okay, this what I do; these are my songs.'

"He just picked up the guitar, didn't really look at who was in the room, and started playing some stuff. At one point he looked to get quite affected by it – almost looked like he was going to cry – and then fell over onto his knee, and, like, the guitar slipped, but he just kept playing the song, and I was, like: okay, this guy means it, you know?

"And Patrick came in and we started talking about playing some gigs, and he said: 'I'm not sure if I'm going to be doing this Libertines thing for much longer.' And Patrick went: 'Well, I've got this bass player, this is Drew.' And I went to shake his hand, and he just looked at me and then looked back at Patrick and went: 'Is he any good?' Fucking charming! I said: 'Mate, I've met you a bunch of times and I lent you guitars when I worked in Rooz', and he was, like: 'Okay, hi, whatever.'"

The trio jammed, Peter later telling Drew – as he had done Patrick before him – that he was the best bassist he'd ever played with, and that he could become a member of Babyshambles if he had the band's name tattooed on his body. The tattoo never materialised, but Drew nonetheless joined the embryonic outfit, learning eleven songs in an afternoon in readiness for his first gig, at the Rhythm Factory.

He immediately warmed to Peter's idiosyncratic means of communicating with his fans, as the band played to frenzied audiences up and down the country: "Those kind of gigs were in venues where they were unprepared for a couple of hundred kids going absolutely apeshit. Obviously no barriers or security guards or anything like that, and it was absolute carnage."

Drew — "We started doing a bunch of gigs. We started doing little jaunts out of town – going up north, playing places like Preston. And, another thing I liked initially about it, was he was hell-bent on playing – not just playing, like, the main towns, the main cities, where other people would play. He'd want to go to weird towns and play in, like, Wetherspoons. The shows were always different somehow.

"And then the fans – which I guess were then kind of inherited from The Libertines – they were just completely rabid. They were utterly rabid; I hadn't really seen that kind of adulation before. I'd seen close, but in, like, big, big venues with massive bands.

"At this point Peter was with The Libertines and the beginnings of Babyshambles, he wasn't that hugely commercially successful, or even well known, but the kids that were into him were into him in such an all-consuming, obsessive way you can't help but be impressed by that and think that there must be a reason for that… I rapidly realised that I'd become part of something really exciting and different."

Patrick — "Rough Trade and The Libertines had decided that their differences were irreconcilable – they weren't going to get back together – so he [Peter] got offered a record deal. We'd done a few gigs and a few tours – we done a lot of tours – and it was Petermania at the time: every gig we played was a riot…

"It felt like we were a part of something special, it really did. I know it was [all about] Peter, but I felt part of it. Especially later on, when I started writing as well, and we started getting our own fans… there were stage invasions every single night, kids dancing with us. We were playing songs and the whole stage was full of kids. It was brilliant – they were very euphoric times.

"We were the most exciting band in London at the time – it was like Guns 'n' Roses or the Happy Mondays or something… it was very exciting. We started playing bigger shows. It was mad. Every single show was mobbed. One show we were playing, there were so many people, we all got thrown off the stage backwards. It was amazing. Amazing times."

Patrick, while acknowledging fans' fondness for Libertines numbers, wanted Babyshambles to be taken as a band in its own right. Tolerating rather than truly embracing fans' favourites such as "Time For Heroes", he wanted to play the new songs that he and Peter had penned: "He acknowledged his past by playing them [Libertines songs], but we tried to get as much new shit in there as we could."

James Mullord started to spend more of his time with Babyshambles, whose public profile was steadily increasing, and with White Sport fizzling out following a fall-out with vocalist Andrew Aveling, a decamp to Peter's band seemed the most sensible course of action. A few months down the line, he became Babyshambles' first manager.

His contribution to the cause was, Patrick believes, immense: "When Peter was getting ostracised [from The Libertines], James was there for him, he believed in him… He really believed in Peter's talent… He was Peter's friend and he was there for him. He gave him the opportunity to make music. There was no contract signed – like: 'I'll look after you on my label' – which is what he did."

Matt Bates, current Babyshambles agent, who formerly promoted the band as well, remembers first meeting Peter in April 2004, booking him for a gig in Stoke-on-Trent, on the 21st of that month – marking the launch of the "Babyshambles" single – which he described as "the birth of Babyshambles."

Matt Bates — "After I left uni I bought a club called The Underground, and one of the first shows we put on was a Babyshambles show. It was when Pete was kind of doing bits and bobs aside from The Libertines, though it wasn't official.

"The crowd went absolutely mental. A ceiling collapsed. A wall collapsed. There was a very friendly riot, and the gig ended up being outside in the car park, on top of a van, rather than in a venue. It was one of the most amazing things I've ever seen and an amazing atmosphere, and the police didn't mind, laughing and joking with people, letting them get on with it."

Peter — "At one point I was in The Libertines and Babyshambles. I remember a gig at Stoke Underground. There was actually a riot afterwards – it all kicked right off, and you got kids weighing into the police and that… it was an absolute belter of a show… the roof came off…

"It was actually Babyshambles supported by The Libertines, all really strange; there was this dual personality going on. The Libertines, which was… becoming quite a big band, and then Babyshambles, which was in my heart and in my soul, and I had real expression within myself, and I knew that that was it really.

"I even asked him [Carl] to join Babyshambles, but he was scared. It had taken so long to get a deal with The Libertines that he didn't want to risk it all… He wanted a little comfort."

Patrick — "It was amazing. I mean, amazing in the sense that I'd never experienced – just, like, stuff you read about. You know bands that capture a generation? I feel like I was part of something like that, because the kids didn't give a fuck – they ripped down a fucking brick wall! How do you do that – three hundred kids tear down a brick wall?!

"And so many kids couldn't get in, it was just chaos. It was pretty noisy. We rocked it like barbarians, we rocked the show. And then afterwards, we borrowed this Mercedes van… and we had a gig on top of it. And there were hundreds of kids around us…

there were cars getting booted, it was crazy... it was a magical moment, though... I guess you could say it was a riot, but more a celebratory riot... It was chaos and it was a bit dangerous, but it was great... Peter had such a charisma then – he still does – but it was a bit more untainted. There was something in the air; it was like Beatlemania. It was like saying to me: 'Why d'you think The Beatles had such a massive success in Japan?' I don't know – there was something in the air... This geezer caught a moment – like Oasis in 1994, or whatever year they came out...

"There was something needed. I think it was just the guitars and people meaning it; they were living it. And he was so open and, like, the whole internet thing – he'd do it if he was skint! But you'd get good value for money – he was so close to his fans. He had people in his house, d'you know what I mean? He had people in his lounge. It was a different thing. It was very, very strange, but it was very touching; it was lovely."

Adam — "White Sport were supporting at Stoke that night. I remember seeing Carl turn up in a hoodie with his security guard. I thought: Peter's either going to smack him or play a corker of a Libs set."

Carl Barât — "It was grand. It was a grand old fucking shindig."

Matt Bates immediately invited Peter back for another show a week later, after which he was asked to book a number of gigs for the fledging Babyshambles line-up. Before he knew it, he had "organically" become their agent, acknowledging the advances the band made once Drew settled in: "The band were a lot better, because, before that, Babyshambles were famous, especially in the early days, for being a complete shambolic mess on stage. But when Drew came in – he's a very accomplished musician – he helped steady the ship, being one member of the band who was always with it. In the rhythm section, he always made sure that at least something was consistent. That's when the band became a lot more professional, [were] taken a lot more seriously, and actually started to be a Babyshambles band and not Peter's side project from The Libertines."

Matt remembers Peter's acoustic tour, stretching July to August 2004 with support from, among others, Dot Allison, Selfish Cunt and White Sport, "going round really small venues, performing some of the best shows Pete ever did; this really special thing after The Libertines, just him and a guitar, doing these tiny shows.

"It's when I actually realised myself what a good songwriter Pete was. It was even before the second Libertines album came out. He was playing a lot of the songs off that second Libertines album. A lot of songs that finally went on *Down In Albion*. A lot of covers."

In the meantime, Patrick and Drew continued to rehearse, working on arrangements and a handful of songs that were to feature on *Down In Albion*, and other that didn't make the final cut, such as "The Man Who Came To Stay".

Their efforts would soon be put to good use during Babyshambles' 24-date UK tour in September and October – culminating in two sold-out nights at The Scala, King's Cross, that had more people queuing outside than there were inside the venue – which won critical acclaim with performances that helped divert attention from the increasing interest in Peter's intake of drugs, the band mutating, as Patrick Barkham put it when writing for *The Guardian* in December 2004, "from bad joke to musical force within months."

It was during the tour that Matt Bates believes the band came of age: "They became really tight, everyone knew what they could do. Everything sold out. The last two shows were at The Scala, King's Cross – they were quite legendary."

Luca C, who has supported Babyshambles on the road with the Cazals, is another who was captivated by the positive energy engendered on that tour: "Babyshambles at the time were at their best in my opinion, 'cos it was really fresh and everyone was really excited… I remember being on tour and being mesmerised by the gigs – obviously there were a few shambolic ones – but it was pretty constant."

Adam   "I remember touring with them [while in White Sport] and staying in B&Bs. It was very basic, but there was a great sense of community, everyone together. There was this one time when White Sport, Shambles and the Towers of London were all crammed into one room in York. The whole of the B&B's residents ganged-up and tried to kick us out".

Peter —   "Those Babyshambles tours, once they started going, it was different. I felt more with the audience. But considering the way I'd worked to be on a pedestal and be some kind of star, then once I was there I wanted to break it back down again and I wanted people just to come and sit and hear me play my songs, not rushing round from place to place, getting on stage, cranking [it] up as loud as you can and that."

The band would have played 23 gigs played in 24 days but for the infamous Lemon Tree no-show in Aberdeen, on the 29th of September, that sparked a riot and evacuation, with seven arrests made, and police escorting Drew, Patrick and Gemma to their hotel, as infuriated fans gathered outside.

Matt Bates —   "Pete, being Pete, hadn't slept for a few days, for whatever reason, and I think he took something thinking they were Ecstasy, but I've been told that they were actually sleeping tablets. He was out cold, we couldn't wake him up at all. I remember chucking a glass of water in his face as he lay on the sofa, and he still didn't even flinch, so we made a really shit excuse on the spot: that he'd fallen down the stairs.

"No-one was going to believe that; I couldn't believe they were going to come out with that. Fair play to James Mullord to have the guts to stand on stage and say: 'Pete's not coming, he's fallen down the stairs.'"

Drew, whose idea it was to create the falsification pertaining to Peter's condition – "I couldn't think of anything else to say… the kids had seen him that day… the kids knew he was on the bus" – remembers being amazed at the sheer number of pills crowding a shelf on the tour bus; such was Peter's vulnerability at the time that he considered it tantamount to "putting sweets in front of a kid."

Confessing that "that was one of the first times that I really got worried about Peter's ability to be quite reckless with his own safety and his own health", Drew recalls how some people attempted to carry Peter off the bus in the hope they could find some way of reviving him enough to perform, even though throwing water on his face and yelling at him had failed to return him from his stupor. "I was, like: 'Listen, you can't do that. Even if you wake him up, he's still zonked; he's in no fit state to do the gig.'"

Once James announced that Peter wouldn't be able to perform, the band's instruments were hurriedly gathered up and thrown in the tour bus, though attempts at a speedy getaway were thwarted by the Aberdeen rioters, who rocked the double-decker bus and hurled stones, the band's driver, an intrepid Welshman going by the pseudonym Deano, providing the band's sole means of defence, brandishing a baseball bat to ward off their assailants.

Patrick — "Peter took shitloads of temazepams – these big yellow fuckers that you can only get in Scotland, I think… James Mullord tried to get him down the stairs… and there was no way. They put him in a shower and put cold water on him; there was no way.

"So we got him in bed, and it's eight o'clock, we're in the venue now. The staff are getting worried. It's getting late, and the kids are starting to scream: 'Cunts!'… He [James Mullord] got hailed with about five hundred to a thousand drugs, bottles and beer. And he goes: 'Pat, just run!', so we ran to the bus. Got on the bus – Gemma was crying her eyes out, scared shitless. And looking down I saw Peter, sleeping, thinking: you're a cunt, you are. When I saw him the next day he said: 'What went on?' I said: 'You were sleeping like a baby.'

"Anyway, we were getting rocked back and forth – it was pretty dangerous, there were a lot of kids, angry kids. The riot police come on horses… So it was full-on… But I was unhappy for the kids obviously, because even if they get their door money back, they lost a booking fee. But that's not Pete's intention anyway – he just had too many temazepams, which is his fault, but what can you do, man?"

A spokesman later explained that the band had played every other date on their tour, "and have done 14 shows on the trot without a day off", adding that the axed Aberdeen gig would be rescheduled as soon as possible. As it turned out, the band missed a rescheduled gig in the Scottish city, but have since played on a couple of occasions. And apologised for the Lemon Tree mishap.

Drew believes that the negative press coverage of the catastrophe detracted from a tour that had been a success: "As the band got bigger and people got more excited about it, there was a sense the whole time that people were on tenterhooks, waiting for the first opportunity to knock us down again – 'See, I told you they were a bunch of fuck-ups. Junkie cunts, they don't know what they're doing'… Because he'd been so vilified beforehand, people weren't comfortable with the fact that, you know, he was coming good and the band could play."

Gigs at The Scala, King's Cross, on 6th and 7th October, reinforced the band's growing pedigree, helping put the Aberdeen disaster behind them. Described as "the best shows of my life" by Patrick, *The Guardian*'s David Peschek deemed the "new look Babyshambles" a "muscular and tight" outfit, achieved "in a way the (sic) Libertines – a tense, nervy and notoriously unreliable live band – have yet to master." The yet-to-be-recorded "Fuck Forever" was, in his opinion, "a future anthem, a peculiarly English echo of "Smells Like Teen Spirit" that is monumental."

Peter —
"I remember being thrilled that that had sold out. They were the biggest gigs we'd ever done more or less and I remember a real buzz about the place. I was bricking it! But the crowd went mental and it was possibly the first time I've seen a proper mosh pit at a Shambles gig.

"I remember riding a scooter there with Chev. Pat was on great form and me and Mullord walked off together afterwards. Happy memories from the black hole of the Shambles past."

Patrick —
"It was such a scene, it was so vibrant. There was a lot of positivity and creativity. It was intense. I remember coming off stage and my mate going: 'Man, there's more people on the stage than the audience, people hanging everywhere.' It was just great. I've never done gigs like those early Babyshambles gigs… Everyone was together and the roar you'd get from the crowd was deafening. It was buzzing, it was fucking great."

Drew —
"It was the end of the tour, and we'd been playing for 24 days. And I don't think there was a day off – there might have been one odd day off or two days off – but it was pretty much back-to-back, and if you put any band on the road for that amount of time at the end of it they're gonna be playing well, and they're gonna be firing on all the right cylinders. It was an exciting time because everything had built up, with the tour going well and proving ourselves as a real band and not just a bunch of junkies. And we did two days, man, and it was like a triumphant homecoming, I suppose. Very exciting."

Anthony Thornton —
"There were all these doubters as to whether or not he could make any decent music without The Libertines, and they played this Scala show and they were great. The Scala

shows were a turning point – earlier on the tour, particularly in Brighton, it had become obvious that this wasn't a hastily assembled band of ne'er-do-wells; it was a tight unit who could put on a great show with a sound genuinely different from before.

"By the time the Scala came around, some of the more wised-up parts of the music media had grasped it, but for some Libertines fans experiencing it for the first time it was a shock: I was surprised to see some fans crying, and so I asked them what was wrong; surely the gig was a good one. 'That's the point', one of them sniffed. 'Because they are good, The Libertines will never get back together.'"

As far as Patrick was concerned, Babyshambles were long overdue the acclamation bestowed upon the band by hacks he felt had been overly harsh in their criticism of the band's early shows: "A lot of it was saying how sloppy we were, which I didn't agree with. A lot of it was: we're part of a movement, and some of it is really positive."

It was "Killamangiro", Drew claims, that signalled the band's intent, producer Paul Epworth's touch bringing the best out of the record, preventing it from, as he put it, "meandering," Paul exerting a calm authority that didn't challenge anyone's ego. Drew was disappointed, though, that one of the track's intended B-sides, "Gang Of Gin", wasn't released, Peter's stream of consciousness rant at the end of the song considered too libellous.

Drew —

"Before that ["Killamangiro"], there was the kind of perception of the band as being a bunch of hopeless junkies, and the songs being songs that weren't good enough to be used in The Libertines. And no-one really took it seriously. And then all of a sudden we've got this amazing single that sounds the bollocks, by the producer who did Futureheads and Bloc Party and The Rakes, and he's just a really well-respected guy… people expect that, because of Peter's musical tastes, Babyshambles should be more effete, to have less balls."

Peter —

"The song will always be special to me. Just because its release was the only time we ever rehearsed and we had a grand old time doing it on a few TV shows. I remember a punch-up with the crowd at *Top Of The Pops* and stage-diving on some kids' TV show, but they all moved out the way and I flattened some poor 14-year-old.

"The video captured the song well, grainy and blue. For the first time we were a band in the public's eye and I was as good as anything else out there at the time."

The Observer's Garry Mulholland wrote that "'Killamangiro' contains all the reasons why this band is attracting as much as devotion as The Libertines, and why The

---

Opposite: Babyshambles wrap up their first full UK tour at Scala on October 6, 2004 in London.

Libs may never reform", the track showing Peter "riffing on one of The Libertines' major themes – the pointlessness of British male street violence, the fear and the running away, and the defiance of the weak or the poor or the freaks who are so often the guiltless victims… And, just in case we forget there's a brilliant young band involved, drummer Gemma Clarke and bassist Drew McConnell create a charging but subtle rhythm, and, a little over a minute in, Patrick Walden does something so split-second brilliant on his guitar that it never fails to make me jump and laugh."

The *NME*, which made it Runner-up Single of the Week, may have expressed a faint longing for Carl, John and Gary to be "bashing away in the background", but arrived at the "awkward truth… that, right now, Babyshambles sound more like The Libertines than The Libertines… No matter how Peter chooses to spend his leisure time, his music remains frightfully articulate, spitting at the music industry with a frighteningly genuine bile."

In November, Carl announced that The Libertines were to disband before the year was out, while "Killamangiro" reached number eight in the UK Singles Chart in early December. An appearance at the Xfm Winter Wonderland, Hammersmith Apollo, went less well, the four-piece told that they couldn't perform owing to Peter's lateness.

Missing their soundcheck – the source of the organisers' anger – the band nonetheless played an acoustic version of "Killamangiro" after Peter started a "Babyshambles! Babyshambles!" chant that the crowd took up. Once the song was finished, the band were expressly told to sling their hook. Which they did. But as Drew says: "We weren't that bothered. We'd just found out that our single had gone in at number eight – the first single that we recorded together – and it was in the top ten."

The band also kicked-off their *32nd of December* UK tour that month. Described by Matt Bates as "the tour of death" and "an evil place to be around", the tour's opening show was held at The Limelight, Belfast, after an appearance on *Top of the Pops* that saw an altercation between Peter and a member of the audience.

Patrick, who dived in with Drew to add some muscle, believed that the troublemaker had been planted there by a redtop to incite the brawl, deriding the band as junkies and forcing the BBC to use rehearsal footage, the corporation fearing the consequences of a live performance.

With the technical rehearsal behind them, the audience were allowed into the studio. Then, as the track started rolling, Peter quickly became, in his own words, the victim of "a load of drug-related abuse", including the question: "Have you had a hit today, Pete?" – "So I just launched myself at him", Peter remembers. "He was a big fucker as well."

Drew — "He said something like: 'Oi, crackhead, how much skag have you had today?' or something like that. And then he started doing the wanker gesture, and Peter just went: 'Right!' and dove into the crowd to clump him, and then Patrick and I saw it and just tore our guitars off and we went in there as well, and he was there with some mates. And the whole time this was happening, Gemma was looking really freaked out, because all of a sudden she's playing drums on an empty stage.

"So it kind of got quashed, and we got back on stage just in time for all the vocals to come in. And we weren't allowed back in to do the filming, because they were, like: 'We've never had a band punch the audience in *Top Of The Pops* before, and we think maybe it'd be a little irresponsible to let you do it. But we filmed the dress rehearsal and we're gonna air that.' So if you watch it on YouTube or whatever, at some point at the beginning you just see Gemma looking really scared, playing drums on her own because we were in the crowd punching people.

"And then when you see me walk on stage, in shot, you can see me putting my bass on, you can see me putting the strap over my head, and Patrick as well. And because it was a rehearsal, Patrick and I were walking around talking to each other – 'What the fuck was that all about?', because it's miming, isn't it, except for the vocals, and just chatting to one another – 'Who the fuck was that cunt?' 'I dunno, but he wants sorting out.' 'Where is he? Is he still there?'"

It didn't take long for more chaos to break out after leaving the Beeb's studios for Belfast, a furious exchange of words resulting in James' girlfriend being thrown out of the tour bus onto the hard shoulder, 35 miles from Manchester, in the middle of the night, along with Anne McCloy, who James invited onto the tour to open the band's shows in Belfast and Dublin.

The incident set the tone for much of what was to follow during the tour, and delayed the bus so much that the ferry to Ireland was nearly missed.

Matt Bates — "Within an hour-and-a-half of being on that bus there'd been a fight, [people] kicked off the bus, people crying, blood. It was probably the most stressing week of my life… Looking back now, I'm still shocked that no-one actually died on that tour. Not necessarily through drugs – just through the bad feelings that everyone had towards each other.

"There were fists flying and threats, rifts, all the way through that tour. Looking back now, it's, like: how [did] no-one get seriously hurt somewhere? How we actually stayed together as a band and how the band survived is beyond me."

Patrick — "The tour of death. It was just, like, everyone was taking way too much drugs, everyone was way too paranoid. Everyone was just very ill. And there was a lot of obscene, strange behaviour going on… I got into a fight with James Mullord because I asked him for some dinner! That's how fucked up he was on those temazepams. You don't really know what you're doing on those. It was crazy shit… The crack and the drugs started to really screw everything up – not just on everyone else's part, but on my part as well; I fucked up as well."

The tour would perhaps be best remembered for what many regard as Peter's worst performance, on the 15th of December at Blackpool's Empress Ballroom, and for another of his no-shows – and another riot – at London's Astoria, three days later.

In Blackpool, Peter took to the stage in a stupor, at one point falling asleep and, later, removing his coat to reveal a rolled-up sleeve and belt tied around his arm, Patrick storming off moments later, followed by Gemma and Drew.

The gig also spawned the moniker Johnny Headlock, after Jonathan Jeannevol, who worked intermittently as Peter's minder, was asked by James Mullord to haul Peter off stage. Johnny, though, effected the request more literally than intended, dragging him off in a headlock, witnessed by a rapidly diminishing audience, the venue half-full at the time – a move responsible for his ensuing dismissal, despite being brought back into the fold shortly afterwards.

Patrick — "Peter turned up to play, and we started a song, and I looked over and he was just going [murmuring noise] – he was too fucked... so I turned around and looked at Pete, and – this is after about the second or third song – so I fucking took my guitar off and flung it at him. I missed, and walked off the stage, and Pete just goes: 'Uuurgh?' … saw the guitar and starts playing no chords, dribbling on the stage… he looked like a zombie…

"By that time, we had all the tabloid people coming to watch our band as well. They were quite amused by it – I think they wanted their money's worth! But it was quite sad really."

Luca C— "He was pretty much unable to perform, and it was a bit of a shambolic moment, especially 'cos the tour had been great. And, all of a sudden, we were in this amazing venue and had played a really good show, were on a real high, and were, like: 'Right, let's watch Babyshambles now.'

"And the band goes on, and everything just falls apart. A few people left, which I thought was the right thing to do… And I thought the right thing to happen was to get him off stage and not carry on with the show. But, as you do, you get a lot of people who seem to enjoy watching the car-crash. I didn't like that; I just went backstage and tried to cheer-up Gemma, who was crying her eyes out, and everyone, obviously, was really upset.

Matt Bates — "The Blackpool gig was probably the most out of it that Pete's ever been on stage. And I remember being on the bus, and just begging Pete to come on the stage, with James Mullord – just begging him to get on stage.

"That's the only time I wish he hadn't succeeded. I think it would've been best if he hadn't of done that show. He didn't know his words, he didn't really know where he was, he slurred. After about three songs, the rest of the band walked off."

Mik Whitnall, a friend of Peter's for almost a decade, and later a guitar tech and co-manager of the band, prior to taking Patrick Walden's place as guitarist, reckons Peter's estrangement from The Libertines was still playing heavily on his mind at the time of the Blackpool gig: "I've seen that one on video. I know Pete's not proud of it, like. But it was a rough time for him then; he didn't have much belief in himself, and The Libs were still going without him."

Not that the Blackpool fiasco curbed Peter's tendency to perform under the influence, when, still jaded from the previous night's intake, he necked temazepams during a soundcheck before the tour's penultimate date in Sheffield the following night.

Drew —

"Peter was still fucked from the night before, and he was falling asleep in the soundcheck. And afterwards he looked up to me with, like, a guilty puppy dog look in his face and said: 'You're not happy with me are you?' And I was, like: 'It's not that I'm not happy with you, man – I'm worried about you. You haven't had any more of those temazepams have you?' And he goes: 'Yeah, I took eight.' 'Why'd you take so many?' 'Well, you know, one for each dead boy.' We've got a song called "Eight Dead Boys".

"We started [the Sheffield show] with "Killamangiro". And there's a line in "Killamangiro" that goes: 'Why would you pay to see me in a cage? And why would you pay to see me in a cage? Some men call the stage.' And he changed the line to: 'If I fall asleep on the stage, don't listen.' And when he said that, he tripped over and fell flat on his face, and looked down, and… knocked himself out."

The Sheffield date was to be Gemma's last with the band, the events of 18th December, when the band were due to play at London's Astoria, helping make her mind up to leave, exacerbating pre-existing concerns that centred on the burgeoning narcotic mayhem and the dangerous situations engendered as a consequence.

It was to prove a defining moment in the Babyshambles story.

The scrutiny on the band would intensify dramatically. And Peter would soon become a marked man, the events that were to follow catapulting him into wider public consciousness in dramatic fashion.

3

Riot at the Astoria

Originally intended as a Christmas party, featuring a selection of the band's friends, The Noisettes and Towers of London among them, The Astoria night should have been a merry celebration marking what would soon be the end of another incident-strewn year of peaks and troughs.

Added onto the end of the tour after Matt Bates reassured the band that it would be a good money-spinner, Drew harboured doubts from the offset: "I didn't want to do it. I thought that we were burning out or burning up, whatever way you want to look at it, and I thought it was just being greedy. If we'd not done it, we would have finished the tour and it would've been fine."

Drew —
"We hired the GAY night at The Astoria, and they've got a licence until about three in the morning. It was going to be, like, a Christmas thing. And kids were there from, like, seven o'clock, drinking cans of lager.

"We were supposed to go on at midnight, and a lot of bands had been on, and I guess the kids were there to see us. For one reason or another, possibly best explained by Peter, he didn't come."

On what Matt Bates describes as "probably the worst day in my professional life", rioters rushed the stage destroying equipment.

With no sign of Peter by 11pm – the band had been pencilled in for a 1am slot – Matt set about trying to track him down. Accompanied by mutual friend Robert Chevalley, they found him at one of his hideaways – friend Gill's in Homerton, Hackney – though, according to Bates, Peter seemed more interested in catching a flight to Moscow than a cab to greater London.

Matt Bates —
"I got there and Pete was begging me: 'Have you got a passport?' I said: 'Yeah'. He said: 'Come with me to St Petersburg, come with me to St Petersburg.' And I said: 'We can't, Pete, we've got a gig to do.' He said: 'If I do the gig will you come with me to St Petersburg?' It was, like, three days before Christmas, and I said: 'If you do the gig, I'll come with you to St Petersburg', thinking: my mum's gonna kill me if I go there for Christmas. I said: 'Whatever, Pete. Whatever you want, do the show and I'll come with you to St Petersburg. If that's what you want we'll do it. But after the show, after the show'."

In the event, Peter made it to neither St Petersburg nor The Astoria, jumping out of a taxi that Matt and Chev had persuaded him to get into, when stationary at traffic lights, and running off into the night, pursued by Chev, who failed to make up the lost ground, leaving Matt to settle the fare.

Alone, he made his way to The Astoria and advised the show's promoters to consider calling the gig off, but their insistence on delaying a decision, in the vague hope of Peter showing up, left the audience with little else to do but drink copious amounts of alcohol, which doubtless played a part in the events that followed.

When James Mullord announced that the show wouldn't be going ahead a furore exploded, would-be revellers' frustrations boiling over as they stormed the stage, taking the band's equipment apart in a matter of minutes.

Matt
Bates — "I had to go to The Astoria, and obviously tell people what had happened, The Astoria going: 'Just pull it, he's done this, he's not turning up.' But the promoters were going: 'No, let's give him another ten minutes, make it half-hour', and I knew in my heart of hearts that this was a really bad idea. And I was going: 'Look, if they're drinking out there, this is going to get worse and worse. The more you make them wait, the worse it's gonna get.'

"They made the decision, and I remember saying to them: 'Phone the police.' 'No, we never have any trouble in here', and I said: 'Listen, get a van, there's gonna be trouble.' And the venue said: 'Don't be daft, we can handle this.'"

Drew — "You open the doors to the gig and actually let the kids in, let them watch four support bands, and let them get tanked up on beer, and then cancel it. It was unprecedented territory for most people. I'm sure it probably happened at some point in the history of pop music, but no-one there had had to deal with that before, so I think people were just running around panicking."

Patrick — "He actually turned up to the venue, and then drove away again, or ran down the high street. And after about two hours of waiting, there were two thousand kids in there ready to wreck the venue…

"The place was destroyed. I remember we were in a little room, and then they put a brick through, and started smashing the doors down – pretty scary shit.

"But I didn't realise how ill Peter was. It wasn't attention-seeking behaviour, that was the illness… I was beginning to understand the pressure on the band a bit, because I was getting asked to do more stuff, but he was the centre of attention… It was scary. There were two, three thousand kids – I'm talking about kids ranging from fourteen to forty-year-olds – rockers who are into The Clash, because Mick Jones was accompanying him [Peter]. And they were angry. They paid their money, they wanted to see a show, and Peter wasn't there."

Luca C — "I remember just being there, waiting for Peter to turn up, and all of a sudden someone comes into the dressing room, saying: 'Everything's going fucking mental, bloody hell!' And I remember seeing my guitarist on the drum riser, swinging a mic stand around him to keep the kids away from Gemma's drumkit.

"It was a pretty sad moment in the history of Babyshambles. I remember things getting nicked and going on eBay, and finding Pat's pedals and stuff – 'as used by Babyshambles guitarist Patrick Walden'. Some people took the piss. Drew lost a bass, I think… We were lucky: we had all our equipment stolen a few months before that, from HQ – that's a different story! – but if we'd had our equipment stolen on that night as well, it would probably have been the end of the band."

Anthony Thornton — "There had already been a riot in Aberdeen. But this was a powder keg waiting to go off. There had been bands. The crowd had to endure a fairly unexceptional evening of bands, and they'd been in there since the early evening.

"The other thing was that this audience wasn't a typical show of industry types waiting to catch a glimpse/pass judgement on the next big thing. This was a band that had grown under the radar, that was big in its own right and inspired passion. Passion plus booze plus bad bands, plus being told hours after that Babyshambles weren't coming.

"Remember, these were people who'd missed the last train home deliberately to see their heroes. These were fans who would be sleeping rough that night. So why not the riot? It was the only human course of action."

Ben Bailey — "It was just fucking mayhem. It's always disappointing, I suppose, because the whole point of the thing is that he [Peter] sets himself out to be a real musical troubadour and then he doesn't turn up. It's a real shame. It'd be like going to see Bob Dylan and him not turning up. When you go and see someone that's held in that much esteem, it's a letdown, and I suppose that's why all the riots happen, isn't it? Because people want to see it and just go mad."

Matt Bates — "I stood there on the balcony looking down, never feeling so depressed about anything in my life… that this had all happened. I remember going in the dressing room after that and trying to talk to Gemma, Pat and Drew. I couldn't really console them; they didn't know what to do, what to think or what was going to happen in the future. If you asked me then if Babyshambles'd ever play again, I'd have said no chance."

Fan Abi Roter, a friend of Peter's since jumping on stage at the Hammersmith Apollo, recalls fans' frustrations at not being told what was going on: "I remember being at the door, and them not letting Pat in – and Pat was getting very angry about that – and eventually letting him in. And there was a sort of air about the night from that moment for me; you could tell things weren't quite right… And then I was walking out and everyone was going: 'Right, let's start a riot!', so they were all well up for kicking off that night. I just wanted to get out of there, to be honest, before anyone got hurt. It was a bit harsh really; you know, everyone pretty angry with the band at that point – not the band, but Peter mainly, I think."

Those who managed to give security the slip rushed backstage, keen to vent their anger on Astoria management and anyone with anything to do with Babyshambles, getting to within spitting distance of their targets before being repelled. By now, Gemma was the only backstage member no longer at risk, ushered to safety, along with her parents, out of the back door and into a waiting car.

Drew —   "Patrick, Gemma and I were upstairs in the production office, which is, like, two or three stories up, and we heard, like, a low mumbling coming over the PA saying that the gig was cancelled, and then the whole building shook. It was like a tidal wave, and then this roar.

"The wave actually subsided right outside, and we were two or three stories up. We heard bottles smashing and security holding kids back. Getting backstage and past two stories of security, they just went ballistic and tore the place to fucking shreds; ripping out seats in the top balcony and throwing them down…

"If you look closely at the lyrics to the second version of "Up The Morning", on *Down In Albion*, he talks about it. I don't know if anyone's ever noticed that before, but something about someone waiting on the door for him. I don't know if I've said too much already, but that's why he didn't come: he was scared to come. Someone had made him scared to come – i.e. 'If you come, this is going to happen'."

Adam —   "I remember calling Pat up the day after. I didn't know anything about it and was calling to see how he was. When he told me I thought: God, what a manic band to be in. About a month later, there I was, in the eye of the storm."

Peter disappeared to his parents' in the aftermath of the aborted Astoria gig, spending Christmas getting himself straight and returning to London in a calmer state, staying at a friend's.

Matt Bates remembers the time they spent together as the year drew to a close, "sitting there with Pete in his bedroom, and that's the closest I've ever been to Pete; the most normal I've ever seen him. He was just like the Pete I'd grown to love and really respected, rather than the monster I remember from The Astoria show. I remember sitting there and him playing me "Up The Morning", which he'd just started writing for the *Down In Albion* album, saying: 'What d'you think of this line, what d'you think of that line?… it was really nice to see him like that."

This good mood was carried, quite literally, into 2005, Peter playing four gigs, in Birmingham, Stoke, Oldham and Manchester, on New Year's Eve, Matt remembering: "I was thinking: my God, we've gone from missing shows to doing four shows in one night. And it was a really amazing night, the best New Year's I've ever had, driving down the motorway with Pete, watching these kids just go mad, just him and a guitar… James Mullord and I were literally stood there, arms around Pete, just trying to keep enough space… to actually play and sing. But it's fantastic. No other artist would do that; you wouldn't experience that with anyone else."

The following day, though, he failed to turn up for an acoustic show at the Return to New York club night at the Great Eastern Hotel, and the intimacy he shared with fans would increasingly become a thing of the past, the media's obsession with Peter, commonly depicted as an anti-hero masterminding his own destruction, erupting when he started dating supermodel, Kate Moss.

Anthony Thornton — "They went from quite an interesting, albeit unpredictable, band to being Pete Doherty and some other fellows, to Pete Doherty, Kate Moss' boyfriend, and that was overnight. It was unbelievable. This is a guy who'd play in front of thirty people with an acoustic guitar, and then suddenly he's all over the papers.

"I've got to say, Babyshambles did fucking good to keep it together, because a lot of other bands would have imploded. They did fucking well to keep it together. I think Adam and Drew in particular were keeping their heads while everybody else was coming in all battered and everything."

Patrick — "It [media attention] intensified. It was just a lot more tabloidy and paparazzi. I don't think it was particularly healthy. It wasn't focused on the music, it was focused on drugs and controversy. In some ways it did the band a favour, made the band bigger. I'm sure Pete knew what he was getting into. They were in love with each other, though. It wasn't a publicity stunt."

Tayo Ogidan, from the Duke of Clarence pub, was another struck at the way in which Peter's dating of Kate brought such a storm of press interest: "On taking over the Duke, the plan was primarily to have it as a music venue with a few famous bands always willing to play private gigs. Hence, the Duke had its own cult following, which was like a 'Duke/Tayo' bandwagon. It became legendary and cultish, and all of this coincided with the early days of Pete and Kate.

"A few times Pete turned up to play impromptu gigs, explaining that he'd put it on his website just prior. The surprising thing is that within a few minutes we had a full house. As that situation continued, the Duke had a constant stream of Babyshambles fans coming on spec that he might be dropping in for a drink and then playing afterwards. No press, though.

"Then we did the first Pete and Kate duo/acoustic set. That was the first time that we were mobbed by both the fans and the paps. As it was an impromptu gig, there was no late license in place, and it wasn't strictly necessary as it was also a private event. Standing behind the bar, my most vivid memory of the night was flashbulbs going off everywhere.

"That was the night that the neighbours complained, as there seemed to be so much commotion outside; with Kate being whisked out the back door as the police stormed the Duke. As it turned out, the band's equipment were confiscated by the council, with some of the cops having to throw a wall around Pete as he proceeded to play a few tunes out on the street."

Kate and Peter had met before, backstage at a Dazed and Confused gig in Shepherd's Bush that Babyshambles played, and when Kate decided to put a supergroup together to play at her 31st birthday party on the 16th of January, Peter was invited along.

Typically missing rehearsals with other members of a one-off line-up that included Dan Goffey of Supergrass, Paul Simonon and Mick Jones of The Clash, Jason Pierce of Spiritualised, and Siobhan Fahey of Bananarama, Peter showed up at the birthday bash armed with a present for Kate: the framed lyrics to "What Katie Did Next", a song that would later the same year appear on *Down In Albion*.

January was also to be a month signalling a major change within the Babyshambles camp, when drummer Gemma Clarke quit, citing disagreements with management, White Sport's Adam Ficek came in as her replacement.

Peter —   "Gemma was a continual worry for me. With Adam things calmed down. I saw him as dependable and creative, and we all gelled well.

"At the time, Gemma's heart wasn't in it for whatever reason, and Adam was hungry for action, as I still was. He came into things in the midst of a fucking hurricane and I thought: if he can put up with this, he can withstand anything. Danny from Supergrass wanted to join the same night, but I always did like Ficek's dress sense."

Considered by Matt Bates to be "too sweet" to be in a band so embroiled in controversy, Gemma left wishing the band well, her driving, powerhouse style of drumming replaced by Adam's more measured delivery of intricate, measured strokes: "I'm not sure she was really ready, at 20 years old, to be amongst that stuff. It used to be so funny on tour: an upstairs lounge and a downstairs lounge on the bus. The upstairs lounge was drugs, party lounge, and the downstairs lounge was Gemma watching *Finding Nemo*.

"And that's seriously how it was split. They're upstairs, drinking, smoking, doing coke, doing drugs; Gemma sat downstairs watching *Finding Nemo*. And that's the spectrum of how different a lot of the band were to Gemma."

Adam, who would have to win over Gemma's legions of fans, who, as Abi Roter put it, would have to "get used to there being a bloke instead of a lovely little girl sitting behind the drums", received his call to arms on 26th January 2005, while watching Rough Trade's Hal in The Monarch, Camden.

A loose acquaintance of Peter's since the spring of the previous year, Peter had initially arrived at the conclusion that Adam had taken a dislike to him – which hadn't been the case at all.

Adam —   "I met Peter in the Lower Street office of PPQ, where James Mullord was running his High Society label. He looked pretty dishevelled and turned to me without any prompting, saying to James: 'See, even he doesn't like me.' To which I replied: 'I don't even know you, mate.' I think I ended up leaving James to it, and returned later."

They were to bump into each other on other occasions, a willo-the-wisp-esque Peter invariably showing up to borrow a guitar, before vanishing into thin air.

"I remember being in HQ once with all the Mains Ignition boys", says Adam of one particularly confusing occasion. "Suddenly this ghost-like character stumbles in, mumbling: 'I need to borrow a guitar.' Everyone looked at each other: who the fuck? Within seconds he'd gone – God knows how he got in or out, as the door had a high security lock on it. Well, that's Peter – enigmatic to the core".

Had their encounters been warmer, Adam might have taken Gemma's place in the fledgling version of the band, though his ostensibly guarded manner convinced Peter that it would be a bad idea, suspecting that they'd clash, creating instability when the opposite was needed – this despite James Mullord's constant championing of Adam, who, he insisted, should have been there from the start.

"I think you've got to be yourself, so I was", remembers Adam. "I suppose, in hindsight, if I'd have joined then, maybe I wouldn't be around now. Sometimes these things are made to happen at certain times."

Less than a year on, Peter's change of heart freed Adam of the teaching job he'd been forced to retain to pay the rent, at a stage in his life when any spare time was largely spent playing and rehearsing with White Sport – for whom Peter had played bass on a couple of occasions. As Adam recalls: "I didn't know about The Libertines and had no preconceptions. I didn't know whether he expected us all to go: 'Woah, there's Pete from The Libertines!' I don't know much about that."

When the art punk band supported Babyshambles on tour, Adam witnessed at close quarters certain band members' penchant for intoxication: "When we were supporting I'd have to work during the day, so I'd make my own way there – thank God I did: when the van-full of band, support and friends arrived, they just fell out, stumbling after four hours being locked in an airtight opiate and crack chamber."

Patrick, who called Adam to break the news of his drastic career change, credits James Mullord for supporting him when insisting that his friend had what it took to cut the mustard at the highest level: "He listened to me a lot about who should be in the band, he backed me when I said Adam should be in the band and Pete was saying he shouldn't. I had to fight to get him in the band until he proved himself, 'cos Adam's an amazing drummer – I've always thought that…

"I knew exactly what he could do and that once he was comfortable he'd be fucking great. 'Cos I wanted to take the band in other styles. We weren't just a punk rock band… Adam's jazz, ska… so we went off on a tangent there."

Adam was told by Patrick that in a few weeks' time he'd be playing in front of thousands at the Brixton Academy, for which he'd receive a sizeable pay cheque – a sum that, incidentally, failed to arrive.

Racked with nerves, he immediately embarked on a period of frenetic rehearsing with Drew, sandwiched between his earliest shows, tirelessly thrashing songs out in a desperate bid to familiarise himself with their form, spurred on by the fear of public humiliation.

Adam —   "It was a totally different approach to playing to what I was used to. At the same time, I was quite a technical, studious type, playing loads of different styles. But this band just needed pure emotion and it was a very welcome release for me.

"It sounds quite full of myself, but I knew I could take care of business equally as well as Gemma had done… The only thing I thought was that she was quite a powerful rock drummer, and I wasn't; I'd come from a jazz/indie/pop background, so I had to put a lot more energy into it, lift my sticks higher, just 'cos that's the nature of the band – it's quite a fiery band, and they move fast; there's a lot of energy there…

"In those situations, I know I can slip easily into giving myself a hundred reasons why I shouldn't do something, so I tend to just ignore that and jump in two feet first, 'cos I know I'll sink or swim… I knew it was going to be hard, but I thought: fuck it; didn't really give it much thought."

Drew —   "I spent two weeks with Adam, going every day and going through the songs, showing him the songs, working on the parts, and the guy picked it up really quickly. He was getting quite a few songs learnt in a day, so by the time Peter came along, Adam had, just bass and drums, gotten to know pretty much most of the songs that we play live, and most of the songs that we were thinking of doing for the album."

Next page: Peter and Drew fronting Babyshambles at The Forum, London, 13th May 2008.

Taking to the stage for the first time at The George, Whitechapel, on 27th January, with just one band rehearsal behind him, Adam put in, as he called it, "an abysmal performance", his unfamiliarity with the songs evident. "I remember Jake Fior speaking to me and saying how it was 'ok', that I just needed to work on not moving with the rest of the band so much. I suppose it was a polite way of saying: 'You played shit.'

"Those first few days were a really difficult time. My mother had only just been diagnosed with terminal cancer and, here I was, totally dropping any sense of job security I had. Literally a life-changing few months."

Patrick saw the night somewhat differently, applauding his friend's efforts in light of his lack of preparation time: "I remember thinking: I wish we had more rehearsal time, 'cos I really wanted Adam to prove himself. 'Cos Peter, at the beginning, didn't gel with Adam. Not 'cos Adam's a horrible character, but he's a bit reserved. And he didn't kiss his arse, not that he should… He did really well considering, but I know he wasn't happy. He sets high standards for himself, he's a bit of a perfectionist."

Adam at first felt uncomfortable being thrust into the limelight, staunch fans scrutinising the newcomer's every stroke – a far cry from his days in the support slot with White Sport, when he'd been greeted with indifference, polite applause considered a result, the crowd reserving their energy for the main event.

But while White Sport's efforts had gone largely unrewarded, failing to gather any real momentum, their lukewarm reception was soon forgotten, replaced by outright chaos, fuelled by Peter's reputation for erratic, reckless behaviour.

It was at his next show, at The Garage, Islington, in benefit of the tsunami disaster, that Adam grasped a little more of the band's true nature, "panicking, blindly panicking" at Peter's lateness. This time, Peter had been delayed in Paris, and though he made it there eventually, Adam said of the moment: "We were all waiting round Matt Bates' house in Dove Road. It was then that I thought about not quitting my job so eagerly… I should have learnt then and there that this was the way it was going to be."

The band's equipment had been blagged and borrowed and the 400-odd-strong crowd seemed gargantuan, his mistakes, and the band's "wobbly" showing going unnoticed in an *NME* review that thought Adam "had a relatively stress free night settling into his new band almost unnoticed."

It was at The Garage gig that Peter introduced him to the crowd for the first time, "which I felt was a nice gesture, although he did say Babyshambles were just 'trying me out'. Cheeky shit", says Adam.

A few name-calls emanated from the crowd, promoting more by way of assurance, and Adam "started to feel a bit more embraced by it all." Just days later, though, he was met with uncertainty again as news broke of Peter's arrest, along with that of Alan Wass, guitarist with Left Hand, following an altercation with Max

Carlish, who had been tracking Peter for a documentary that was aired on Channel 4 in May, entitled *Stalking Pete Doherty*.

Carlish sold pictures of Peter taking heroin to *The Sunday Mirror*, and the pair clashed in the Rookery Hotel, Farringdon, amid conflicting reports of what actually happened to spark the incident.

Carlish had been allowed into the inner sanctum with promises of a fat pay cheque, on condition that, if everyone in the Babyshambles camp was happy with the results of his work, a deal could proceed.

Peter —   "First of all, he wasn't a friend of mine – that's one thing I've always wanted to clear up… Mullord turned up one day, and said: 'There's a man who's gonna give us a million quid for letting us be filmed. So we were, like: 'Hooray!' Especially Muggins here. 'Yeah, he can film what he wants.'"

Gathering footage between June and October 2004, Carlish was occasionally invited on stage, assuming the role of, as Max himself put it in an article given to *The Guardian* in February 2005, "some kind of demented, posh Bez figure… a kind of idiot savant to Pete and his familiars."

Max allowed the line between professionalism and obsession to blur, shadowing Peter with such intensity that, for the most part, he earned a reputation as a menace.

According to Max, access to Peter started to dry up in the wake of a night of humiliation at Southampton, when, after joining the band on stage for his "Bez impression", he was pelted with bottles once Peter disclosed that he was in the process of making a documentary for Channel 4. Max, hurt at this public show of rejection, fell into a depression, his hopes of completing the documentary fading by the day.

A few months passed with little contact between the two parties, but when Peter started seeing Kate, interest in the documentary grew.

Max re-established contact with James Mullord to try and complete the project. But when nothing happened, Max claims that he took the advice of a friend, who, having seen footage of Peter taking heroin, suggested that he ease his financial burden – Carlish had been subsidising himself entirely while filming – by selling the images.

A bidding war erupted. Max, who maintained that he had no desire to sell the photos, confessed that: "I did want to use them as leverage to meet up with Pete again and complete the film." He phoned James, proposing that his footage be held back in exchange for his being able to resume filming, but when he didn't hear anything back, he accepted an offer from *The Sunday Mirror*, convinced that his work on the documentary had been wasted.

It was to prove a horrendous error in judgement that not only tarnished his own reputation irrevocably, but set in motion a dramatic chain of events that culminated in another spell behind bars for Peter.

Peter — "I was in love and nothing could bring me down, and then the next minute – bang! A picture of me smoking smack, banging up – and it's, like, what the fuck? This cunt's selling me down the river!

"And he received all this money for selling those photos. Now, the way my mind works – I'm only human – my thought was: well, he's stitched me up and he's received all this money, and I've got nothing…

"So I received a message saying: 'Come and meet me at the hotel, let me do a bit more filming, and you can have half the money.' I was, like: 'No, I tell you what: I'll meet you at the hotel, and you give me half the money anyway, and I won't hurt you. Fuck any more interviews, you've just sold me down the river' – I think he got thirty-five, forty grand – 'You give me half of that and we're sweet.' And he said: 'No problem'."

On 2nd February, Peter booked a room for he and Kate at The Rookery, where he had arranged to meet Carlish to receive his cut of the *Mirror* money. Eager to impress Kate, he was in the process of sprucing himself up for their date when he heard a knock on the door. An hour before their planned meeting, Max Carlish stood before him. When Peter asked for his money, Carlish "throws a comedy fiver in my face and says: 'Feed your habit with that'."

Shortly afterwards, Carlish was sporting a pair of black eyes and a broken nose. He told Peter that the money had already been spent, and was later taken to UCL Hospital, London, for treatment, where he was discharged a little later. Peter, meanwhile, was held on charges of actual bodily harm and theft, spending the next six days in Pentonville Prison following struggles to raise bond money.

Matt Bates had from the start considered it an odd decision to grant Carlish unlimited access: "Max Carlish, what a character… He was given unlimited access to the band, which seemed absolutely ludicrous to me, which it obviously did become… If you've watched the documentary, it's the guy having a nervous breakdown – that's what it is; it's not nice to watch. It doesn't make Pete look bad in the least."

Carlish, "a shining example of how Peter's too trustworthy", according to Drew, would often hide in the studio during takes, adding to his collection of footage: "I'd be in the middle of a bass take, and I'd feel a clunking, and see one of the baffles moving, and then I'd see this fucking curly hair and wild eyes and spectacles, cursing because he couldn't get his camera to work."

Matt Bates, who had at the time been sharing a flat with Drew, next to Peter's place in Dove Road, Angel, remembers the media circus at the height of the Carlish furore: "I couldn't walk out of my house without the flash of the cameras, just in case I was Pete Doherty coming out, and it was much the same for all the residents in the block; they must have had the same.

"And I kept thinking: God, that's annoying me, how much must that annoy Pete Doherty to have that many people outside your house, day in, day out, these cameras just waiting for you to do anything?"

It was Peter's involvement with Kate, Matt believes, that helped whip-up such a media frenzy: "That's the reason the story was newsworthy. Other musicians caught doing drugs may have got a few column inches in *The Sport* or something, but suddenly this was Kate Moss' new boyfriend on the front page of the *Mirror*, or whatever, smoking heroin."

He remains astounded by the amount of access that the band continues to permit outsiders, but doesn't anticipate Peter shying away from an honesty that far too often encourages negative press coverage: "The fact that a camera's pointing at him doesn't seem to stop him being who he wants to be. You can applaud it or condemn it, but at least he never lies in front of the camera: what you see in front of the camera is normally what Pete Doherty is. He doesn't put any pretensions up about who he is and who he isn't, so in that kind of way you've got to respect him."

Tony Linkin — "Well, if I'm being honest, I couldn't understand why they were doing it in the first place. I really couldn't understand. Max was a bit of a buffoon, but he's probably quite an alright kind of guy. But… in my meetings with him, he didn't seem quite right somehow…

"He was just always so full of himself as well, and it just seemed to me that, you know, it didn't seem like the right type of person to be doing a film on Pete, really. At all… I mean, it is different when you're filming around Pete, with everything going on, anyway; you've got to have total control, I suppose, of the situation. I didn't think they did particularly."

Drew — "Countless times I've seen him [Peter] mistrust the people he should trust, and in his mind there's a reality where someone who is there for the right reasons, and is doing a good job, and is completely trustworthy and is really his friend, he decides that they're evil and they're manipulative and they're untrustworthy. And, conversely, I've seen countless examples of him trusting people that he shouldn't. And the more you try and tell him that he shouldn't trust that person, the more he obstinately insists that he should… We just have to be a lot more careful about who's following us around with a camera, you know?"

After five nights in Pentonville, Peter was on 8th February released on bail, raised via a combination of Rough Trade and James Mullord, on condition that he attend rehabilitation. Peter subsequently entered the Florence Nightingale Clinic, where he was instructed to remain until an appearance at Snaresbrook Crown Court on 21st February, his enforced rehab preventing him from attending the *NME* Awards on

17th February, where Babyshambles were up for the Best New Band and Best Live Band gongs.

For Adam, the night was a window into an entirely new, superficial world: "It was weird for me, 'cos I was stepping into this whole fucking environment, looking around seeing all these people I'd seen in the press. It was, like: oh, wow. You're a bit star-struck when you first go to these places, but it was probably that night when I thought: this is all a load of bollocks, I don't want to be part of this. You see all these guys swanning about, really giving it, 'cos you see them in *NME*... It's really not for me, this scene. Some people love it. It gets boring after a while. I'm into this to play music, not be a peacock."

Had Peter made it to the awards show, he would have been reunited with Carl for the first time since their fall-out the previous summer. Carl, who collected the Best British Band award for The Libertines – the band had also been nominated for Best British Band, Best Live Band, Best Album for *The Libertines*, which débuted at number one in the UK album charts the previous August, and Best Track for "Can't Stand Me Now" – spoke warmly of Peter, who had an opiate-blocking implant fitted on the 18th, the day before walking out of rehab to begin a twelve-week programme of counselling and therapy.

When the 21st arrived, his case was adjourned to 18th April at Snaresbrook Crown Court, Mr Justice Radford relaxing his bail conditions, which had imposed a curfew confining him to home between 10pm–7am. The ruling freed Peter to play at the Brixton Academy the following night, though he was warned that if he failed to abide by the conditions of his release, he would face likely arrest and revoking of bail.

The band were, in fact, reunited before then, appearing at The Garage that night, Peter's wayward tendencies kept under observation by a pair of burly security guards, supposedly brought in on Rough Trade's tab to protect the label's investment and enforce bail conditions, though the band later discovered that it was they who'd footed the bill.

The attentions of the paparazzi had been of particular concern, and the extra muscle would help keep them from Peter, and Peter from them, Adam noting that "he doesn't tend to himself in situations like that".

The Garage show – performed under curfew, security hauling him from the stage at 8.50pm to ensure bail conditions weren't broken – spawned the series of photos splashed across the tabloids the following morning, showing a wan, zombie-like Peter, eyes rolled back into their sockets.

The truth, on this occasion, was that Peter was sober, Drew recalling: "That famous photograph of him with his eyes rolled back in his head, that's just him thrashing about in the middle of a punk song."

Opposite: Kate and Peter at the National Arts Club in New York City, September 2005.

Adam —   "Turning up at The Garage that night was a real eye opener to how maliciously the paps treat people. As soon as we arrived they were all over us – well, Peter – scrambling over cars and pushing through people just to get photos. One of the security stopped the car and threatened to dismember a pap, as he'd scratched his car."

The following night's show, at Brixton Academy, introduced by Clash legend Mick Jones, had to be stopped twice – firstly, when overcrowding led to a crush in the front rows; and a second time because of a brawl between Peter and Patrick, security wrenching the warring bandmates apart before things turned any nastier.

Five minutes later, their differences resolved following a backstage slanging match, the band took to the stage again. Once the dust had settled, the rumour mill had it that the scrap had been staged as a publicity stunt.

Peter —   "Basically, I spent about forty minutes in a taxi journey, telling him that if he cared anything about me – and at the time it was quite a sensitive subject, because he hadn't been to two of the rehearsals... Adam... and Drew... were both showing a lot more commitment than either me or Pat when it came to rehearsing, and so I was basically just questioning his commitment, and said to him: '...Prove to me that you care about this band. I want you to smash me round the face as hard as you can with your guitar, halfway through the set.' And he said 'no', and I said: 'Well... then they was right... you're no good to us, man. You don't care. I'm asking you to do something for the band, for us, and you won't do it.'

"You know, it was going to be a glorious moment, when you see him fucking smashing every bone in my face with his guitar. He said it's half what I deserve. I think... I had an enforced implant, basically. So, yes, I was really nervous, as I always am, before gigs... beyond climbing walls, beyond paranoia or fear of not performing well. It's like full-on, blood-curdling, obsessive... I don't know what it is; a lot of it's to do with self-consciousness and a fear of the crowd and all that. For the wrong reasons.

"It's a Shakesperian comedy, where they're... paying their money to take out abuse on someone, you know? I'm a QPR fan... and my dad used to sometimes take me to The Shed and watch these blokes – thousands of blokes – paying, like, paying all of their money to abuse people. Not to enjoy their football, just to abuse people. Funny, that particular day there was an eighteen-year-old black kid called Carlton Palmer, who made his début. Soon as he came onto the pitch, man, woman and child were going 'ough ough ough ough', making monkey noises and that. It's really weird, you know? That's how I feel. People aren't going 'cos they like music – they're going... for a laugh, and jeer, and throw fruit...

"So I like to make sure I put a little twist on things and make sure something happens that's going to guarantee a genuine musical spectacular. Like, I dunno,

Shane McGowan would come on for a number, or, I dunno… when I was with Kate, Kate would come on and sing her one little line, and skip off. But it's just something fucking memorable. You know, if you like… a trick!…

"I don't actually like gimmicks and tricks, but still I had to create these illusions. So I thought that a good punch-up would look good, it would do it. But he was crying and saying: 'Peter, I don't want to hurt you', and: 'Why are you making me hit you…?' …And then he did actually swing for me… backstage, he did swing for me, and then he says: 'Why did you say all that? And if you want me to I'll break your fucking neck, you stupid cunt…!' And so that just spilled over on stage, really.

"But Pat really did lose it… I remember Mick Jones, like, came in and was, like: 'Look, boys, you're gonna have to calm this one down… get out there playing… you're brothers, you're brothers.' Pat was going: 'He's not my fucking brother, he's a fucking idiot! He wanted me to hit him, and I didn't, and then… he thinks he's got one over me… ' It was always like that with Pat. That I was trying to get one over on him and that, somehow."

Patrick —   "It wasn't pre-planned. We were in the cab on the way there, and he'd been up for days, going: 'Let's have a scrap tonight.' And I said: 'I don't really want to, I'd rather play music.' 'Come on, let's have a fucking good old fight.' I said: 'Pete, if you want to fight me I'll fight you, but I don't really want to fight on stage in front of my dad – my dad was ill and he didn't have long to live; he died a few months after that – and he'd been up for days and he was in a different reality.

"In the middle of a song he started whispering shit in my ear, really abusive stuff: 'Cunt', this and that – stuff that he knew would wind me up; he'd done too much crack… I took my guitar off in the middle of a song, and… I kicked him up the arse; I get him first, he swings at me and misses, and falls onto the monitor. The lights go on, and then there's five thousand kids going crazy.

"And we got backstage, man, and had this massive, massive row – I just wanted to kill someone – but he was going: 'It'll be in the papers the next day!' I was, like: 'I don't give two fucks – I'm here to play music!' It *was* in the papers the next day. Mick [Jones] came in and said: 'Go back, boys.' It wasn't pre-planned, though, but a lot of people think it was. It was funny."

Adam —   "That first Brixton date was also an eye opener. We were sitting round Peter's flat and he suddenly turned to Drew and myself and said: 'I don't really want to do this.' I think I just kept quiet, thinking: oh. It was Drew that reassured him and explained about the kids turning up and that."

Drew —   "Peter hadn't slept for, I think, six days, and there's just something that happens to Peter when he doesn't sleep sometimes: everything's a fight and it's him against the world, and there's this kind of psychosis that develops that is really hard to break him out of. And he was just in one of those moods, and I think that, married with the stress and nervous tension of playing after he got out of rehab, resulted in him behaving like that.

"The second song, he threw a microphone at my head. The microphone fell over, and it was near me and I was singing a part. And I looked down, and I looked at him, and he had this fucking vicious look on his face. And he kicked the microphone [stand] and it came up and twatted me in the head.

"I dunno, when someone's acting crazy – especially if a very good friend of yours is acting crazy – and you know it's crazy and it's not really born of anything real, then sometimes the best thing to do is to let it go. Especially when you're playing in front of five thousand people. The professional in me said: 'Okay, he just kicked a microphone [stand] in your head and you're in a lot of pain right now, but fuck it. Wrapping a bass round his head isn't gonna help matters, is it?'

"So I just let it go, and then later the fight happened. But fair play to Adam, man: we got there and the tenuous infrastructure that James had built around the touring Babyshambles entity was crumbling rapidly – mates of mates were hired to do backline, and they'd never done it before; people who had never really played guitar before were guitar-teching, fumbling about with tuners. We got there and Adam's drumkit wasn't there, and Patrick's guitar wasn't there; Patrick's amp wasn't there, and we'd gone past soundcheck time and there wasn't time to go and get it…

"I think everyone has a life drive and a death drive, and, like, a survival instinct and a self-destructive instinct. And some people, when things are getting good, as soon as they're starting to go really well, it's almost like on some subconscious level you don't really believe that you deserve it, and so you sabotage it without maybe even realising you're doing it. I dunno, I'm not a psychologist, but that seemed to be what was happening with Peter and Patrick."

Ben Bailey — "It was the first time I'd properly seen them with Adam drumming, and I was quite taken aback, because the last time I'd seen them play was about a year previous, and it was all kind of, like, ramshackle and the band didn't know the songs, and he obviously hadn't taken the time to teach the rest of the band the songs. But this time around he really had, and they were really tight.

"I saw them afterwards, and I was, like: 'Well done.' Because it's difficult to go from being in The Libertines, such an influential band. It was always going to be difficult for him to build himself up again, and that night I thought: he's built himself up, so well done to him."

For Adam, the interruption came as welcome relief – "a bit like when a fire alarm goes off in the middle of an exam" – and temporary refuge from the "blind, sheer fucking fright" that held him back during his early gigs: "I got on stage and realised that the drums were all at the wrong heights and too far or too close. It was just very hard work playing that set-up; I kept hitting my legs and fingers and thinking: just one more song.

"I was in agony, so when the fight broke out I was quite relieved. I'm not really sure why it happened – something to do with Peter asking Pat to hit him or thereabouts. I put it down to too many chemicals, coupled with pressure of performance."

Peter's ongoing curfew restrictions meant that shows at London's 100 Club on the 26th, and on the 27th in Stoke, were restricted to matinees, his drug rehabilitation treatment taking its toll.

Drew, Patrick and Adam wanted to keep him on track and out of trouble, but the recording of *Down In Albion* provided ample opportunity to fall into bad habits again.

Not that Peter was the only one who would suffer in a predominantly traumatic period that somehow managed to encompass moments of warmth and laughter; though these would prove to be few and far between. A potent fusion of bereavement, bizarre behaviour and outright chaos saw to it that the weeks to follow threw a mountain of obstacles onto an already congested path.

A great album was waiting to be made, but the huge reserves of persistence and patience required to fulfil Mick Jones' vision for the record were such that it nearly proved beyond those involved in its production.

Wales, and, later, an intrigued public, awaited.

4

Misadventures in Wales

The month of March opened on a tragic note, the loss of Adam's mother marring his richly deserved elevation from White Sport to Babyshambles. The support slot with The Streets, slated for 11th March, was axed as a mark of respect, Peter putting on a solo show at Alexandra Palace instead, so as not to disappoint fans.

A week later, still reeling from his bereavement, Adam had been set to join his bandmates for performances at London's Boogaloo and Koko venues, but with Peter losing his voice, the shows were put on ice.

A couple of days later, with his power of speech restored, the Rhythm Factory staged a gig that sold out in minutes. A couple of days after that, the boys left for Wales, the idea being that, cut off from the outside world, they would be free to record their first, eagerly awaited album in peace and tranquillity.

Peace and tranquillity, however, would be off limits, the band and their entourage bringing with them a unique brand of mayhem never seen before in the wilderness of Brecon Beacons National Park, South Wales, sandwiched between two reservoirs and enveloped by trees and waterfalls, the region's tallest mountains off to the north.

Setting off in the early hours of March the 21st, the ordering, delivery and consumption of Class As were responsible for delaying a departure originally intended for the day before. The travelling party eventually hit the road at about two in the morning, washing up in a Holiday Inn near Caerphilly after being turned away from a number of full hotels, trashing a room in the three hours or so that they were there.

When they eventually made it to Twin Peaks, James was comatose in the back of the van, to the dismay of Twin Peaks studio owners Adele Nozedar and Adam Fuest, who had signed legal documents consenting that Peter could use their premises as a bail address for the duration of the recording as part of conditions under which he was allowed to leave London.

A respectful couple with a palate for organic, vegan cuisine, they were about as far removed as you could get from the irreverent excess exhibited by Peter and James in particular during the coming weeks. Indeed, the latter wasted no time in rubbing them up the wrong way, delivering a foul-mouthed tirade of such intensity that he was very nearly banished from their grounds immediately.

It was an inauspicious start, and as Adam put it: "They didn't know what the fuck they'd let themselves in for. I felt quite sorry for them."

Peter —   "She came in halfway from making a cup of tea and he thought that she was the cook or something… and she said: 'Right, that man is not welcome at this studio anymore.' And it was, like: 'Well, hang on, he's our manager. What do you mean: he's not welcome? He's not welcome, he's rude – tell him to fuck off.' James completely denied that this had happened… and so there was a lot of confusion."

Drew —   "James, when I first met him, was a very passive, intelligent, articulate, gentle man, and over the next few years he morphed into Raging Jim. He was almost, in our minds, this kind of cartoon character… He had rage problems, he had problems with his temper, and he didn't really hide it. He'd become indignant and angry very easily and start smashing things up and yelling. And I guess you kind of just get used to it. But Adele wasn't having that at all."

Adam —   "I don't really know what was said, but after our arrival Adele seemed very upset at the thought of James being anywhere near the band, so the whole thing got off to a very shaky start."

The next morning, Adele and Adam Fuest were woken by the paparazzi who had assembled at the entrance to their property and in the woods, Adele writing in her diary: "One guy is in a hired mini-campervan with a standing frame on the top, and is in full camo gear and has a digital Nikon with a colossal telephoto lens. I ask him what he's up to. 'I'm a bird watcher.'

"I explain to Peter that unless he's going to start smoking crack amongst the flower beds, the worst they can get would be a picture of him having a cuppa, sitting on a bench. However, the notion of 'outside' is anathema and, accordingly, curtains are put up in the bathroom window. Later, a pic of Peter on the balcony, holding a toothbrush, will make the redtops."

Rough Trade supplied a minder to effect close scrutiny of Peter, this unlikely pairing placed in rooms opposite one another, above the studio, with producer Mick Jones and engineer Bill Price joining up later, returning to London at the weekends.

As Adam explains: "The minder's room was meticulous, everything in its place to the finest detail, and on the other side was Peter's – imagine a bomb had gone off in the middle of a well-trodden squat. The owners subsequently took up the carpet and had to burn it."

Peter –   "My heart was suffocated, anyway, by what had gone on – for the love, like, with that particular girl. To Kate. It brought so many sweet and wonderful and cherished events and memories, and rendezvous' and jaunts and japes and dancing and singing and just, you know, pure love in some ways. But with it, too, came this world that I knew existed, 'cos I saw it everyday on the newsstand in red and white and those words on the *Mirror* and *Sun* and the *Star*. I knew it existed and that, but it never really affected me.

"Occasionally there would be something like, you know: 'Drug Addict Has Punch-Up With Fish', or something, you know? But it wasn't on a daily intrusion. No one really gave a toss. And it was, like, you open the door and there's thirty or forty blokes there going 'click click' etcetera etcetera… So, I dunno, it felt like I'd sold myself to the devil in exchange for true love; I was gonna have to deal with this wicked world. And then the first thing that happened was, I ended up on this ridiculous court order where I was given the choice between jail or having a twenty-four-hour security team.

"Now, some people might say that was fair, given that I have, like, committed violent crime, but I was on a charge of robbery and blackmail, I was on a curfew, I was… awaiting trial. It was quite a precarious, very volatile scenario. But the fact is that money was coming out of my own pocket as well, you know? So I was very resentful and very angry, and they were getting more and more involved in my everyday personal life. And at that time I was quite a happy young man: I was in a band I loved and believed in, I was with a girl I loved and believed in. And they were, like, just intruding. They were, like, taking my drug dealers aside and just, you know, explaining in no uncertain terms that: 'You sell any more drugs to this lad and we'll put you in a fucking wooden box, you little cunt.' And it wasn't on, you know what I mean? As it happened the little cunt got his own back…

"It wasn't on. They were getting too involved, they were there too much…I remember the bigger one kept saying to me: 'You're wasting it, you're throwing it away. You owe it to England, you owe it to the kids of England. Just clean-up, sort yourself out.' And I said: 'Hold on a minute, you're breaking my heart here and… you're a hired goon.'"

Four days in, Adele reported the first in a lengthy list of damages – "headphones literally crunched underfoot" – and, by the next, threats to expel James from their land were cemented, their already fraught relations exacerbated further when he showed up with drugs for, among others, Patrick, whose withdrawl syptoms were so severe that he offered one of the minders a couple of grand to knock him out and spare any additional pain.

Adam Fuest met James at the gate, hauling him out of his car and spreadeagling him on the bonnet, checking his pockets, Adele writing: "When it became very quickly apparent that Mullord was not so much a manager as a … and after he told me to 'fuck off' and that he wasn't going to pay the bills, I decided life was too short; and that, even if anyone ELSE seemed to be terrified of him, I wasn't!"

Afforded an ill-deserved stay of execution in the studio with an associate until the following morning, James' aggression remained undimmed, however: when

Adele went to wake him up and move the pair on, he told her that he had no intention of contributing anything whatsoever towards the band's stay.

He also barked out another expletive at her, and issued threats alluding to threats of imminent death at the hands of some unfavourable characters hailing from Ballymena, an area with a reputation for hard men and hard drugs.

Later Peter tried to persuade Adele to reverse her decision, reasoning: "You don't know what he's like. I know he was rude to you, but he can't remember it and he's sorry. He's rational now. We have a bond. We are brothers, and he's going to kill me if you don't let him in. He brought drugs, but he threw them all in the river – that's how sorry he is."

Adele and Adam Fuest were, though, unshakable in their resolve to try and ensure that their time with the band was as trouble-free as possible. James' warning, meanwhile, was enough to persuade Rough Trade to fork out for another security guard, in the wake of a request by Twin Peaks, Adele now fearing a violent invasion of her property by gun-toting, drug-crazed gangsters ready to bring about their demise.

Not that they'd have got very far, faced with what would soon become a phalanx of seasoned war vets who charged about with camo on their faces, binoculars and night vision-enabling apparatus in one hand and a baton in the other, while possessing an encyclopaedic knowledge of pressure points.

Drew — "She [Adele] had made a decision to move to some really remote part of Wales called Brecon Beacons, buy a house, do it up, and get back to kind of basic, simple values, and she was really spiritual about everything and stuff, so a bunch of gibbering crackheads turning up, flanked by ex-military security guards, was a bit of a shock to her…

"We had these security guards with us who were complete meathooks. Solid brawn from the neck up. They just didn't make us feel comfortable. It was an awkward time, because… no-one would like to have a curfew and have squaddies following you around, making sure that you don't do something wrong or whatever, and things were getting really dark with Patrick… His [Peter's] very philosophy is based around freedom and liberty, so for him to have meatheads monitoring his every move – yeah, it was very suffocating for him."

Matt Bates — "The guy who was in charge, any time he shook my hand I couldn't grip a pen for about two days afterwards. I've never met a guy so over-aggressive in my life. He kind of meant well, but… I remember introducing him to a girl once, and the girl goes: 'Oh my God, I can't feel my fingers!' No matter who it was, he'd crush your hand. Any gig you went to they'd be there, flanking him [Peter] either side, arms around him as he's leaving the building; that's not what Babyshambles are about – it's a band for the people. The kids can get close to Pete – that's why he's so loved.

"People have been to his flat, people have been on the tour bus, people have been to the dressing room. He lets anyone into his life. Sometimes for the worse, if stories get out, but on the whole for the better – and that's why people love him. And they [security] weren't letting any of that happen."

Patrick —   "We were messy and we were disorganised, and it was chaotic – Peter was being outrageously badly behaved at the time; paparazzi everywhere, bail conditions. Reports of James Mullord hanging out with gangsters – nonsense; Rough Trade was trying to drive a wedge between us and Mullord, 'cos they didn't like Mullord."

Rare interludes in what was, for the most part, an extremely dark period, included the purchasing of Wellington boots, to assist the boys' growing appreciation of the great outdoors.

To help them embrace the elements further, Adele booked a boat ride along the Brecon and Monmouth Canal, though their reputation for wreaking havoc dissuaded a new arrival from joining them. In her diary, Adele wrote: "One of the security guards' girlfriend arrives. They only met a fortnight ago and, to be honest, it's not the sort of date I'd invite anyone on, especially a nice girl who works for a recruitment agency in Southampton, whose only experience of crack is something that happens to the china occasionally. I don't hold out much hope for the sound of wedding bells.

"I do ask her on the Saturday if she's going to join the boat trip, but she gives me a look which says, 'they're a bunch of fucking imbeciles, what do you think?', and departs shortly after...

"Most of the band have a massive dinner at The Travellers after the boat trip, which was a big success, apparently. It was a shame the paparazzi weren't there to see that one: all of them in their brand new wellies, still with the price tags on, and Peter in a souvenir captain's hat."

Postponing the arrival of a professor due to carry out an experiment into the vibrational frequencies of trees, on the basis that, as Adele put it: "the random nature of the 'moods' people might be in could preclude any conclusive results", the feel-good factor rapidly disintegrated.

The swelling team of security – three of whom were given the monikers Big Ox, Little Ox and Goldilox – added to the tension, sleeping in shifts to maintain their round-the-clock surveillance. Understandably, the Babyshambles camp were less than impressed with the security arrangements – especially Peter, who took advantage of what Adele called "an inexplicable lapse for a close surveillance and security expert" to pilfer some of Big Ox's belongings when he left the car boot open.

Slipping his unwanted observer's underpants and bulletproof vest on, and screaming about a snake being in the boot, an alternative energy expert, who had arrived unexpectedly and witnessed the unfolding scene, was "looking, but pretending not to look, at Peter, whose method of walking is getting to be a little on the John Cleese side… and his big pants are sliding down", remembers Adele.

Adam and Drew were left frustrated in their efforts to get on with making the album, jamming together while waiting for their bandmates to recover some level of lucidity, amid scenes of prolific drug-taking; and in their desire to structure the recording process in such a way that it included a profusion of takes, enabling them to layer tracks more efficiently, making for a tighter, sleeker finish.

Mick favoured live takes – a far riskier strategy with a gaggle of musicians who struggled to consistently hit top form, hampered by scant rehearsal time and recording sessions typically conducted in the wee hours, by which time sobriety had become a distant memory.

And with the apparently simple task of convening the four-piece proving troublesome in itself, Adam and Drew increasingly found themselves listening to stories regaled by the security guards. To add to the confusion, Alan Wass turned up wearing a cowboy hat and no shirt, despite the sub-zero temperatures, promising to sort things out and staying on for several days.

Adam — "It was a frustrating time, recording in Wales. At times it felt like it was only me and Drew holding the whole process together, and I'd only been in the band five minutes. There was a lot of drug consumption going on, people in and out of the studio – it was fucking frustrating, 'cos I'm the sort of person who just wants to get the job done and done really well. And we've got the opportunity to make a really good album, and it frustrated me how that was just slipping.

"Me and Drew were trying to hold it together, and everyone else just wasn't as focused as us. And it's really frustrating when you're not working from the same page. Me, I'd just got in the band, and wanted to make a really good go of it – not just learning the songs, but putting something really good together, and it seemed to get harder and harder and harder. Towards the end we were scraping stuff together, trying to build an album from what we had. It shouldn't be like that. It should be: 'This isn't good enough, let's do it again', but it turned into an uphill struggle."

Tony
Linkin — "Everything was out of control – not in a nice way, in a scary way… It [*Down In Albion*] cost a lot of money to make, but it should have been really easy: the songs were all there."

Drew — "It was a dark cloud hanging over us the whole time. The sun never seemed to come out – it was perpetually twilight, grey mist everywhere – and there was no phone signal. You'd wake up in the morning, and one of the security would be out there with these binoculars looking for snipers.

"This feeling of just being in this place, and all the barriers around you kind of looming in on you, and this really kind of barren, sort of rustic terrain. Not much seemed to go grow there – a few shrubs here and, like, patches of forest – and you'd go for a walk and you'd hear the snap of a twig, and you'd expect to see paps running away in camo gear. We were in a valley, and anywhere you looked there was any number of vantage points they could photograph from, so you felt really claustrophobic."

Peter –   "I don't think it [*Down In Albion*] was a statement of that time. Not at all. On the whole, it was quite an upbeat affair, I think. Where we were at that time, we were trying to come down from somewhere. From some precipice. They say classical music is the worst music to drive to, because it relaxes you and it makes you unprepared for needing quick reactions. Kinda like a car coming round a bend real quickly, you gotta be on your toes to be able to miss it, you know? You got heavy metal blaring out, you're gonna swerve and you're gonna miss it. You're not gonna be monged-out, listening to something mellow.

"We needed to come down; we needed to really fucking come down. I was desperate just to make a *Harvest*. To make a *Harvest*, to make something a bit like… the Stone Roses record, the first one… "Fuck Forever", "Pipe Down" – songs like that. Real fucking, fuck off, get yourself on the dance floor, put another dime in the jukebox – like the good time rock 'n' roll. I wanted to strip it down and… sing a lot of angry songs, a lot of fucked-up, angry songs, like "Eight Dead Boys". [Sings:] 'When it suits you, you're a friend of mine!' You know? Those were venomous lyrics… but, as I said at the time, I was in love. I didn't really feel that much venom a lot of the time. I felt quite loved-up. I wanted people to come together and make love, you know? Not fight."

What Drew described as the "light and shade of the group dynamic" was affected by the possibility of Peter returning to jail, and he felt that James could have adopted a more responsible attitude in his role as manager: "I don't want to say too much bad stuff about James, but one thing I will say is: that album came out despite – not thanks – to James' efforts.

"At first James was great, and he was in it for the right reasons, and I'm sure, in his heart, he was in it for the right reasons to the end, but his behavioural patterns were more of a hindrance. And it handicapped the process: a manager's supposed to help you get where you're going, not obstruct you from getting where you're going."

In a diary entry for 5th April, Adele recorded how she and Adam Fuest were woken by "crashings and bangings" that came courtesy of Peter, Patrick and Alan. "They have done their best to wreck the studio", she wrote. "And were about to start on each other when two of the security guards came to organise the fighting saying:

'An Englishman's not an Englishman till he's had his brew, so you lot better wait otherwise we'll knock seven shades of shit out of the lot of you.' They then sat down, drinking tea, taking bets on who was going to hit who first. They then directed the rest of the fight outside and started to clear up the broken glass etcetera."

The weekends were particularly trying. Mick Jones would return home, dramatically increasing the chances of Peter and Patrick absconding, though there was no set agenda for further disorder, random moments of mayhem a regular feature in Wales as anywhere else.

Another early wake-up call, courtesy of Peter, who wanted to mess about in the studio, further antagonised relations between the band and Twin Peaks, as did his decision to pursue a howling James into the woods one evening.

Banned from the grounds, James had driven up from London and disappeared into the surrounding forestry, the skills he'd learnt in the army demonstrated to good effect when camping out and building fires. Roaming the woods in a dressing gown, he could be heard projecting wolf-like cries, a similarly-attired Peter pursuing him in a stupor, spaced-out on sleeping pills, sending cries out of his own. And with security on their tail, aided by night goggles, the commotion woke the studio's owners, Adele and Adam, from what had by now become scarce slumber.

Adam — "Peter would love to wind up Adam Fuest by saying: 'You go to bed, I'll just stay down here and have a little play.' Obviously, Adam was becoming more and more anxious about his recording equipment and studio.

"I'm not really sure exactly what happened [with James], but from what I gathered, he'd arrived and set about trying to communicate with Peter. James felt that the security were there not only to keep Peter from leaving, but to push him out of his managerial position, instigated by Rough Trade.

"So it ended up with Peter wandering around the surrounding woods in a dressing gown following the wolf cries made by James. I've subsequently found out that Wolfman was also there with James. So we ended up having security following Peter. Following Wolfman. Following James. I'm glad I was in another cottage."

Patrick — "He felt heartbroken he couldn't see us. But he wasn't fit to be our manager at that time; he was ill. He is fit to be a band manager, he's got the skills and the brainpower."

Drew — "It's like *Lord of the Flies*! You can imagine him, starting fires and hooting manically to himself. And there's Mick Jones trying to make a record in the middle of all this,

---

Next page: Peter at a press shoot for Get Loaded in Turnmill's basement.

and me just sat there going: 'Right, I'm gonna have a cup of tea, this is all getting a bit weird.'"

Soon enough, the band would join James in leaving Twin Peaks, a couple of incidents persuading the owners that it was time for them to move on.

In the first instance, Peter's frustrations received another airing, when, enraged at the security guards' continued presence – despite a court order ruling that their shadowing of him was no longer a condition of bail – he drove off into the night, his unfamiliarity with the surrounding terrain soon becoming evident.

On the way back to Wales from Peter's London hearing, after a pleasant afternoon getting pissed in London, in celebration of his not having to go back to jail, a mobile phone call informed Drew that security were, in fact, awaiting their arrival the other end.

The news provoked dismay – especially so for Peter, who refused to believe it, until seeing the burly lot for himself in the Twin Peaks studio, by which stage he'd whipped himself into a veritable frenzy, the journey from the capital spent getting increasingly hammered.

Storming back out of the studio, he insisted on driving immediately back to London, pleas for reason ignored as he seized control of a seven-seater off-roader, before speeding off into the darkness and before very long finding himself in a ditch – which, as it turned out, was a far more comfortable alternative than the fate he would have met had he careered off in the opposite direction.

Drew —

"Peter went into the studio, and I sat in the front seat, and I said to our technician, Mike: 'When Peter gets back, do not get out of the driving seat, no matter what he says.' He's, like: 'Alright, course.' I said, 'He's fucked, he's not going to be able to drive, and he's going to go in and see security there, and he's going to come back and he's going to demand that you drive him to London. And when you refuse, he's going to tell you to get out of the car, so he can drive.' He said: 'Right.'

"Right fucking on cue, Peter comes back in a rage, demands that Mike drives him back to London, and Mike refuses. And he goes: 'Well get out!' Mike jumps out of the car, everyone else jumps out of the car, and I opened the door and put my foot out, so he wouldn't drive off. I was, like: 'Don't go, mate.' He said: 'Don't get out of the car, you're coming with me. Don't let me go on my own. Stay.' I was trying to say to Peter: 'Mate, come on: get out of the car. You're too fucked. You're not going to drive back to London.'

"And then he just started screaming: 'In or out! In or out! In or out!' And I'm still [going]: 'Get out of the car, mate.' He goes: 'Fuck you, then!' Slams the car in reverse – I'm halfway out of the car, hopping on one foot, backwards, as the car accelerates – and the car's going towards a wall, and the door's open, so I'm about to get squashed between the wall and the door of the car, and managed to jump out in time, slam the door shut before it hit the wall, and he reverses off up this driveway that heads down to the studio.

"And on one side of the driveway is a lake, and on the other side is this steep cliff, and he kind of careered off backwards until we couldn't see the car anymore, and we heard the sound of him doing a kind of dramatic sort of handbrake turn, to kind of turn the car the right way round. And we just heard a big noise, but fortunately he'd turned the car so he went into a ditch.

"And so I'm walking up, kind of dreading what I'm going to see, and the car was face down in the ditch, and he's revving like a maniac. The wheels are spinning, but the car's not going anywhere. And I walked down to the car and looked in the window, and he looked up at me with this stupid little grin, just shrugged, and started singing a song and went [intimates smoking a pipe]: 'Pipey McGraw'."

Attempts to push the vehicle back out proved fruitless, so it remained where it was, forgotten about until the next morning, when Adam Fuest made his latest unsavoury discovery during the band's tenure, arranging for it to be towed away.

The straw that broke the camel's back, the numerous threats to kick the band out materialised, and they were told to pack their stuff and leave the following day. Allowed to stay in a guests' cottage overnight, an already costly album ran up an even larger slate when Peter, inebriated, and frustrated by the restrictions placed upon him, smashed the property up. Adam, who had seen enough carnage for one day, consequently bagged a cottage all to himself "and wedged a chair under the doorknob in true horror-movie style", wrote Adele.

Drew —   "They were, like: 'That's it, he's almost driven a car into a lake. You can go and stay in the guest cottage, but you're gonna have to sling your hook tomorrow.'

"The drugs just drive some people crazy, the drugs and sleep deprivation. You take the most sane person, keep them awake for four days and give them crack, and they're gonna smash things up… It's what happens – you lose your mind."

Adam —   "I knew it was gonna kick-off. In the car he was getting more and more anxious – I think he'd been doing a lot of sherbet.

"So we get there and he walks round the cottage angrily, saying how he feels trapped by security and Rough Trade, while systematically smashing every picture, mirror and ornament in the place. I honestly thought it was going to end in a brawl.

"The whole thing was mayhem. I spent most of my energy applying diplomacy between James, Peter and everyone else. James was extremely angry at that time, making threats and generally getting very paranoid."

Adele thought that Peter had by this stage "crossed the line between playful destruction to violence and dangerous behaviour", with "nothing to stop the insanity being contained within the environs of the studio. We are told that Peter was apparently launching himself at the windows, trying to smash them. He smashed a mirror and some furniture, then fell into a fitful sleep."

But before leaving, Peter expressed the warmth so frequently pummelled into submission by his mushrooming drugs ingestion, finding Adele, giving her a big hug, and saying: "Thank you for having us."

Peter –   "I've got some real fond memories of that time… Getting up in the morning and strolling down by the little brook, an actual bubbling brook, believe it or not… Everyone was amazed by how hospitable they were to us – despite the fact that we were a bit of a rag-tag bunch. And, you know, quite rightly so, we were not really trusted by anyone at that time to be left to a recording studio… and they did. They trusted us."

Despite regretting the inconvenience their hosts had sustained, everybody in the Babyshambles camp agreed that, having outstayed their welcome, London was where they needed to be – especially now that the charges of robbery and blackmail had been dropped against Peter, who was hankering for a return to the capital.

The decision to plump for Wales had been an unwise one, questioning the wisdom of putting the boys in a studio so remote and with a reputation for clean, healthy, organic living – the polar opposite of the tumult and disarray embroiling Babyshambles at the time.

Brecon Beacons had, nonetheless, garnered the nucleus of *Down In Albion*, while providing the setting for a deal struck to produce *Who The F**k Is Pete Doherty?*, a documentary by film-maker Roger Pomphrey, director of *The Jimi Hendrix Experience: Electric Ladyland* – considered one of the finest documentaries ever made about the musical genius.

A former guitarist with The Eurythmics who has recorded with Terence Trent D'Arby, now known as Sananda Maitreya, and UB40, and played with, among others, Mick Jagger, Bono and The Edge, Joe Strummer, Suggs and Chrissie Hynde, Roger was no stranger to the world of narcotics, the destruction it wreaks and the way it more readily suffocates creativity than encourages it. So for him, the prospect of working with the band held no fear; if anything, he was more accustomed to the chaotic, unrestrained extremes of libertarian life than those artists operating in a less volatile, more tempered environment.

In the wake of the Max Carlish fiasco, James and Peter were keen to see an intelligent documentary made that would showcase Peter's talents and counter any misrepresentations of his person.

Contact was made as far back as August 2004 – nearly six months before the tabloid explosion sparked by Peter and Kate's relationship – through Paul Roundhill, a mutual friend of Peter and Roger, and another who was anxious that Peter be seen in his true light.

Roger, who at the time was living in Bristol, received an invitation to join the band in the city on the 25th. Babyshambles had been offered a last-minute slot at Filton Polytechnic's Freshers' Ball, where they would compete with, among other attractions, fairground rides for revellers' attention, and so Roger drove to meet them.

It was important that everybody felt comfortable in each other's presence and that any filming be conducted in a climate of outright trust – a firm tenet of Roger's methodology.

It soon became clear that he was the right man for the job. At the Bristol gig, he joined the band onstage for a rendition of "Wolfman", after spending several hours on the tour bus, getting to know the boys and participating in the kind of party that featured heavily at the time.

A decision was taken to try and get the prospective film funded. Roger proposed that the best way of going about it would be for him to hit the road with the band for a couple of days to gather footage – a suggestion that met with everyone's approval – and so he travelled to Stoke for a couple of gigs at The Underground on 4th October, and to Shrewsbury for the following night's gig at the Music Hall, recording up to fifteen hours' intimate footage.

Roger Pomphrey — "It was actually those two shows [at The Underground] that really confirmed that I wanted to get involved, because there was a kind of audience involvement and a kind of excited mayhem, the like of which I haven't seen really since possibly even the punk era. It wasn't just the stage invasion, it was the frenzy into which the Babyshambles whipped the audience up. I hadn't seen Oasis do that, and I hadn't seen a lot of other bands do that.

"It was just a sort of feverish pitch that the band were capable of taking the audience to – they took them to a place of genuine excitement, and it was that excitement, along with my intrigue with Doherty, that confirmed to me that I did want to get involved and make a film about him and them, because it was pretty unusual; it was definitely unusual."

It was time to head back to London.

The band had a record to finish, and spring would soon cede to summer, heralding another festival season in which Babyshambles would play a large, if controversial, part.

5

Festival Season

Adam —   "There was a point after Twin Peaks when I actually thought the album wouldn't get made. It was just so touch and go – total mayhem – then somehow we managed to get into Doghouse."

Free from round-the-clock observation, some feared that Peter would quickly readopt bad habits to the detriment of the as yet unfinished album. Such concerns, though understandable, were in this instance largely unfounded, and the recording process continued at the Doghouse, Henley-on-Thames in May 2005, with Peter revelling in being spared the presence of security guards who had stuck to him like a second skin.

Set in the serene countryside, on the banks of the River Thames, the Doghouse provided a much calmer environment in which to knock the album into shape, owing primarily to its proximity to London.

Technician Bill Price was too busy with other engagements to commit any more time to the project, so Iain Gore was hired to bring the recording of *Down In Albion* to a belated conclusion at the Doghouse and, in August, at Metropolis Studios, Chiswick.

Iain
Gore —   "Everything was turned up to ten in the control room. From an engineer's point of view it was really hard work, because it was up so loud just trying to hear what was going to tape, and then you've got Pete rolling around on the floor, doing vocal takes, knocking chairs over. That was always quite amusing. And he liked to try and operate the computer as well sometimes. If I left the room to go for a piss he'd go back to the computer and stop recording, and he'd be stood over the computer looking round."

Comparing the process to working in "some kind of a soap opera", the weeks Iain spent on the album flashed by in a haze, each day peppered with folly, including Peter's threats to neck a potent solvent capable of inflicting serious damage: "There was this one point where he did try to drink the Isopropyl alcohol, which is used for cleaning tape machine heads. It's, like, ninety-eight, ninety-nine per cent proof alcohol, if not more, so that had to be removed from the studio. It can make you go blind if you drink it. Whether he would have drunk it or not, if we'd have let him follow through with it… he probably would have actually. I think he would have."

And while the daily shenanigans occasionally tested his patience, Iain considers the atmosphere more positive than that generated in the recording of the second

Libertines album, when Peter had been "really withdrawn from people", explaining: "It was definitely a different recording process to that second Libertines session; it just felt that he was more involved in making the record... I think the whole process of *Down In Albion* was just a freer spirit... it was just allowed to develop into its own record.

"I learnt so much from Mick Jones and the way he approaches production. It's always a creative environment; there's never any pressure to do anything – not for the band anyway...

"It might not be a conventional or a modern production, or how people would want to do a production, but Mick always knew what the band were doing. He knew what he was doing – it wasn't like he just hit a recorder and said: 'Go'... He'd listen to the record a lot, he'd take the mixes home and he'd be up most of the night, listening to stuff and working it out in his head.

"Quite a lot of this album was kind of coming together in the recording stage as well... It wasn't like some bands that go in extensive rehearsal and get their set together and go: 'Right, we're going to do this track...'; they were still playing stuff and rehearsing it as the album went on.

"Mick would always do nice little things – like at the start of "Up The Morning", we recorded them boiling a kettle and making a cup of tea. Mick would always visualise sort of around the song and the context of the lyrics, and always saw Pete's records as a story from start to finish about what was happening in his life, and the running order does follow that.

"It's like at the end of "Merry Go Round" as well: I don't know if you can hear Pete actually fall over in the studio. If you listen right up to the end... apparently he was walking round the studio, playing his guitar, so you kind of hear him come off mic as it gets more roomy, and then there's this noise as he falls over...

"I can't even remember which track it is, but Pete's singing slightly out of tune, and in a modern environment, where someone might autotune it or doctor it somehow, Mick actually put in really low BVs [backing vocals], but in tune, and it kind of gave the effect of the vocal being in tune or gave it more tuning. He used to do things like that."

Adam —   "That cup of tea [in "Up The Morning"] caused so much bother. For some reason we couldn't get a tea pot, so I suggested we just use a kettle and make coffee. Mick was having none of it – it had to be tea."

Sandwiched between the album sessions were a pot-pourri of gigs, including one at the University of London Union, for Carling Live 24 on 30th April, at which a fire alarm was set off – allegedly by the event's security, to clear the venue – after a bodyguard stopped fans getting on stage.

Patrick —
"We all got evacuated, and the guy's grabbed Doherty, and I go: 'Don't grab him and pull him like that!' And he goes: 'Fuck off!', and pushed me. Pete says: 'You don't wanna be doing that, mate, he's my songwriter, band partner.'

"So we all got bundled into the car, and I said to him: 'You're a cunt!' And he said: 'What?' I said: 'You're a fucking cunt!' He said: 'Get out of the car and say it to me!' And because I was so out of my nut – this guy could have crushed me in a second, d'you know what I mean? I was skinny then – I said: 'You're a fucking cunt!' and walked right straight up to him, and he didn't do anything. I don't know why. Maybe it's because I looked so mad, I dunno."

Subsequent performances at London's KoKo on the 29th, and at Dublin's Trinity Ball, Ambassador Theatre and Mandela Hall, on the 13th, 14th and 15th May respectively, passed without major incident; as did the Joiners gig in Southampton on the 27th, before the Homelands Festival, Winchester, the following night.

The pairing of Babyshambles and Homelands seemed an odd one, given the festival's traditional dance following. "Homelands was always going to be odd, but in the end they kept pushing our time further and further back. We ended up only playing for about twenty minutes, then smashed the stage up", says Adam.

Peter requested an early slot at Homelands, giving him enough time to make it to Scotland for the Burns An' A' That poetry festival later that night, in honour of celebrated bard Robert Burns, though not before *NME* journalist Tim Jonze had been threatened with being thrown out of a car whose driver was pegging it down the motorway in order that the flight from the airport be made in time.

Unable to record the interview he needed prior to Homelands, owing to the band's tardiness, Tim joined Peter and James on the drive to the airport.

As far as Drew is aware, Peter's insistence on smoking a pipe lay behind what could have turned out to be another catastrophe: "James turned around and said: 'You can't do that, mate!' And he's, like: 'Why the fuck not?' And he's, like: 'You can't do it in front of Tim, he's an *NME* journalist!' He's, like: 'Alright, well we'll kick him out then!', and he opened the door and went to push him out, but he didn't actually push him out.

"I think he was probably just trying to make some kind of point, as in: 'I'm gonna smoke this anyway, and if that's the reason why I can't then…' Extreme Peter, twisted logic, but he didn't actually throw him out. I think young Tim might have died if he'd been thrown out of a car at 120 miles-per-hour down the motorway."

Tim Jonze —
"We'd spent two full days trying to get Pete Doherty to sit down for half an hour for an *NME* cover story. That's two days of hanging around in hotel lobbies, playing Playstation with the rest of Babyshambles and, er, well, there's not all that much to do in Southampton.

"Now we were at Homelands Festival, watching Dior designer Hedi Slimane run around trying to offload his latest collection of skinny suits onto Pete (who thanked him by putting them in his bag, which kept flapping open and dropping its contents in the mud). Anyway, Pete had to get a flight up to Scotland in a few hours for a Burns Night poetry reading, so we ended up agreeing to do the interview in the taxi to Heathrow.

"Me and Pete didn't exactly hit it off. I don't think he likes journalists who aren't obsessed with his visions of Arcadia and don't want to spend the entire interview time blowing smoke up his arse. But you know what? I was kind of in awe of the chaotic, drug-fogged way he lived his life. Watching him stumble around Homelands with his bag spilling valuable possessions (lyric sheets, trinkets, books) and lumps of crack across the site… well, it wasn't like this hanging out with Editors.

"So anyway, we all got in the taxi and headed to Heathrow. It was pretty surreal. At one point we pulled into a garage and Pete played me a preview of the first album.

"We managed to get something resembling an interview done. Reading it back, it's pretty funny in print – Pete claimed he'd smoked tampons and mumbled about hypnotising giraffes. But in reality our 'chat' was all over the place because Pete kept falling asleep, muttering nonsense to himself and getting in a strop. After an hour of this, I was getting pretty bored, truth be told.

"Then chaos broke out. The most ludicrously childish whinge-fest between James and Pete started up. Our driver missed the turning for the airport and we started swerving all over the road. Everyone started yelling at each other. Pete kept saying he was getting out the car, opening the door and pretending to climb out. Me? I just sat there staring out the window whilst my teeth went numb from the crack fumes.

"God knows how we didn't crash. God knows how we made it to Heathrow in time for Pete's flight. And God knows how Pete and James made it onto their flights, seeing as their bags seemed to be littered with crack and heroin.

"I went home to write up the piece – the taxi-ride bit is still probably the most entertaining thing I ever wrote for *NME*. Looking back now, I don't remember sitting in the taxi bored out of my brain as Pete wandered in and out of consciousness. I remember chaos and crack fumes and Pete asking James if he could ditch me on the hard shoulder of the M25. I still don't know if he was joking."

Once at the festival itself, Peter gave readings of his own work, but with his audience more interested in his skills with an acoustic, he duly obliged, belting out a number of crowd pleasers, among them "Can't Stand Me Now".

Matt Bates realised that night just what Peter means to his followers, likening him to another outsider who polarised opinion, Kurt Cobain, for the manner in which he inspired such a deep level of loyalty, often obsessive, in his devotees: "He read this poetry, played some songs, and it became apparent to me then just how much he was hero-worshipped, and the people obviously love him. Really, really love him, really worship him."

Peter —   "It was an honour, and we did ol' Burns himself proud with a real old school debauch that night in town. Lucky to leave Scotland alive the next day."

June was a month of busy festival activity that took in the Isle of Wight on the 11th, Glastonbury on the 24th and 25th, and the Wireless in Hyde Park on the 30th.

It was at the Isle of Wight Festival that Matt Bates grasped how much Peter's life had changed in the time that they'd known each other: "I remember having to go out in a car to meet Pete and Kate in a farmer's field, because they came by helicopter, rather than bus like the rest of us – that's when I realised things were changing. It was no longer about doing it in the back of a green transit van; Pete now gets a helicopter to a gig. A year ago we were literally driving around in a green transit van, and now he just gets a helicopter!"

He also recalls the criticism directed at the band at Glastonbury, at a time of heightening opposition to Peter and his Babyshambles cohorts: "I think everyone had got to the point where they wanted to knock Babyshambles down. I mean, they got to the point that whatever they did, it wasn't good enough."

The two Glastonbury shows – the band played the Other stage on the 24th, and the Leftfield Stage the day after, when headlining Love Music Hate Racism day – showed that, despite the largely negative press Babyshambles were garnering, they were still considered worthy of the risk of a no-show.

With the band's sets over, Adam and his girlfriend started making their way back to London, leaving everyone else – save for Peter and Kate, who were staying in a caravan in the festival grounds – to follow them back to the capital in the tour bus. But with habits to feed, the tour bus took off without Drew and Sally, depriving them of their essentials.

Drew, incidentally, had opted to stay behind to watch recently reformed The La's play, though Sally would sooner have had the option of a ride back to London.

In the open in the early hours of the morning, Drew crashed out, pissed and a little stoned, with no shirt on, the ground his mattress for the night. When he came to some eleven hours later, just before The La's were due on, his typically Irish complexion, coupled with the sheer amount of time he'd been laying under a scorching sun, left him vulnerable to the worst of its rays – to the extent that he suffered third degree burns.

Opposite: At home with Babyshambles.

To this day, he bears the marks of nearly half a day lying in the sweltering heat, each of the freckles dotting his chest formerly a blister.

Drew —

"God bless Sally: she was like Florence Nightingale, man. She totally looked after me, got me the right ointments and what have you and looked after me for a week. She got me out of there as well. We got to the end of The La's set, and Tabitha from the Queens of Noize and her mate, they were wearing pyjamas, and they saw me like a fucking beetroot, with this sunburn, and they just thought this was the most hysterical thing in the world. Which, you know: 'Yeah yeah, it's very funny. Yes, I'm very sunburnt – yes, yes. Yes, I'm in an awful lot of pain – yes, that's funny, too.' And they just kept creasing up.

"It's quite funny now in hindsight. But I was, like: 'You know what? I can't deal with this.' And I was either gonna clump Tabitha's mate, who was a guy, or, like, cry or something. Plus I was incredibly hung over, and so Sally and I just went and got a taxi back home. It was horrible. Really bad sunburn is horrible."

Drew was forced to sport his unwanted radish-red hue when playing the Wireless date, which had been on the brink of being pulled due to Peter's dismal timekeeping, meaning that the band had to rush a shortened twenty-five minute set, amid threats of banning the ensemble for future events.

To exacerbate his discomfort, he had to face 40,000-odd people when trying to account for Peter's lateness, and absorb their aggression when the inevitable round of boos rang out. "People were waiting for us, they were booing, and then it started raining", Drew explains. "I can't remember how late it was – fifteen, twenty minutes late? – I get a call from Peter, and he's in the car and he's on his way, and he's going: 'Go and tell them I've been nicked! Go and tell them that I'm stuck in traffic! Tell them I can't find my shoes!', just trying to get me to go on stage in front of, I dunno, 40,000 booing people pissed off in the rain. And I did it. I went up on stage.

"I can't remember what I said – something equally stupid as Peter's fallen down the stairs, like that time on the bus. I said something about him being late, that he's on his way. I can't remember exactly what I said. And all of Hyde Park booed at me in unison, and I was, like: 'You motherfucker'."

Organisers might have wished they'd gone ahead with the threatened cancellation, an uninspiring display drawing criticism once Peter eventually made it on stage, assisted by The General, who became friends with Peter in Pentonville Prison, and who would later appear on "Pentonville", which features on *Down In Albion*.

Drew's frustration was such that, at the end of the set, he took his bass off, grabbed it by the neck, swung it around his head, and smashed it up on the stage, in two.

Drew — "I was the most unpopular guy in London for a day, and smashed my beloved bass in half because I was in such a rage. It takes a lot for me to lose my temper, but sometimes enough's enough… That was the first bass I ever bought, and it's the bass I still play now, but for a year I had to play other basses because I'd smashed this one in two. I eventually managed to get it fixed. But I remember that gig because all of Hyde Park booed at *me*!"

Adam — "Drew had been absent from the studio for a few days, which was a pain as we needed him for some vocals. His reason for this was sunburn. Yeah, yeah, I thought. When I saw him at Wireless I couldn't believe it: the poor fucker was boiled… Wireless was a nightmare. General was only meant to come on for one song, but stayed the whole set, freestyling over everything. I felt a bit sorry for him… he didn't know where to turn."

Away from Babyshambles, Peter met more controversy on 2nd July 2005 at Live8. The event – organised by Bob Geldof to try and persuade world leaders to cancel the poorest nations' debt, increase the aid they received and improve fair trade rules – marked the 20th anniversary of Live Aid and preceded the G8 Conference and Summit, Gleaneagles Hotel, Auchterarder, Scotland, held between the 6th and 8th of July.

Peter was roundly condemned for what was widely received as a shaky showing during a duet with Elton John on "Children Of The Revolution", at one stage appearing to forget the words to the T-Rex number, though Sir Elton blamed nerves, claiming that rehearsals had seen them polish the track until it was "tip-top, perfect".

As for press allusions that he was out of his head, Peter said afterwards that he was high only "on adrenaline and nerves", and that while he'd made mistakes, "the idea that I might be all right now seems to be absolutely appalling to some of the papers". If nothing else, critics had focused – albeit fleetingly – on the music: "Normally it's hype this and that."

Peter — "It'd taken such a hammering, hadn't it? Such a hammering. Jesus Christ. It was, like – what the fuck's going on here? The crowd were horrible to me. There was no fucking love from the crowd. The band – Elton John's band, right? I mean, really, and I don't talk like this about anybody, ever, you know – even when people have really done me up; I'd rather forget about it and get on with my life. But on this occasion I will say: what a bunch of fucking wankers. What a bunch of sausage-sucking, session, slaphead, ponytailed pricks, you know?

"They knew that I needed their help, right? We had a rehearsal the day before at Watford Football Stadium. I'd gone up there with Kate and friends of Elton, who kind of organised the thing and encouraged me to do it. And to an empty Vicarage Road, we went through "Children Of The Revolution", and the band were great –

they were, like: 'Is this tempo alright for you? Do you need, like, a little note here to know if you're going to be in tune or not? Do you need help? Do you need this, d'you need that?' They couldn't have been nicer. And we had a fucking stonking version of "Children Of The Revolution". The whole of Watford must've heard it. It was blazing out of the fucking speakers. And we fucking smashed it, right? During the rehearsal this is, you know? Even managed to have a quick bit of fucking pipe in the Watford first team dressing room. Which I was quite proud of.

"But, on the day, I dunno. I came on, you know, alright, fine. I made an effort. I dolled myself up. But they thought I was being a prima donna. They thought I was trying to do some sort of show. It was Elton John's gig. I was a guest. And they thought I was coming on and giving it the big 'un. I wasn't. I was coming on and wanting to do a fucking fabulous song. They didn't even greet me. No one nodded or said hello. They just blanked me and I thought: that's it. They didn't give me that little extra note in the intro that was gonna keep me in tune.

"They left me to fucking die, right, and I don't understand it. I don't know why, to this day. Even Elton John, you know, I gave him a big smacker of a kiss. That lingered on the lips that little bit too long for comfort. So. Alas. Alas they did that to "Children Of The Revolution". [Sings:] 'But you can bump and grind, if it's good for your mind. Twist and shout. Let it all hang out, but you won't fool… a team of session musicians, no you won't fool…'

"It felt like they'd decided beforehand that the make-up was too much, the little sailor-boy, queer-as-a-bicycle look was too much, and that I didn't deserve to bask in Elton's glory. I deserved to go down the fucking pan."

Adam, who had already flown out to Ibiza with Drew for the forthcoming Ibiza Rocks festival, was surprised at this latest backlash against Peter, considering his performance an entertaining one that merely stood out as unique for the wrong reasons.

Had he been watching as an impressionable teenager, he reckons he'd have been drawn to an intriguing artist offering something different to the more manufactured sound of some of the other acts on show, demonstrating an edge so often lacking in a largely manufactured industry.

Adam — "I didn't understand what all the fuss was about. I thought it was excellent, pure Peter. He did look extremely nervous, though, but I suppose anyone would in front of a crowd that size. It didn't help having to perform with a session band instead of us. It's a shame we couldn't play; we were all up for it, but the organiser didn't give us a chance."

Patrick — "He kind of looked like a gay biker, but give him credit: I think it put all the music that was made that day – plush, perfect pop music – to shame. It was good to see someone singing out of tune with a bit of a rock 'n' roll attitude. He's my man, Pete, he is. Bad choice of make-up, though."

Anthony Thornton — "I thought it was brilliant. I think it was absolutely brilliant. I thought the event was awful, back-slapping, infinitely predictable and pretentious. Even with Live Aid, whatever you think about Live Aid, those who played put a lot of heart and soul into it. I don't think they put their heart and soul into that, apart from Pete…

"I thought he was blinding. I just thought: that's his one chance to appear in front of millions and millions of people, and he just does what he wants to do. He wasn't like everyone else: bland and trying to get every tiny nuance right and make sure the light show was working… he just went out and did it.

"He looked fantastic as well. I think a nation of mums and dads went: 'That's the bloke going out with Kate Moss, he looks a bloody mess! And what's that song he's singing? He sounds awful!' And that was it: that was brilliant, because he managed to upset people. It was ballsy, it was exciting, it was unpredictable. In a weird way, everybody there thought they were rock stars, and he *was* a rock star, because he's what you always wanted a rock star to be. I thought Elton John was great as well…

"The other thing about it is if you ask almost anyone about that show, there's two things they'll remember: one is Pink Floyd – fair enough, they haven't played together for, I don't know, twenty-seven years or something – then Pete. There's loads of people far, far more famous, who sell millions more records, and that's what people remember."

Danny Cliford — "You've got a situation where it's the tail wagging the dog a lot of the time. The press were making decisions on behalf of the public, and it depends on how they wanna write it. Pete gets up there and does a T-Rex song, and muddles through it the same way he muddles through all his things.

"It's not his own song… It's another song, and he's performing it with someone who's quite pristine. Sir Elton John is quite together, so it's a bit of chalk and cheese there – Sir Elton John giving it large and doing what he does best. He was trying to coach Pete along, but he's a buccaneer, he does it his own way, and he did."

Tom Atkins (The Paddingtons) — "I say: hats off, me. He's got some fucking balls to go out there; I'd probably need a fucking crack pipe to go out there and do that, to be honest. He did look like he was a bit nervous, but wouldn't anybody?

"It's Pete again, going against the grain. Every tabloid's writing fucking horrible shit about him, but he didn't have to be there at all; he could have not been there.

Next Page: Peter performing with Sir Elton John during the Live8 concert in Hyde Park, London, 2005.

But he went out there and went: 'Look, fuck you all.' It just so happened that it went a bit tits-up… But he got through it, just forgot a few words. It's all for the greater good, innit?"

Drew —

"When you have a Naltrexone implant, your body has to have been clean for more than seven days, I think it is, and if it isn't, something weird happens to your chemical balance, and you go through a lot of pain and go a bit mental.

"The first time Peter had an implant he *had* been clean for seven days – longer, much longer – and the second time he had an implant, he hadn't; he'd been lying or pretending that he had. It was quite a quick thing – I think they just jetted off to the Isle of Wight and boshed it in. I think you're supposed to be there for a few days before it gets boshed in; I think they put it in pretty much straight away, and he went a bit loopy for a while, and that was shortly before the Live8 thing.

"He's a sensitive guy, you know? He's a strong guy, he's quite hard, but he's a whole spectrum of things, and one of those things is he can be fragile and sensitive, and you put anyone under the kind of spotlight that Peter was in, coupled with his drug problems and the looming menace of going back to jail, which would scare the fucking shit out of anyone – having all of your freedom taken away from you – and, again, he hadn't slept for a very long time, and I just think he wasn't in the right headspace to do it… That wasn't an isolated incident: at that period in time he was behaving very erratically, and not quite being himself, and I think he was fucked – he was out of his mind.

"In the rehearsal, apparently, it went swimmingly. I think I'd be pretty fucking nervous if I was walking on stage to sing a T-Rex song with Elton John in front of however many millions of people watching on television worldwide, and even if I was in the most stable mental state, I'd still have butterflies and my voice might be a bit shaky, so I think that was it – it was all a bit too much for someone in the state that he was in. But, at the same time, some people, when they talk about it to me, they say it was fucking great."

According to Ben Bailey, Peter spent the entire night before the Live8 show getting hammered with His Lost Boys bassist Stef Benson, not leaving until around eight the next morning: "Apparently, they were absolutely fucked all night… Peter's like: 'I'm singing with Elton John. Singing "Children Of The Revolution"!', and Stef goes: 'You do know the words to the song?' And he goes: 'Yeah, yeah, yeah, yeah, yeah.'

"And it comes to the next day and it's patently obvious that he didn't have a fucking clue what the words were! But I think that's half the genius of him: how many people do you know that would get up on stage in front of, like, two billion people and not know the words to the song you're singing? I think that's amazing! Absolutely genius moment!"

Sally, who was forced to miss her best friend's Las Vegas wedding as a consequence of trying to help track Peter down, remembers a fatigued young man, starved of sleep for four days, who, taking exception to a friend's criticism of his apparently slipshod guitar playing, took refuge in a drugs haze.

Self-doubt had crept in, and Peter was in no mood to do anything he didn't want to. But with an extensive collection of no-shows threatening to compromise the growing respect the band's music was attracting, Sally and James talked him round.

The sheer scale of derision aimed at Peter was yet another demonstration of the misunderstanding surrounding him. He was never going to give a note-perfect, synchronised performance. Instead, he delivered a typically edgy burst of spontaneity that, had more observers been more aware of the artist, as opposed to the tabloid caricature, would surely have received a more sympathetic press.

Not that Peter was too bothered either way. Straight after the gig, he treated himself to a vintage guitar in Denmark Street and hopped into a black cab to spend the night at Kate's – hardly the worst way to prepare himself for the inevitable media backlash the next day.

6

Fuck Forever

A couple of days after Live8, Babyshambles announced an eleven-date UK tour, stretching 26th July to 6th August, in support of "*Fuck Forever*", originally slated for release on 25th July.

On the 4th of July, Peter and James joined Patrick, Drew and Adam in San Antonio for the Ibiza Rocks festival, and in spite of keeping fans waiting again, Babyshambles put on a mesmeric display that had organisers Andy and Mike McKay singing their praises, claiming they'd kick-started the event and that the island "had never been rocked so hard."

Peter — "It's like Noel Gallagher said: he said, during the rave era, people go out raving all night and then they end up back at some flat, and he'd be, like: 'Come on, man, stick on a bit of fucking Neil Young.' You've gotta have variety, and it's the same in Ibiza. Two different vibes, isn't it? And sometimes you just wanna, as they say, get your fucking rocks off. So we went over there and we had it right up, mate. I was trying things that I didn't even know existed. Quite a few people were. In every sense of the word. And say no more. But, yeah, I wanted to stay forever."

Drew — "Sometimes we play great shows, sometimes we play bad shows. I thought that was a really good one. It was just weird because of the context, the environment that we were in, and watching people trying to rave to it.

"There was a handful of kids in Shambles T-shirts who'd obviously bought flights to Ibiza to come and watch us, but then the rest of the ring was full of people who were there for, like, a normal evening…

"The numbers were falling and the indie scene was getting exciting again, so they thought that they'd invest in the future and the way that they saw music going; that they should start being the first people bringing bands to Ibiza."

Adam — "Ibiza was a weird one. I hadn't slept the previous evening and we were all worse for wear. I think we might have played the Duke [of Clarence] the night before. The show itself was an awkward, dream-like affair for me."

The band stayed at the Manumission villa, a secluded, gargantuan property with marble floors, enveloped by sprawling meadows grazed by goats. "When we first got there it was beautiful in the garden by the pool, sprinkler systems and all that. All melons, apples, strawberries and other fruit", says Adam. "The next day there were strawberries lobbed at the window, melons lobbed at the goats… this poor old place just got wrecked."

Another time, goldfish were carried by a couple of "friends" from a pond into a massive swimming pool, whereupon the villa's cat would leap in in search of a catch, remembering after a couple of lengths chasing orange flashes that the girth of the pool's lip left it with an uphill struggle when pawing itself back out again.

Adam — "They kept getting the fish from the pond and putting the fuckers in the swimming pool – the goldfish like they're on fire, with the chlorine boiling their faces. So me and Drew are trying to get these poor fuckers out – they were so big. And you can see their eyes popping out of their heads – it's like bleach to them."

Drew — "I get really pissed off when people are inhumane to animals. That fucking well pisses me off. To take a goldfish and put it in a pool of chlorine, and all manner of chemicals, it's going to be in a lot of pain. That's not one of the most pleasant memories from that trip."

A burgeoning reputation for let-downs was enhanced when Babyshambles failed to appear in Berlin, Germany, on 22nd July, at London's Big Gay Out on 23rd July, and, earlier that month, when another of Peter's no-shows cost the band a support slot on Oasis' UK tour.

Of the various explanations as to Peter's failure to turn up at Southampton's Rose Bowl on 6th July, for the Oasis gig, the truth is he was marooned in Paris, in the wake of fashion designer Hedi Slimane's birthday party, missing all of the Eurostar trains that would have seen him make the gig, sleeping through them, unaware of the many phone calls made to try and salvage the situation.

Peter — "James Mullord actually came out to France to get me, and I think he had an inkling about what was going on. It's all bollocks, though; it's all boring bollocks. I should have played that gig. 'Cos that would have been the highlight of my fucking life. I mean… I really don't give a toss what the media think of me. More and more, as I'm making my way in the music industry, I have more and more respect and admiration for Noel Gallagher from Oasis.

"It passed me by completely. At the time I was at school, I was fifteen, sixteen, and it should have hit me right between the eyes, like one of them boxing gloves on a spring. But it didn't. It annoyed me. My sister liked them. My sister used to go to Maine Road and all those gigs, and go on and on about them. People at school were always getting their hair cut like Liam Gallagher and learning to play guitar, and I was just like, you know: 'What?' I was just QPR, and QPR and QPR. A bit of Chas 'n' Dave.

"But then, yeah, I think I got it. I got it. The thing that I never got and why it didn't appeal to me was because I wasn't really a rock 'n' roll mythologiser. I'd never read books about swagger, I'd never been to gigs… I thought it was a sub-standard form of poetical expression until I heard The Smiths, and then it became the foremost poetical expression in contemporary culture. It was the most succinct and powerful way of getting your point across – whatever that point is. Whether it's: 'I'm fucking good-looking and you should shag me while you've got the chance,' or whether it's, you know: 'You should get yourself on this dance floor. Now. Quickly.' Or: 'You're gonna remember this moment for the rest of your life, and this is gonna be the soundtrack that you're gonna remember for the rest of your life.'

"This started to occur to me around that time and, unfortunately, I got brainwashed by joining in. Everything else became redundant. Utterly redundant. I blame my sister. She made me listen to the fucking devil. I wouldn't have known it if it had come up and slapped me in the face."

Drew — "God, that was a tough day. That was the last time I took magic mushrooms actually, because I was so depressed about what had happened. We were supposed to be playing with Oasis and we were all – everyone, except for Peter – on this little minibus driving down to Southampton…

"There was a party on the bus [and we're] going: 'I'm fucking supporting Oasis!' – punching the air – and we were almost at the venue, and we get a call saying: 'Peter's still asleep in a hotel in Paris.'"

Repetitive calls to Peter's mobile were made in a desperate bid to salvage the gig. But as the day wore on, it became obvious that he wouldn't make it, despite the fact that the Eurostar could have shuttled him back to London in not much more than a couple of hours.

The Babyshambles entourage tried to fend off Oasis management's concerns, insisting that their vocalist was on his way, but they were sent packing when it became clear that these were empty assurances, axed from the Mancunians' gig at the Milton Keynes Bowl on 9th July.

Unwilling to risk any more letdowns, Oasis replaced Babyshambles with The Zutons, frontman Liam Gallagher saying shortly after: "It's not a question of professionalism. It's much more simple than that. This is the greatest group in the world and what we're not going to do is let anyone – Pete Doherty, Liam Gallagher or Elvis – fuck it all up."

Drew, Patrick and Adam were totally despondent – especially the latter, who, born and bred in Milton Keynes, had to come to terms with the fact that his much-anticipated homecoming at the MK Bowl was out of reach. They felt that, through circumstances beyond their control, they'd let themselves down and lost a golden opportunity to play in front of a huge audience; they'd missed out on the biggest gig of their lives to date, and hadn't even received an apology.

By the time James and Peter surfaced, separately, that night, any possibility of rescuing the situation had been lost.

Adam — "The Oasis thing was a major disappointment. I was gutted – who knows what really happened? The blame was being passed from James to Peter to Kate; I suppose we'll never really know.

"The Oasis support was another nail in the coffin for James as a manager: whether he was to blame or not, he took the shit. It was a frustrating time. Peter was telling us James was not involved any more, and the next day James would ring us and tell us he's still managing. No-one knew what the fuck was going on."

Drew — "Whatever the actual reason was, what matters is that it didn't happen; what matters is that we didn't support Oasis. I'm still so gutted about that, I guess. Every time I think about that I just get this horrible sinking feeling of wasted opportunity. So, yeah, that was a drag, man…

"The thing is, Peter's a grown man… He's a grown man and he should be able to turn up at his own gigs – that's the bottom line, you know? The real reason Peter didn't turn up is because Peter didn't turn up. Ultimately, it's Peter's fault. You've gotta take responsibility for your actions at some point."

Just over a week later, the Fuck Forever tour was shelved. The official line was that the band were back in the studio to finish off *Down In Albion*; the rumour mill, however, said different: that Peter had sacked his bandmates.

At the heart of the uncertainty was a breakdown in communications between Peter and the rest of the band – or, rather, no communication at all – leaving them to fear the worst.

Peter had at the time been staying at a hotel to escape the burden of his uninvited status as public enemy number one. The last thing he needed was James firing questions at him about what type of press to commit to in the coming weeks.

When he eventually snapped, James angrily proposed that they throw in the towel and sack the band. Enraged and tired of being pressured, Peter flippantly agreed, not for a moment thinking that his words would be taken seriously and acted upon.

Sally
Anchasi — "I heard about it, and I just knew, because I know Peter, that it was ridiculous – he wouldn't fucking do that – but James had just rung up the rest of the company and told them [to] pull everything, put a stop on everything; nothing's coming out, which was ridiculous. And then I called Peter and I said: 'What's going on?'

And he said: 'Well, I just wanted a break for a couple of weeks', but it was his need at the time.

"You know when you're just tired and you're, like: 'I don't want to do anything, I just wanna forget it all, I wanna stay with my girlfriend and have picnics.' James just blew it all out of proportion, and before you knew it he'd called up everyone and said: 'You're sacked, by the way: Peter sacked you.' And he called the record company; it was just something small that got blown out of proportion."

James' insistence that "Fuck Forever" be remixed by Nellee Hooper, considering it to be of insufficient quality to hold its own in the charts in its current format, as good as sealed his departure, his decision upsetting Mick Jones, who was anxious to discover whether any more of the as-yet unfinished *Down In Albion* was to be tampered with.

With Peter nowhere to be seen, the rest of the band only agreed to James' request once assured that Mick was happy with the decision – a fabrication that Drew believes James adopted after Mick clashed with him over the remix, the uncertainty only resolved once Drew and Peter discussed the matter in the Rhythm Factory, Whitechapel Road, where Drew was heading to watch a gig.

Drew —   "Basically, James was also going a bit crazy at that time, and they were arguing, arguing, arguing, and it was just horrible. And James didn't like the sound of "Fuck Forever": he didn't think it sounded good enough for radio, and went in with Patrick and an engineer and had a quick remix to make it sound better. Mick got upset about it, said he [James] was the manager not a producer; James flew into a rage and asked Nellee Hooper to produce the single. Which I thought was a bad idea because of the politics…

"So James called us all up and said: 'I've spoken to Peter, he's happy for us, not to do the whole album, but to try "Fuck Forever" with Nellee Hooper.' I went, 'Really?' and James said, 'Yeah, yeah, I spoke to him. See you at Nellee's studio on Monday.' 'Wow, okay.'

"So we went there. First day, Peter didn't turn up. Second day, Peter didn't turn up. Third day, Peter didn't turn up. And then on Thursday, I called Mick Jones, and he was, like, almost crying, and he was, like: 'So, are you doing the whole album? What are you doing?' Because we'd just found out. James had also told us that Mick was okay with it. I don't know exactly what the truth is, but on the face of it, James was mad at Mick Jones for challenging him for wanting to make "Fuck Forever" sound better, and Peter *hadn't* said it was okay, and hadn't agreed to it…

"What Peter told me is that he sacked James, and what James did was call us up and say that Peter had sacked us. And then James went and told everyone that – called up all the press, called up our press officers to tell everyone that Peter had sacked the band – when in reality, according to Peter, it was just James that had been sacked.

"I didn't see Peter for a couple of weeks, and then I was in east London on my way to see The Things playing the Rhythm Factory, and I saw a couple of mutual friends, and they were on their way to see Peter. I was, like: 'I'm going down the Rhythm Factory, can you come on there?'

"I went to the gig, and there was a tap on my shoulder, and it was Peter. And so we went back out to the bar area, sat down and had a chat. He said: 'I never sacked you. It's not true.' His chemical balance hadn't quite settled from the Naltrexone implant. And he's, like: 'I never sacked you, I sacked James. James didn't tell me anything. I told James I would never do that. Fuck that, I'd *never* do that!'

"And we hung out that night and then I called Adam the next day and told him what Peter said, and that was the beginning of the end for James, really."

Peter — "I hope they all know this: that if I sack someone, then I sack them to their face. I tell them I can't work with them no more... With Mullord it wasn't like that. He said: 'Do you want to do this thing with Nellee Hooper?' You know, with his legs apart in his comfy chair in his flat. And telling me how he'd been doing this and that with this and that fella, and Nellee Hooper had done Madonna, Radiohead.

"And Pat was in awe... as always, if some famous bloke was involved. Pat was well up for doing it. And Mick Jones was absolutely fucking gutted. He was, like: 'What the fuck?' He hasn't been asked, and I said to James: 'I don't care who he's done. It doesn't matter who he's done. It doesn't matter who he is. The point is: what we're doing is betraying Mick Jones, d'you know what I mean? If you were going to take Mick Jones in, right, or you've got Mick Jones' permission, right, for that track to be released, then that's different. But Mick Jones is our producer... We made this album with him, we done "Fuck Forever" with him. I'm not going. You book it, but I'm not going. I tell you that now. So let's just see how much you really care about what I think.' And he didn't. He didn't care about what I thought in the slightest. He thought he could do an amazing mix of it with Nellee Hooper.

"I can't remember if he did or he didn't. In the end, I think it was a bit shit. I can't remember. But it really upset me. It really rocked the boat, I thought... And there was no fucking remix. It was James' idea. It was James playing at being producer, writer, entrepreneurial Machiavellian genius. Plans. Plans. America and all of that...

"Maybe, I think, I said if they turn up to do this, knowing that I don't wanna do this, then they can all fuck off, you know?... But it happened that, apparently, they didn't know that was how I felt. James had said that I wanted to do it. So it's all very confusing, really, isn't it?"

Patrick —   "I wrote that song with Peter. I wasn't happy with the production; it should have been a bit faster and a lot better. Looking back on it now, it's raw and that, but it's a much better song than the version that was released. It did cause a lot of grief.

"I went into the studio. Pete never turned up to do his vocals… And Nellee Hooper, he knows how to make a hit record, man – and it sounds great. He got me playing guitar like a motherfucker, he produced me… The only reason it didn't come out was because Pete had a loyalty with Mick Jones at that point – he didn't want to upset him."

As far as Iain Gore was concerned, the track had already been laboured over enough, the mere mention of it enough to promote nausea: "A mix normally takes between one and two days to do; normally a day-and-a-half to two days. "Fuck Forever" was up on the desk for seven days…

"I can't listen to "Fuck Forever" now. To have a song up on the desk for seven days is, like, insane – well, it is for me. It made me go insane: to the point where, when we were printing the mixes, putting the final versions down, if I heard it I would feel physically sick."

Iain Gore —   "Bill Price had recorded that down in Twin Peaks in Wales, and I'd done the overdubs in Reading, Henley-on-Thames. We'd mixed it in one studio, and the band weren't happy with it… Bill wasn't working on the Friday, and Mick wasn't, and they wanted me to go in and work with the band, and do some extra bits to it, which meant, basically, making it a bit more pristine… So I didn't really do that much to it, and then James was, like: 'No, we want you to do this to it.' And I'm, like: 'Well, you have to book a studio through Rough Trade', and all that stuff. 'I can't book a studio.'

"So it never happened. And then on the Monday we were in the studio with Mick Jones, still waiting for the band to turn up to finish the mix, and a phone call came through – I think it was from Rough Trade – but it wasn't their decision; they said Nellee Hooper's producing the track. This was the first that anyone had heard of it…

"Basically, the track had gone off to be produced by Nellee Hooper. Everything had been recorded, but the mixing process came to a stop then, while everyone decided what was going on. But, apparently, Pete was not into this idea at all. Rough Trade didn't like the version. Various people from the whole Shambles lot were saying it was good, some were saying it was bad. It was up in the air, and it was meant to be the forthcoming single.

"Anyway, I think in the end Pete said Mick Jones was producing it. I'm not sure how aware he was of what was actually happening in that situation. I think a lot of management were shitting themselves about Pete having a release… and everyone lost the plot a little bit."

The "Fuck Forever" furore made it impossible for James' tenure as manager to continue. It would be nearly a year before Babyshambles would seek a replacement; in the meantime, the band would have to muddle through as best they could.

A gig at Stoke's Underground on 1st August marked Babyshambles' first appearance since cancelling their "Fuck Forever" UK tour, dispelling rumours of a split.

With London a hive of press activity, The Underground was the perfect venue to give a public display of unity. The club was a regular pit-stop for the band and, mistakenly assuming that there would be equipment waiting for them the other side, they caught a cab to Stoke – to the obvious delight of owner Matt Bates, who had to find nearly five hundred pounds for the round trip, another taxi driving them back to London after the show. Matt also arranged for a local band to lend equipment, enabling the band to play at all.

Underground regulars, who paid just a couple of quid entrance fee, expecting the standard weekly indie night, had no idea that the band were to play – the gig hadn't been advertised in advance; it had, in true Babyshambles style, been a last-minute decision – but were treated to three sets.

Fans who'd learned of the gig from those inside, via mobile phones, quickly descended upon The Underground. And though few of the couple of hundred waiting anxiously outside actually made it in through the door, compensation came in the form of Peter, who chatted to them between sets, signing autographs and posing for photos.

Drew — "I remember driving back that night, with all four of us in the car, just with broad smiles and everyone really happy and really singing from the same hymn sheet. And it was, like: well, when we're together everything's fine, it's when we're not together we're hearing bits of hearsay – Adam reckons this or Drew said that, and Peter said this and Patrick did this, or whatever. That's where people get confused and, in our case, anyway, the trick is to just cut out the middle man and spend more time together, is what we realised at that point."

Failure to obtain permission for another secret gig at the Duke of Clarence pub, north London, on the 11th – owner Tayo Ogidan hadn't secured a licence permitting a performance exceeding certain noise levels – saw police confiscate equipment that left the band unsure whether they'd be able to make Norway's Oya Festival, Oslo, the next day. Borrowed instruments remedied that particular problem; another presented itself when the authorities stepped in to prevent a swift passage through customs at Oslo airport.

Looking far from their best, an absurdly early flight was missed as a result of being directed towards the wrong checking-in queue, so a later one had to do.

Making the show remained a possibility: the flight was due to land in Norway around an hour before Babyshambles were due to perform; and with the venue about half-an-hour's drive away by car, it would have been a case of clearing customs, racing to the festival and performing pretty much without pause.

Their good intentions were, however, wrecked by their latest encounter with the law, on a day when Patrick, looking particularly ill, had to be taken off the carrier in a wheelchair, attracting the attentions of customs, who demanded that all band members, bar Adam, be strip-searched, before placing them in what Adam described as "microwave ovens" – silver throughout and with just a small bench for company.

Barred from using their phones, Adam nonetheless managed to send a text message to Matt Bates, who, unaware of the unfolding drama, went on ahead to ensure that their car was ready to take them to the festival.

Adam urged a perplexed Matt to get in touch with lawyer Sean Curran, who expressed little hope of Peter's release when told of the incident, underscoring the country's strict stance when it came to narcotics.

Adam —   "I had a bad feeling as soon as we'd got off the plane. Pat had been shouting and screaming back at Heathrow, so our cards were already marked from the start. The problem, as always, had come from certain individuals panicking about leaving the country and not being able to score, so, last minute, an associate was called to deliver to Heathrow.

"Within the hour almost all was consumed, so some of us were more lucid than others. Upon arriving in Norway, the authorities didn't need to look too closely at our party – two of whom were a green colour at that point. As Pat was quite 'unfit', we decided that a wheelchair might be a good idea. Well, it wasn't – it drew even more attention to us and resulted in us being rounded up before we reached the exit.

"These serious-looking guards led us into their room, separated us into small silver cubicles, and began their searches. I think Drew and I were first. I remember being first out, trying to sneak a message to Matt, who had got through and was oblivious to what was happening. Every time I tried to reach for my phone this huge woman shouted: 'Stop! Don't move!'

"I managed to text him anyway, and he set about sorting out lawyers etcetera. Back in the search room, I was let out, then Drew; then I heard groans from both Peter and Pat, so God only knows where they were hiding their booty.

"Drew, myself and Matt spent the next three hours wanting to hear what was happening. They [Peter and Patrick] eventually got released with a fine."

Opposite: Patrick at the 2005 Nokia Isle of Wight Festival, in Seaclose Park, Newport, Isle of Wight.

Drew —

"There was a whole period – over a year and a half, maybe – when we didn't have management, and we were booking shows in festivals around Europe and going on these little jaunts, and not always making all the dates that had been booked, because people would get trapped in a black hole in a hotel room in Barcelona or something, or Patrick would go missing in Berlin for a day or something.

"And so we were booked for this festival – Patrick and I were really excited because Sonic Youth were playing – and we were supposed to play the main stage about four o'clock. Patrick took some brown with him, and I think he got nervous about carrying it over, so he took it all – a couple of bags' worth – before he got on the plane, and by the time he got off the plane he was so mullered he could barely walk; he was kind of stumbling along.

"At this airport there were two sets of customs, and we thought we'd got through all these checks. And we were just walking down to the door, and we put Patrick in a wheelchair that was in the middle of the corridor – Patrick wasn't doing very well with walking, so we put him in the wheelchair – and we were charging about with him, semi-conscious, in a wheelchair being pushed by Peter – not the most inconspicuous sight at three in the afternoon at Oslo airport.

"And the boys were carrying more stuff, and we walked past customs, and they took one look at us and thought: okay. And so they pulled us in, and Patrick's there like that [out of it]. And they were, like: 'Sir, have you been taking any form of medication or illegal drugs?' And he's, like: 'No, I promise', his teeth all brown, lips all brown. And this guy gets a torch out, shines it into his eyes: no reaction. 'Sir, I think that you have been taking heroin.' 'Nah. Promise.'

"And for some reason, we all got strip-searched apart from Adam – go figure! I think Adam took off his flat cap and his jacket, and he [customs] was going: 'No, you're all right, mate.'

"We got strip-searched and threatened. Luckily we didn't get the glove treatment, but we had to do this thing where you lift and cup yourself. And there's this really humiliating thing, where you have to touch your toes, while they're stood behind you. Not pleasant, man. And I didn't have anything on me, but Peter and Patrick both did.

"In front of them, Peter took a rock and claimed that he needed it to rub on his wound, and took the bandage of his implant off, and with about, like, a two hundred quid rock, started rubbing it, and then tried to slip it inside, in front of them. And then that was it: it was all over."

Peter —

"I think about that sometimes. I always think about that when we're travelling abroad. What were we doing? We'd already… drawn far too much attention to ourselves on the fucking plane as it was, and we just thought that we were untouchable. You know, going through the airport, stopping, hiding under tables, smoking pipes. And he does this thing – it is very good, very realistic. Not quite as good as Mik's, but he does an impression of a spastic walking. It is highly disturbing, but so realistic.

"So we put him in a wheelchair and he was giving it all this: the old 'mmenneee' – makes grunting noises – and, surprise surprise, they pulled us over. And we all got a thorough arse-probing. Er, yeah. They actually arrested me and Pat. He's like Wolfie, actually: he takes it really bad. He really suffers. 'Oh no, man, I'm clucking and I've got nothing.' And I had a nice little stash. And in the end someone bribed someone, and we got let out. And we didn't go to prison. I don't know how that happened."

Patrick —   "We were just messing around, and then customs came along and found heroin in my pocket, and crack. We started panicking. I was just out of my nut and started sleeping, and the woman kept coming up to me, going: 'Wake up – are you dead?' They didn't know what crack was; they thought it was cocaine.

"I remember her going next-door to Peter: 'Your friend next-door, he's not very well.' He goes: 'He's fine, he's just asleep – leave him!' I remember we had to pay money to get out of there... If you had no money, you'd be fucked wouldn't you? It's out of order.

"They were waiting for us. I mean, it wasn't a stitch-up because we had the drugs in our pocket, which was absolutely fucking stupid, but there was press for two days... the monsters were coming. The Babyshambles are coming, the drug fiends are coming, so those fuckers were waiting for us. And turning up in a wheelchair, doing pipes before, wasn't good."

Matt Bates— "I wanted to make sure our car was waiting for us when we got out, so I ran out of the departure lounge, got the car... turned around and thought: where is everybody? [I] waited five minutes, waited ten minutes, tried phoning, [but] no-one was answering their phone. [I] finally got a phone call from Adam, going: 'We're being strip-searched.' And I was thinking: thank God I walked ahead!...

"I didn't know what to do. Kate Moss kept phoning me to speak to Peter, but I couldn't tell her her boyfriend's been pulled in Norway... And then I phoned Sean, Peter's solicitor, and I'm going: 'Sean, what happened?' He goes: 'Matt, I don't know, it's really bad. I think you could be in a lot of trouble over there – Norway's quite strict for drugs and stuff'...

"I honestly thought that if I'd been interviewed in, like, two years' time, I'd be talking about how Pete had been in a Norwegian prison for three years or something. I can't believe how they got away with that – it's amazing."

Remarkably, Peter and Patrick, collared for stashing small quantities of heroin and crack cocaine up their respective arses, escaped further action upon payment of penalties totalling the best part of £1,500. But by the time the band eventually made it to the festival, some five hours behind schedule, they'd missed their main stage slot, coming on at 10.30pm instead and putting on a short show, truncated by an electricity shutdown, that included Peter throwing up on stage.

On 26th August, the band set off to play the Rock En Seine Festival. Once the band had played their set, a couple of thousand kids wrecked the festival's flimsy fencing to reach them, clashing with security, who lacked the manpower to prevent them getting to within touching distance of their idols.

Adam —

"We all came out backstage and sat down on the grass. Loads of kids then spotted us and set about trying to rock the security fence to get to us. We then noticed loads of security getting quite heavy-handed with the kids, so we all steamed over to the fence.

"At this point security are grabbing us, so it turns into a bit of a brawl on both sides of the fence. Suddenly the fence breaks and the kids are all joining us, trying to rumble with the security. Eventually it died down, and we got loaded into the minibus from the backstage area. A few bums got smacked, but no-one really got hurt, I don't think."

Drew —

"We were just behind the stage that we played on and there was this grassy verge and we kind of stumbled off the stage, tour our shirts off because we were so hot, and just laid on the grass. And all the kids – they were watching us – could see, because it sloped upwards. And they were, like: 'They're right there.' And that was it: they just bumrushed the fence and we watched it come down. I thought someone was gonna kill themselves, actually."

The following day, the band flew back to England for the Carling Weekend, spanning the Reading and Leeds festivals on 27th and 28th of August, for which they were forced to hire instruments to replace their own, still impounded by Islington Council.

At Reading, Peter came to blows with a security guard, who took exception to his attempts to lift a youngster out of the crowd, after encouraging a stage invasion that quickly saw scores of fans flood the stage. At one point, a peculiar tug-of-war occurred when, as Peter and Wolfman helped people up onto the stage, security pulled them the other way.

The hired equipment, meanwhile, ended up in the audience, a cymbal sent flying through the air by Peter, followed by his guitar and the entire drum kit, leaving Matt Bates with the job of having to find replacements in time for the Leeds gig.

"Wolfman comes along, wriggles about a bit, trying to pick up my drum, realises it's far too heavy, and goes back – then Peter sees it," says Adam. "So, anyway, I've got no drum, so I'm whacking something I've got on the floor."

Drew — "Security guards in general tend to be fucking meatheads. If you're a meathead and you like fighting and you want to do security, then go and do security at a football match, because indie kids are small and peace-loving. People dance and people get excited because it's a release. They're not causing trouble, they're not trying to ruin the place. And from the stage you see these security guards – these guys are fucking seven feet tall and six feet wide – getting some little kid in a headlock, and his mates are giving them digs on the way out...

"Peter lamped one of the security guards. I'm not saying that I want the band to be known for violence, but something kind of snaps when you see someone that size beating a little kid up. It's hard not to react."

Organisers of the Leeds Festival, at which the band arrived late, were the latest in a bulging line of those issuing warnings that Babyshambles would never play at their shows again.

Patrick was responsible in this instance, returning to London after the Reading show to score. By the time he reached Leeds, he was an hour behind schedule, on a day that Peter headbutted Razorlight vocalist Johnny Borrell, a former fellow Libertine – an incident that, perhaps not unsurprisingly, given their earlier warning, resulted in a subsequent ban from the site.

Told that Borrell had badmouthed him, Peter made for the Razorlight tent along with Alan and The General, sticking one on his antagonist, who he later described as a "fucking cunt" and a "poisonous snake" totally deserving of his comeuppance.

Peter — "I caught him with an absolute fucking stonker, mate. His nose went like a ripe tomato, man – whoosh! Just like that. We'd been quite close, me and Johnnie... And he was good. He was a good songwriter. I always believed in him from the start. I saw him play and heard him sing, and sat round with him. And knew there was something special, and that it would come out one day as well. And it will come out one day... away from Razorlight. Away from all that industry bollocks. It will come out: him, Johnny Borrell, with an acoustic guitar, maybe; harmonica, some gospel singers. It will come out – this beautiful beautiful Dylan-esque album. It will, it has to. It can't sit in his soul for too long.

"We were kind of muckas. He was just one of the gang, really. So when he became famous – slightly after that – I was pretty much of the same mentality that I was before: very much live and let live. Wanting to make music all the time, not judging, you know? I was quite unnerved and angry by the way he'd become very successful, Razorlight a very popular band. A very big band, and he was mugging me off. He was saying shit about me in the press. To be fair, I found that out after I headbutted him.

"What it was: Alan Wass was with me at Reading. Johnny was supposed to have chatted-up his bird or snogged his bird or something. Alan was going to go around and beat him up. In the end we got round there and it was all handbags at dawn, with Alan going: 'Listen, you don't know who I am – I'll come and have you wrapped up', and Johnny's going: 'You cunt, I've been boxing on the Holloway Road'. And in the end I just went: 'You know what? Have some of this,' and put one right on him…

"The General had fly-kicked a chair. That was his contribution. As you can imagine, Alan's giving it the big 'un in his trench coat, I've nutted Johnny, who is is down on the ground, writhing, and The General jumps in the other direction – fly-kicks a plastic chair… And he [Johnny] wore sunglasses for a month. So I must have caught him a right good 'un."

With the twice-postponed "Fuck Forever" – which entered the UK Singles chart at number four on the 22nd of August – finally released, Roger Pomphrey's documentary, *Who The F**k Is Pete Doherty?*, was given its first airing on the 28th, on BBC3.

In interviews given at the time, Roger spoke warmly of his time with the band and expressed how Peter had inspired both admiration and concern in him. He had, he said, witnessed at first hand a genius at work, but was unable to ignore the many destructive forces at work around him, subsidising their own existences by using Peter to their own advantage.

Roger Pomphrey — "He needed protection from some of the darker influences in his life. However, ultimately, the only person that can protect Pete from that is Pete himself, and that rule applies to any person with any addictive qualities at all, whether it's alcohol or drugs or gambling or sex addiction, or any addiction. Ultimately, the only person who can conquer that addiction is the person that is in possession of the addiction. So although I figured that his management should have been more protective of him, I know the band – Patrick, and Drew and Adam especially – were trying their hardest to protect him – you can't chain a person down, you can't stop a person from hanging with certain other people. So I fear for him continuously, because it's really, really easy to make a mistake. And you've only got to make that mistake once and it's all over.

"I never, ever, ever felt that Pete had a death wish. People say that he wants to kill himself or he wants to be dead by twenty-seven – that's fucking nonsense to me; it was blatantly obvious to me [that] the guy really enjoys life. He loves life.

"There were a lot of people around Pete that were really just a very, very bad influence, and who were there for one reason and one reason alone: to take. That's not unique to Pete Doherty. I was in The Eurythmics, and I've played with a lot of very famous household names, and all famous people and celebrities, for want of a better word, suffer from that.

"And it's a complex issue: it's all to do with the stroking of ego and the confirmation of one's standing within the collective celebrity community. And Pete would allow the darker influences in his life to really prevail, and in some senses he kind of kept me at a distance. And I think he's a very, very intelligent man, and I think he knew that given half the chance I'd sit him down and say: 'Pete, what the fuck are you doing? You've got an absolute God-given talent and yet you're pissing it against the wall. Why are you doing this?'

"But it's all part of addiction – it's a fear, it's an insecurity. In a lot of artists, if you have a fear of really, really, really committing to your talent, there's a fear that it might fail. If you don't commit to that talent, if you just kind of live it to a three-quarters degree, you can say to yourself: 'Well, I never really tried, so it don't matter.'

"If you really try and it don't work, you've then got to live with failure, and I think that's part of the problem. I think a lot of addicts suffer from that mindset. I'm no psychologist, but I can see that in myself. When you get to a point where you have to put all your cards on the table, you're then going to expose your hand. If you don't play all your cards, you're not exposing your hand, and it cannot by the very nature of that fail for you, because you haven't committed to it. Non-commitment, can't fail."

Roger also acknowledged how alcohol and drug intake were detrimental to the quality of music. Generally, the tighter, more impressive gigs were fuelled by little more than adrenaline; their sloppy, disjointed counterparts were invariably the ones where too many substances had been ingested.

But whatever state they played in, Roger saw a collection of four individuals making music together, "underlined by the fact that Pete Doherty is unquestionably the motivation and the artistic driving force behind it."

Roger Pomphrey — "They're genuinely a very, very exciting band – when they're on-song they were as fucking good as anybody. Absolutely as good as anybody. There's no doubt in my mind that drugs let the band down, in so much as it made them unpredictable in their level of performance, and that wasn't just a part of Pete Doherty or Babyshambles – that applies to anybody.

"If you're going to be narcotically charged, it's a rollercoaster of how good or bad you're going to be, because you're not in total control of who or what you are. But when they would go on stage and click and gel, and it was as tight as fuck, it was just as kicking as you could get, really – good, good rock n' roll music. Fabulous."

Perhaps the grossest manifestation of the darker influences Roger referred to occurred on 15th September, when the *Daily Mirror* ran an exposé showing pictures of Kate allegedly sniffing cocaine at a Babyshambles recording session, though she did not admit taking drugs and no charges were brought against her.

The fall-out from the story raised urgent questions about who was responsible for the betrayal. Peter immediately pointed the finger at James Mullord, claiming he pocketed £150,000 in return for the story, as the press gleefully reported the number of modelling contracts his girlfriend was said to have lost as a consequence.

James denied any involvement in the affair, protesting his innocence on *The Richard and Judy Show* and in the *Evening Standard*. Talk within the Babyshambles camp linked him to a couple of drug dealers, alluding to their collaboration in selling the footage to the *Daily Mirror*. The dealers, with a poor grasp of English, were thought incapable of possessing the kind of nous required to negotiate with a heavyweight tabloid, which is where many thought James came in.

Other factors pointed to some form of involvement from James, but without definitive proof, any of these could be put down to coincidence. And though many were unshakable in their insistence that the trio under suspicion were culpable, others simply couldn't imagine James stooping so low as to betray a former close friend in Peter, who, despite not being directly implicated in the controversy, was distraught at the malicious, unwarranted treatment his girlfriend was being subjected to.

Adam —

"I was there just before and I know who took the photos."

Tony Linkin —

"Everyone, *everyone*, was under suspicion; no-one was not under suspicion, really. That's why I was so glad I wasn't actually there, because I probably would have been under suspicion as well. I think people just realised they could do it and get away with it… It did look horrible for her [Kate] at one point, but thankfully she came out of it well."

Roger Pomphrey —

"Kate's a very private person, and that's her choice, and you have to respect that… No-one has the right to invade anybody's right to privacy. It was really snide, and that was an example of Pete being surrounded by the wrong people."

Drew —

"The only thing I'll say about the Kate Moss thing is: whoever sold those photographs, you're a spineless, hateful cunt of a human being, and one day you're gonna get yours."

Peter —

"I would be more than prepared to tell you who was responsible, and I would ask you to shout it from the rooftops, but I don't know. All I know is: a couple of lads, who I'd owed a fair bit of money to for some time, who I'd been quite close to for a number of years. Not just as, like, a customer. I did buy drugs off them… I stopped seeing them; basically, I'd cleaned up. I got an implant.

"I didn't phone them anymore… We'd spent a lot of time together knocking about in the East End, having a laugh. And we tried to pull a few scams in the past, stupidly

– like setting up things or get cash upfront for a deal and not do it. Or literally rob the journalist. Once he did actually tie-up a journalist and take him off. I thought it was quite funny. I was wrapped up in love. I was spending all of my time with my missus… And then the big one came along and they've done it, and that's it."

Such was the scandal already associated with Babyshambles that record sales were unlikely to be damaged by their involvement with drugs. Put simply, people expected nothing else. On a more disquieting note, they had been betrayed by a member of the inner sanctum, by people they had regarded as their own. In future, they would try and vet more stringently those given close-quarters access; though, inevitably, there would continue to be violations of trust.

Babyshambles had lost a friend and manager in James Mullord. From now on, their guard would be raised. But the real loser in this sorry affair was Kate.

Her relationship with a man earning a reputation as an embodiment of declining moral standards, in spite of the fictitious nature of much of what has been written about him, marked her out as a target. And now she was going to have to pay the price.

7

Down In Albion

While the media continued to hound Kate, who would within days take refuge in Arizona, booking herself into The Meadows Clinic, a managerless Babyshambles, minus Patrick, flew back out to Spain to close the Ibiza season at Bar M with another storming performance on the 16th of September.

The show marked the first time the band played as a three-piece, following Patrick's failure to turn up – a consequence of, as he put it: "A mixture of my own stupidity and traffic." Missing all available flights, his absence, despite forcing his bandmates into a corner, demonstrated that they could manage on their own – a realisation that helped ease the gradual parting of the ways that followed a few months down the line. "It was the first time we recognised that we could cope without him", said Adam. "It's horrible to say, but what could we do?"

Peter initially refused to concede that Patrick wouldn't show, but when, during the journey from the Manumission villa to Bar M, it became clear that their worst fears were to be confirmed, the decision was taken to see how they'd fare as a trio, creating what Drew terms "a lot more of an organic, breathing thing."

Drew — "Peter grabbed a guitar, and I grabbed one, and I went through some of the songs that he hadn't played guitar on, and we did it as a three-piece. We ended up playing for, like, two and a half hours, doing a bunch of The Libertines songs and a bunch of Kinks songs and La's songs and Beatles songs, and our songs as well.

"And it got to the point where we'd played for so long that it was almost [like] the way a DJ's set will depend on the crowd reaction and so on, and as it goes on you can shape it to work with the crowd; it kind of became like that… We ended up touring and gigging quite a lot as a three-piece – Adam, Peter on guitar and me on bass. And I quite enjoyed that period. Obviously it's much better with Mik. But as a three-piece, things were really elastic."

Adam — "That Ibiza gig was intense. Before the gig, Andy was telling me how proud he was about this vintage Telecaster he'd managed to borrow and how no-one on the island had any spare gear to lend, but he managed to blag it. Peter subsequently smashed the vintage telecaster up – to Andy's credit he didn't charge us!"

The hire company which provided the guitar obviously had no knowledge of Peter's proclivity for on stage demolition – or chose to ignore it – judging by its choice of instrument: a twenty-thousand pound Telecaster.

Peter had been trying to sporadically tune it throughout the gig, at one point swapping instruments with Drew and playing bass for a while. But with Drew faring no better than Peter had, Peter destroyed it during the band's second set, security quickly pouncing on him to prevent any more damage, as Adam darted out from behind his drums in defence of his mate.

Drew —

"If you're going to hire Babyshambles a guitar, give them the stock guitar. Don't give them the jewel in the crown of your hire guitars. Which is what happened. And as soon as he smashed it, about three lads jumped on stage. One of them looked like he was going to beat the crap out of him. But, yeah, what do you expect?

"I don't know why Babyshambles have always been plagued by guitars with bad intonation, or gigs without tuners. It does my nut in, man. There's nothing worse than everyone playing well, everyone being on form, and it sounding shit because the guitar's out of tune. It just sounds to the crowd like we can't play. 'Cos, despite popular opinion, we can play – quite well. But that gig, like loads of gigs we've played, there were no tuners. We were all having to do it by ear."

Had it not been for Danny Clifford's intervention, Babyshambles would have been presented with a hefty bill for the broken Telecaster. Indeed, by bringing it to Andy McKay's attention that it'd be worth significantly more than that if framed, bearing Peter's signature, the bill was withheld.

Danny, who Peter interrupted a song to speak to when spotting him taking some shots from the side of the stage, remembers tension backstage after the gig, having identified a number of suspicious-looking characters – reporters – hunting for an exclusive. Among these was the journalist who broke the *Daily Mirror*'s story about Kate, whose safety Danny feared for if Peter got wind of the situation: "Pete would really have had a go – he was out to kill anyone with anything to do with the *Mirror*."

As for the other journalists present, it was patently obvious to Danny that their intentions were purely predatory: "I looked at them and thought: these guys are not punters for this club; these guys and women here, they're not locals – they're British journalists, all in their late thirties and forties."

Fortunately for these hacks, Peter didn't manage to get his hands on them, though the Manumission villa, which Andy and Mike McKay had lent the band for the night, suffered another trashing.

Danny Clifford —

"Everyone disappeared to different parts of the villa, and there's just Pete and me together in this sort of, like, lounge area. And it was kind of my fault – I didn't mean to do this – but I said – we were looking at all the CDs – and I said: 'Ah look, there's the Sex Pistols' *Never Mind The Bollocks*, and then, with that, he thought he was Sid Vicious and he started smashing the room up… He tried to smash the TV and failed, which I thought was pretty funny… He had a vodka bottle and he lobbed that on the walls – it went everywhere."

After challenging Danny to a fight and calming down long enough for an impromptu photo shoot, Peter proceeded to lob full bottles of spirits into the swimming pool as it started to get light.

Having seen enough excitement for one day, Danny decided that it was time to escape the lunacy, hitching a lift into town, from where he caught a cab to San Antonio; not long after, he was on a plane out of Spain, glad to have left such mayhem behind him.

Shortly after returning from Spain, the band embarked on their rescheduled *Pipe Down* tour, which kicked-off at Carlisle's The Brickyard on September the 20th, also taking in Greenock Town Hall, Aberdeen's Moshulu, Dundee's Fat Sams, Sheffield University, Nottingham's Rock City, Northumbria University, Birmingham Academy, The Underground in Stoke-on-Trent and Manchester Academy, before trouble flared up in Shrewsbury on 1st October.

Despite claiming at the start of the tour that it was the "first time in years" that he'd been on the road without using, Peter was arrested for possession of Class A drugs.

Warned for days by Matt Bates that police were set to launch a raid, tour buses were as a consequence significantly tidier and freer from drugs than would normally have been the case.

With the band relaxing backstage, word was put about that the venue they'd just played in, the Music Hall, was to be busted immediately. Officers stormed in seconds later, impounding tour buses and dragging Peter, Wolfman, his girlfriend and support band The Littl'ans – mistaken as Babyshambles members – to Telford police station for questioning, as Patrick slipped away to safety.

Adam also managed to evade the police raid, driving his 15-year-old brothers to Shrewsbury train station to prevent them from getting caught up in the sorry affair. By the time he returned, the police had completed their searches, and despite informing them that he, too, belonged to the band, suggesting that, by association, he should be searched as well, he was turned away.

The force was satisfied with its haul, netting what they suspected was the prize catch: Peter, who was held overnight for possession, the confiscation of tour buses meaning that the rest of the band had to find a hotel for the night.

Peter –   "They were absolutely gutted, the Old Bill. Honestly, I hadn't seen so many blue uniforms since the May Day Riots – they were everywhere. In the end there were

---

Opposite: Peter backstage on the Pipedown Tour, 2006.

only a few of us that got nicked. What I got nicked for was not illegal – it was a prescribed drug. And I had an implant at the time that was going a bit wrong, and had a plaster on it. I think it was that one. And I had everything stashed in my plaster. And I was in the police station, and before anything happened: 'Sarge, look', and I squeezed out a Naltrexone pill, blood. And pus came oozing down my leg, and they were all, like: 'Aaaaaaargh!'

"It didn't occur to them for a second that, you know, that also, in my hand, there was an awful lot of crack and smack. But then they raided the bus. They raided the tour bus of the support bands. They were all, like, vegan non-drug-smokers. They were gutted.

"Me and Wolf, when we heard the police were in the building, we had like, fuck, two minutes to get everything flushed down the bog. And we were, like: 'Nothing is going down that bog.' And we lined-up rocks of crack… stuck 'em in the pipe, and blazed and blazed and blazed.

"It was a stitch-up in that they'd obviously planned it, but it was the most disorganised drugs raid. Because we're drug users, but we're very disorganised. Everything is normally lost or consumed by the end of the evening. It's the wrong time to raid a van, you know – after the gig. They didn't realise that; they presumed that everyone does the gig, then goes out and gets wrecked. It never works with us like that – we go out and get wrecked, and never do the gig."

Drew —   "Ian Blair had launched this new initiative to crack down on upwardly mobile, rich drug users, as opposed to just targeting impoverished street junkies – like he wanted to be seen not victimising the poor drug users, and turning a blind eye to the City boys who have cocaine habits or whatever. And so the media furore that followed this gave the police force an easy way of generating spin and supporting this new Blair initiative.

"After the gig I think someone got nicked or something, and the guy who was tour managing at the time went down to the police station. It was taking a really long time, so I called him. I dunno why he didn't call before, but he was, like: 'They're on their way there now, they're coming right now.' So I put down the phone and ran into the dressing room, and everyone was drinking, and I was, like: 'Hide everything right now. Chuck whatever you've got, chuck it right now.'

"And, luckily, everyone took it seriously, and did, and, like, within thirty seconds the door was kicked in and we were all taken off and put into meatwagons. Speaking to the police who were there, they weren't even from the local constabulary; they didn't really know exactly what was going on… The policemen I spoke to had been drafted in from these neighbouring constabularies. These guys didn't really have an issue; they didn't really understand why they were doing it, either."

Patrick — "I escaped – I said I wasn't in Babyshambles. This police officer said: 'Well, you look like you're in Babyshambles.' I said: 'No, no, it's not me.' I saw Johnny [Headlock] – he was in the background – and I winked at him, and he just played along. I went and stayed in a hotel. I got away with it."

Matt Bates — "We played some great gigs in Scotland, and it all seemed to go swimmingly for the Babyshambles tour until we got to Shrewsbury, which is actually where I grew up. And all my family are still living there, and it wasn't very nice to see the band I looked after being arrested in my home town and in the papers…

"The police thought: this is our chance, our moment of glory – we're going to take down a rock star here. We can get two lines in *The Sunday Mirror* or something. And they found, from what I can make out, fuck-all on the bus. They'd probably have found more if they went down to the local college and searched the common room – they'd *definitely* have found a few wraps of charlie or something."

Tony Linkin — "At that point the police were trying to catch him out. I'd been on the road with them, I think, a few days beforehand, and we all knew that they should be being careful, because there could be a bust at any point. I think everyone was a bit more worried that it couldn't happen again… [because] the tour couldn't work as long as the police were going to come knocking at any moment."

Ronnie Joyce (The Littl'ans) — "After our show at Shrewsbury, we all jumped in our van. Well, except me and Andrew [Aveling] – we were both stopped by kids asking us questions and congratulating us on the shows. Our manager at the time, Josh, then stormed over, shouting at us for taking too long to get in the van – he wanted to miss the traffic and get home to London as quickly as possible… We finally began to drive away, towards the outskirts of Shrewsbury. This was our last show until we re-joined the tour again at Bristol, two days later…

"We were driving along when, all of a sudden, the van stopped. I didn't even have enough time to blink as the van's side door had been flung open. I put my head down and remembered when, earlier in the tour, in Sheffield, driving outside a hotel, some kids had opened our unlocked van side door and tried to get in – thinking Pete was inside. But the noise this time was so violent, I thought we were being robbed by criminals on the side of the road.

"All these thoughts passed through my head and, as I looked up, I felt the wrath of a policeman's truncheon across my left eye. There were at least a dozen policemen, all in riot gear, shouting: 'Put your hands up!' We all complied, except Josh, who, comically, held up a flyer for the "Their Way" single [a collaboration between the Littl'ans and Peter, released by Rough Trade on the 17th of October] and protested: 'We're not Babyshambles! Look, I've got a flyer – I can prove it!'

"But that didn't phase the police – who may also have felt a little gutted that they'd got the wrong van; our quick getaway seemed to have prompted them to chase us, when Pete was still in the venue – and we were all handcuffed in heavy-duty cuffs and split up, and marched into two different vans.

"As we sat twiddling our thumbs, still in handcuffs, two policemen started to engage in conversation with us. It turned out one of the coppers was a fan of Littl'ans, and wondered if he could get our autographs when this was all over. Bizarre as it sounds, I honestly think he was being serious."

Fortunately, Babyshambles' acting lawyer was already in Shrewsbury. While he was racing around trying to resolve the situation, those who'd been collared were taken to Telford police station, sat down in the lobby, and called in one-by-one to a private room where two male police officers stood alongside a chief constable.

Strip-searches were conducted – mercifully, without the dreaded rubber glove treatment – and suspects were released. Peter, they were told, had been taken to another station on his own, which raised concerns about his safety.

A large, costly operation, it had garnered little in the way of results: a small amount of gear on a crack and heroin addict – hardly an alarming find – while the bits and pieces discovered on others didn't exactly make it a resounding success; certainly insufficient to justify such expense and manpower. Put more succinctly, it was a waste of everyone's time and of taxpayers' money, with no names made and no big find.

Detained for over twelve hours, Peter was released on bail until December, claiming that his implant had been mistaken for "the hard stuff". Returning with his bandmates to find the tour buses stinking of sniffer dogs and their belongings strewn about the place, the episode forced the postponement of the tour's next gig, scheduled to take place at Norwich's University of East Anglia the following day.

Unable to make it to Norwich in time, the show was postponed until the 14th of October, the tour resuming at The Chinnery, Southend, on the 4th. Fulfilling dates at Bristol Academy on the 5th of October, The Cornerhouse, Middlesbrough, on the 7th, Leeds' Blank Canvas on the 8th – at which Peter pulled down an entire lighting rig that narrowly missed Drew's head – Liverpool Academy on the 9th and Cardiff University on the 10th, the tour came to an abrupt end the following night at Brixton Academy.

Shows slated for the 14th, 15th and 16th, at Norwich, Coventry and London's KoKo respectively, were cancelled, owing to Peter's reluctance to perform, though the official line fed to the press was exhaustion.

Adam —   "In hindsight, it was a mistake booking extra shows to tag on to the end of the tour. It was Peter's idea in the first place, although he will deny ever agreeing to the extra dates. I heard it through Ronnie [Flynn] that Peter didn't want to do the new dates and, as usual, I approached him. He ummed and aahed, then looked sheepish and said he needed a break. I thought: fair enough, just don't agree if you aren't into it. It was a bit annoying, as it was his idea in the first place."

Peter's lapse into melancholia continued in the run-up to the release of *Down In Albion*, not helped by officers' raiding of the studio featured in the *Mirror* story, and the leaking of the album onto the internet at the end of October.

Lacking universal acclaim, detractors bemoaned unfulfilled potential and a release far too rough round the edges for their tastes, others opting for a muddy middle ground amid accusations of carrying too many fillers, while advocates warmed to its raw, unpolished sound.

John Ford, writing in an xfm.co.uk review, hailed Adam as its driving force, applauding his "no-nonsense" drumming on "A 'rebours" and "The 32nd of December", and the album's "numerous moments of greatness," while claiming that "What Katy Did Next" required "a serious rewrite," and that "it's the low points that sting the most" – too often a case of "good ideas badly executed and tarnished with the Mick Jones production 'sheen'."

The Observer's Jon Savage, writing on 20th November 2005, didn't receive the album any more warmly, accusing it, "somewhere after the cod-reggae Sticks and Stones", of becoming "mired in mid-tempo sludge", with too many tracks seeming "overlong, even if they're not much over three minutes."

Blaming the group's "own conceptual and physical shortcomings", rather than production oversights for the album's perceived lack of punch, he rated it a "misfired grand statement that fans will love, that the curious will find intriguing, and that the general public will ignore."

The Guardian's Dorian Lynskey called it "frustratingly inconclusive", opining that "the album stumbles from peak to trough, testing the listener's patience while retaining its eccentric charm... Many of *Down In Albion's* vices – strained vocals, half-formed ideas, Mick Jones's thin, grey production – are familiar from the final Libertines album, but the portions are bigger."

More grateful reviewers included Pete Paphides. Writing in *The Times* on 11th November, he considered it a better effort "than we could have reasonably expected", warming to the "freewheeling narco-funk" of "The 32nd of December" and the "dissolute swagger" of "Pipe Down" and "Eight Dead Boys". His *Sunday Times* counterpart, Mark Edwards, wrote that while "Doherty's tabloid fame has grown, we've been waiting for some hard evidence that his talent, rather than merely his lifestyle, justifies the attention." "La Belle et la Bête", he thought, "begins a fabulous five-song onslaught that proves he really is worth worrying about".

Andy Gill of *The Independent*, meanwhile, thought it "a far better album than we have right to expect from the tabloids' favourite dissolute folk devil", while warning Peter to avoid becoming "a bright, perhaps brilliant, flame dimmed by dissipation."

Drew —
"Most musicians really want the most people possible to hear their records. And because of how it sounds, and the performances and everything, I think that we didn't achieve the potential that that album had… But it's a warts-and-all, accurate account of the place we were at at the time; it was a fucked-up time, and I think aesthetically and artistically that album is very representative of the place we were in.

"If Mick had let us use some of the cleaner takes, some of the tighter takes, and some of the bits where Peter's vocals were more in tune or where there wasn't a kickdrum out of place here and there, it could have had the same effect and still been a little bit closer to what it could have been.

"The songs, they're still the same songs, you know? And I'm proud of the songs and proud of being in that band at that time, and I'm proud to have worked with Mick Jones. There's a certain method to his madness and it's a rough diamond, I suppose.

"In my mind, what's good about it is the fact that it's really good songs played badly, instead of really bad songs played well, which you get a lot – these awful set-up songs that are on the radio and MTV all the time that have super-slick production, but they're awful songs.

"When I look out the window at a gig and I see a bunch of kids singing the chorus of "Loyalty Song" or "Fuck Forever" or "Eight Dead Boys", you can't hear the production then. Or somebody walking down the road whistling "Albion", you can't hear the overly-laboured Hammond intro."

Adam —
"I have mixed feelings about *Down In Albion*. It has loads of amazing bits of music, but it also has loads of unnecessary mistakes and poor playing, and that's just in the drumming! I mean, it is real and raw, but no-one releases raw and untouched takes. To be honest, I found it quite hard to listen to when it was finished, but now I've learnt to live with the rawness of it.

"I don't blame anyone for the uniqueness of the album. I just wish we'd taken more time and been stronger in the studio. But what's done is done and the album is out there, so ultimately that's an achievement in itself. There were times when I thought the album would never be made. The album got made despite severe drug addictions, deaths, threats, paranoia and, at times, manic psychosis – now that's the real achievement."

Patrick —
"Its strengths are the songs. Some of them came out good – "Pipe Down" did. It could have been a bit heavier. "Up The Morning" is a beautiful song. First time I ever played it with the band. It could have been so much better."

"Its weaknesses are the production and the sound quality. I'd like to go and re-record that album. There's songs on there, like "Loyalty Song", which could be a modern day "There She Goes" if the sounds were right… Basically, what we did: we got in the studio, we plugged the guitars in, recorded it, thought we were warming up, and he [Mick Jones] was recording tapes. Do you know how frustrating that is for an artist, for someone who's worked on his songs for a year? It was like smashing my head against the wall, like sticking a bayonet in my fucking skull. It was really frustrating, ultra frustrating. I was complaining about it all the time."

Tony Linkin — "It's got brilliant songs on it. It's a real mood album, I think, that if you're in the right mood for, then it's a great record. I know a lot of people who love that record; I love it myself. Its weaknesses? Probably some of it was a bit too disjointed, and my biggest problem is probably Pete's vocals on it – the B sides especially – because it just wasn't as beautiful as his voice usually is to me. I didn't think his vocals were great on that album, which is always a pity, because I think he's got such an amazing voice. It was always a bit cracked on that, excuse the pun.

"I think it would've been a better album if they'd have come off the road and gone in and done it… when they did the British tour, they were really good – really, really good – by the time they'd finished that tour. And then they could have gone straight into the studio and made an album, and it could have been made really quickly, because all the songs and everything were there.

"It's something I'm not sure about exactly, but I think there were problems with Rough Trade at the time, or maybe James was trying to get them off Rough Trade, which is part of the reason they didn't go in quite quickly and do it…

"It made them sound more shambolic than they actually were, although in a way it's genius for what it is. But it's not a record I could put on all the time, which is what I want it to be, really, because some of it's quite painful to listen to, for me. Maybe that's because I was quite close to the whole thing as well."

Anthony Thornton — "*Down In Albion*'s main strength and weakness is exactly the same: there's no compromise. They eschewed the temptation to get the latest hot producer in to make a 'product' of its time that would slip down easily because it varied so little from the then current norm.

"It's a difficult record, but only insofar as some of the great records of the '70s were difficult. It required a certain level of dedication, but once given there are plenty of rewards to be had; new things crop up all the time.

"Mick Jones' production has to be praised as well: he's made a record that sounds timeless; it could have been made at pretty much any time from 1969 onwards. For that reason and because it's simultaneously dense and sprawling, it'll endure."

Ben Bailey — "There's some great musicianship on it, [but], I dunno, sometimes there's just a little bit in it where I'm longing for it to be a bit more complete, but then I suppose that's the whole style of the band."

Iain Gore — "I've had some people tell me the record's shit, while others have come up to me and said it's fucking amazing – it depends on what people are into. And I think there's a lot of people who've jumped on the 'it's shit' bandwagon as a record, just because they've heard that from other people, and people generally repeat what other people say. There are people who've said: 'That record's not very good, or it doesn't sound very good, or it's a bit scrappy.' And it's, like: 'Have you listened to it?' And I'd say, like, ninety per cent of those people say no… But I like my music raw; it's, like, if it was done in a different way, would it still have the same charm? You'll never know."

Released on 14th November 2005, *Down In Albion* charted at 10th place in the UK Albums Chart, though once Babyshambles' hardcore fan base stopped buying it in droves it slid out of the top ten – evidence that the group had some way to go before they could count on a wider audience for sales.

Behind the scenes, meanwhile, frantic liaisons were taking place between Rough Trade and Patrick, Drew and Adam, who wanted to ensure a contract was drawn up with their names on it.

As things stood at the time, a fatigued and wayward Peter was the only one set to earn any royalties from the album, despite stating categorically that other contributors be on the payroll. The problem: as so often, he was proving nigh on impossible to pin down.

Rarely in his rooms at the City Hotel, Brick Lane, that Geoff Travis had booked as a favour to him, despite the cost of the stay eventually being taken out of subsequent royalties, Rough Trade instructed its lawyers to advise that Peter's signature was essential in establishing that his bandmates had indeed worked on the album, despite knowing full well that this was the case.

The feeling among the band was that the label had largely turned its back on them, now that it had an album to market, displaying a reluctance to deal with an increasingly distant Peter directly. Rough Trade nonetheless organised, via international label manager Colin Wallace, interviews in Peter's hotel rooms in support of its release.

Peter often requested that journalists follow him to Brick Lane and Spitalfields market in search of trinket shops, in which he'd invite them to purchase items of interest for him, including old cigarette boxes, spoons and vintage record players, indulging his love of, as Adam puts it: "bits and bobs."

He was less forthcoming, however, when it came to James Mullord, who was keen to re-establish ties with the group, putting Adam in a predicament by asking him where Peter could be found. Feeling obliged to massage the truth, Adam opted to protect Peter's whereabouts: "It was really difficult. On the one hand I had Peter saying: 'Don't tell James,' and on the other, James was almost in tears that he'd been blamed for the photos, and was desperate to patch things up with Peter. I just tried to be diplomatic. James eventually tracked Peter down himself."

During this latest period of uncertainty for the band, there were, thankfully, more examples of the high jinks that punctuate the Babyshambles story, including the smuggling of an old white scooter into City Hotel.

Meeting Drew and Adam in a nearby pub to discuss division of royalties, Peter persuaded them to join him for a ride on the scooter, Drew climbing on the front, and Adam on the back.

Spluttering down Brick Lane the wrong way with about as much pace as a lethargic slug, greeting their fellow passengers with lung-busting "yeehaas!", they made it back to the hotel's foyer, to be told that they had to remove the scooter from the premises. Undeterred, the boys shoved it in a lift when the receptionist's back was turned. As soon as the lift arrived at the floor Peter's room was on, he wheeled it out, jumped aboard and rode it up and down the corridor, into the upstairs lounge, and back along the corridor.

When hearing the lift ascending, signalling that the receptionist was on their case, he knocked on another guest's room, asked if it was okay to stash it there for a while to avoid getting rumbled, and then talked the receptionist round when he arrived. Seconds later, with the receptionist on his way back down to the hotel's foyer, Peter retrieved the bike and set off again, revving violently, recalls Adam.

Peter, however, remembers the episode slightly differently: "I didn't have to smuggle it, mate. The bloke on the desk only needed twenty sovs for the entrance I made. Yeah, I got that scooter in, and I was so happy with it, too. It was great… I didn't really have a lock-up for it, you know? And I wasn't leaving it out there. Not in that area at that time of night. Just kept it in my little suite. And everything was sweet, yeah."

The ensuing costs of Peter's expeditions on scooter, allied to those levied as a consequence of his having redecorated the walls of his rooms with spidery scrawls, led to another inflated hotel bill.

A week or two later, with promotion of the album suspended, an elusive Peter decamped to Clapton with Mik Whitnall, with the intention of working on solo recordings, leaving Drew and Adam – increasingly the Babyshambles heartbeat in Peter's mounting absences – wondering whether they had a future with the band, a situation exacerbated by Patrick's gradual disengagement.

Adam — "Peter didn't really know where he was going or what he was doing – he was pretty messed up. He was staying round Gill's for some reason, and avoiding calls, when I eventually managed to get him. He told me that he felt Pat no longer wanted to be in the band, so I called Pat to try and sort it."

Drew and Adam's efforts in steering the good ship Albion in Peter's absence were not lost on Matt Bates, who said of the pair: "Without Drew and Adam, there would be no Babyshambles now, because they held it together between them – especially Adam in times of no management… Without Adam I'd never have got a show organised. I mean, I used to go through Adam all the time. For a drummer to take that responsibility on was quite a lot for him to do. I hold him in great esteem. So it if wasn't for Adam, there'd be no Babyshambles now, definitely."

Under pressure from Rough Trade to pen a solo deal, founder Geoff Travis was believed to have paid for Peter to stay in Bath to continue work on his own material, though it later emerged that, as had been the case with his decamp to City Hotel, the band had in fact footed the bill; and that, for all of the label's enthusiasm for the project, Peter was in no state to withstand another gruelling recording process.

In spite of this, he and Mik still managed to record a number of tracks worthy of release: "We've still got them all," says Peter. "He's still got them all on his digital recorder… We met some bird with a saxophone, actually…She was trying to fucking swap this saxophone for rocks, and we were, like: 'So where d'you nick it from?' And she was, like: 'Oh, no, I play it, but I just need a fix.' So we're, like: fuck that. Gave her some gear and got her to come and play on the demo. And it was pukka, man. It was pukka."

Adam and Drew visited Rough Trade in an effort to try and negotiate another album deal – a more long-term undertaking that Peter could ease himself into, sparing him the immediacy of his solo work – but the label showed little interest.

Sensing that the fragile Babyshambles empire was about to crumble, they decided to act, dragging a reluctant Patrick along with them to Bath, fearing that if ties weren't strengthened soon, particularly those between Patrick and Peter, they'd find themselves in an irretrievable situation.

Their efforts went unrewarded – initially at least – the trio alarmed at the extent to which the drugs were taking their toll on Peter, Adam describing it as "a time of mass drugs consumption and growing egos." As for repairing the damage done to Peter and Patrick's relationship, it was more a case of an already tense situation becoming untenable, one occasion in particular going a long way to driving them even further apart.

A barely coherent Peter decided on a whim to return to London in the early hours of a cold November morning, imploring others to join him in his battered old

---

Opposite: Relaxing in the dressing room.

Jag for "an adventure". Drew and Adam, unwilling to flirt again with danger as a consequence of Peter's inebriation, declined the offer of joining him.

An awkward Patrick, unsure who to side with, opted to join Peter, along with Nuha Razik, an undergraduate who had become friends with Peter since meeting at a gig in Nottingham's Rock City that summer, and who had recorded as-yet-to-be-released footage christened *The Brick Lane Sessions*, the material captured covering a three-week period that included gigs and more intimate moments.

For Patrick and Nuha, their decision was to be an unfortunate one, Peter turfing them out halfway towards the capital, dumping them on the hard shoulder and acting as if nothing had happened when they caught up with him shortly after.

The incident helped widen the gap between Peter and Patrick, who, now assured of the security a share in the recently struck Rough Trade publishing deal, and sick of feeling marginalised, appeared sparingly with Babyshambles in either a social or professional capacity thereafter.

Nuha puts Peter's behaviour down to his latest, impending spell in rehab. Rough Trade's pleas for him to commit to treatment were ignored, and it wasn't until Kate suggested that Peter follow her to The Meadows, Arizona, where she took refuge after the *Daily Mirror* story broke, that he agreed to fly to the States.

Aware of how important it was that Peter made the flight the next day, Nuha and Patrick didn't want to risk him going astray at such a vulnerable time. Pretty soon, however, Peter was playing up, at one point driving down the wrong side of the motorway – "It was just fucking ridiculous, stupid behaviour", Patrick recalls.

Nuha Razik —

"Peter started driving a bit stupidly, just for the hell of it, and Patrick was getting a little bit panicked, and he was, like: 'Calm down, what are you doing? Calm down.'

"And the more that Patrick was getting a bit nervous about things and telling him to just fucking calm it, he was playing up to it a bit more and just being that bit more reckless… so I was just trying to calm everything down… At some point it all went really quiet in the car… [then] something happened that made him flip in a second, and he was, like: 'Right, get out of the car! Get out!' We were, like: 'What? In the middle of a fucking motorway, in the middle of nowhere – somewhere between Bath and London, in the middle of the night, pitch black?'"

Nuha stormed out of the car, followed by Patrick, the pair bemused as to their next move, as Peter sped off. Freezing cold and stranded on the side of the road, and with no idea where they were, Nuha proposed that they keep walking in the direction that Peter had taken off in, figuring that he'd stop at some point.

Sure enough, about ten minutes' later, they came to a side-street illuminated by a set of headlights – Peter's. Peering into the front, they saw his head resting against the steering wheel.

When climbing in to join him, he immediately perked up, greeting them cheerily, Nuha recalling: "He either just pretended what had just happened didn't happen, or he couldn't remember what had just happened… but somehow we just got back in the car and sat there, me and Pat just looking at one another."

Patrick — "I walked up and found him and got back in the car. I was in two minds whether to beat the shit out of him and take five hundred quid out of his pocket so I could get home, or just get back to Adam and Drew. Normally I wouldn't take shit from anyone; for some reason, I was in a bit of a frail state of mind…

"He can't explain it. I asked him about it ages ago and he said: 'I'm really sorry, I can't explain it, Pat.' …I wanted to drag him out and leave him there and drive off, but I'm not a cunt. I said to him: 'Look, if you're gonna leave me here, at least give me some money.'… That was a fucking raw move."

With America, and another spell in rehab, looming large, Peter employed some tried-and-tested tactics to delay the process.

Adam — "A few of us were all just basically trying to pack him off, and as soon as he was ready to go he'd then run back upstairs and get something else, or grab another suitcase – just fucking around, continually packing a case, unpacking it. Just being a maniac, trying to stall going.

"I think in the end it took him about four hours. He went on his own, in his Jag, then me and Drew went home. Then I think he ended up in America somehow."

Finally, Peter was on his way to America. Drew and Adam would be spared their frequent trips to Bath, where their friend's troubled state of mind was garnering little material worthy of recording; and, they hoped, the sight of Peter's "really messy" state, as Adam puts it.

The grip of addiction was tightening, and it was patently clear to those with Peter's best interests at heart that another spell in rehab was the only sensible option.

Quite how long he would remain there was open to debate.

8

Mik Joins The Band

With Peter holed-up in Arizona, "Albion" was released on 28th of November, having been showcased on *Later With Jools Holland* earlier that month along with "Fuck Forever", the single enjoying a similarly impressive début to the album from which it was taken, reaching number eight in the UK Singles Chart.

Adam —   "*Jools Holland* didn't show us in the best of light. Pat's guitar was out of tune, and both he and Peter hadn't slept for days – both had been on a bender. I was in two minds whether we should do it, but we done it. And like most things we perform, it is what it is!"

Adam, who had been promoting "Albion" in tandem with Drew, received a call informing him that Peter was dancing on the bar and waving his arms about in the Brixton Academy, where The Paddingtons were supporting The Bravery.

The news meant that Peter had lasted just over a week of a scheduled four-week spell in rehab – much to Kate's chagrin.

Peter —   "I cancelled rehab in Arizona, the idea being that I'd finish rehab in Arizona and then move to L.A. with the missus… and then we'd live happily ever after. But, nine days of detox in the desert, and I couldn't get out of there quick enough."

Worse was to follow. On 30th of November, he was stopped by police in Ealing for apparently erratic driving, amid suggestions of glazed eyes, and arrested for alleged possession of Class A drugs. Bailed to return in January 2006, the arrest, and in particular his failed rehabilitation attempt, so disappointed Kate that their sometimes tempestuous relationship took another turn for the worse. Peter, shouldering a heavy guilt burden, took off again, feeling that he'd let everyone down.

Back in Clapton, East London, where he was joined by Mik Whitnall and new friend, Purple – later to join the band on stage as a rapper – he resumed work on his solo material, avoiding contact with Drew and Adam for a couple of weeks, and involuntarily reacquainting himself with the law again on 4th December – for "erratic driving" – a search producing drugs; and on the 18th, when he was arrested on suspicion of driving under the influence of drink or drugs.

To the delight of his critics, Peter's latest brush with the law came just less than a fortnight after charges were dropped against him for the Shrewsbury raid. Initially fleeing the car after being flagged down, Peter and three others were outpaced and arrested, leaving traces of both heroin and cocaine behind in the vehicle.

This, and the arrests on 30th November and 4th December, meant that another year opened amid great uncertainty, the threat of another jail sentence hanging over Peter, who nonetheless saw 2006 in with an intimate shindig at his new flat in Laburnum Street, which he'd moved into shortly before Christmas.

Drew and Adam, who only found out about the hastily arranged party at the last minute, left after performing a couple of songs to fulfil their respective engagements. Both were surprised to see James Mullord at the bash, supposing that he and Peter had patched up their differences.

The new year also marked the introduction of Ashtar Alkhirsan into the fold, to garner footage of the band for an *Arena* documentary that was shown towards the end of the year.

Ashtar first met Peter while producing and directing *The Unknown Hancock*, a 90-minute tribute to comedian Tony Hancock. Peter recorded a track entitled *Don't Fall Backwards*, the name of which references a book the comic read in an episode of *Hancock's Half Hour*, and was also interviewed for the documentary, screened on BBC2 on Boxing Day.

Knowing that Peter was a big Hancock fan, Ashtar made contact, with a view to him penning a poem for the show. Peter agreed instantly, and the pair shared a number of conversations – one of which included Peter singing, in a taxi, to a total stranger he'd met in the street – about how they could move the project forward.

As it transpired, Peter decided against a poem, favouring a song he'd been working on about Hancock. Ashtar travelled to Bath, where Peter was staying at the time, to record the song and an interview for the documentary. Peter spoke about how Hancock's work evoked images of a bygone era, an age that he really related to, even though he wasn't sure it ever existed – a dreamscape, if you like – but nonetheless something he connected with on a personal level.

Older Hancock fans may have considered Peter's inclusion a curious one, but Ashtar regarded him as a fresh voice, and one who very probably had more in common with the comic than they were comfortable admitting.

The most obvious thread of connection is addiction. Hancock's alcoholism blighted his life, whereas Peter's struggles with crack cocaine and heroin have cast a shadow that far too regularly detracts from his talents as an artist.

Ashtar recognised a frailty and vulnerability in Peter that had also been part of Hancock's make-up, not to mention the chaos engendered by addiction. She was also taken by how nervous Peter had been about his contribution to the Hancock documentary, and how important it was for him that his input be of worth, his generous nature ensuring that any apprehension she harboured fell quickly away.

Once work began on the *Arena* documentary, Ashtar gained a greater insight into Peter's true nature. Far from the hopeless junkie so often portrayed, she found him to be industrious and disciplined, so engrossed in his work that he was practically oblivious to her presence when left alone together.

His friends for the most part gone by early evening, Peter would use a variety of implements to aid his vast creative output – "he'd have a couple of dictaphones going, he'd be recording it on his laptop, and he'd be playing stuff and then playing it back", Ashtar remembers.

She observed as he crafted songs out of mere kernels of ideas, struck by his lack of preoccupation with how they might be viewed by others, and the freedom she was given to make whatever film she wanted; if she put the camera down at any stage, because she thought someone was too upset or she deemed her presence inappropriate or intrusive, it was Ashtar who took that decision; nobody ever instructed her to do so.

Ashtar Alkhirsan — "What's typical of Peter is that, in certain areas, he'll give you total access; in others you won't get any. Although he appears to give you unrestrained access, in actual fact he knows where the line is, but most musicians, the line would be in the writing process – they wouldn't let you be party to that, so I found that really interesting...

"It's really inspiring that he's not worried about what people think – it doesn't matter to him, he just doesn't care. It's work in progress, and he'll put it out there and let people hear work in progress, whereas most other people are so nervous about being judged and so terrified, and so insecure about their work being seen in a negative way, that it has to be pristine before it'll go out there. Not with him.

"I found that really, really interesting, and a lesson to me that there's no point in protecting your ego in that way – it's just utterly pointless. And I think it's a mark of somebody who's, ironically, incredibly strong. He's fragile, but he's incredibly strong at the same time to have no compunction about that – he doesn't give a fuck.

"That could have ended up on the telly – he wouldn't have cared. Because now, twelve months later, that song is worked through, and is a really good song. But its original incarnation, it was very different and it was a sketch, and now it's become something full and three-dimensional."

And while Peter is clearly the leader of the band, Ashtar saw how Drew, Adam and increasingly, Mik, complimented him perfectly, interlacing their idiosyncrasies to form a vibrant, unified collective, their undervalued contributions essential to the creative process.

Demonstrating a fierce loyalty towards Peter, their emotional intelligence and understanding of the way that he works provides a crucial safety net, freeing him to the take the sort of risks on stage that few artists would feel comfortable with: "They don't know a lot of the time what he's going to play next: they're constantly watching, and sometimes at some stage, because he's so instinctive, he will go out and play a song that he's still working on…

"What they're brilliant at doing is watching him and instinctively trying to understand what it is he needs – they're absolutely brilliant at that – and I think that's indispensable to him. They are exceptional in that way, in their sensitivity to him, and to the music that he's creating."

Not since The Smiths in the '80s had she seen a group of musicians capture a generation in the way that Babyshambles have – not forgetting The Libertines before them – embodying a passion that in particular evoked memories of The Clash and The Jam.

Indeed, watching how followers of the band reacted to their vibrancy and resonance enabled her to recall what fired her as a teenager.

Ashtar Alkhirsan — "I looked out in the audience and I saw in people's faces that devotion and that energy and excitement, and that's exactly what I felt about The Jam. That's exactly what I felt. And I remember looking at those kids' faces just thinking: oh my God, that is it – that is what it was like to be seventeen, eighteen. It was so clear to me that it was a similar experience for them, and that got my adrenaline pumping."

"There is a real, raw energy and a kind of passion which is really intoxicating. For me, being on stage filming them, you're caught between these two sort of tsunamis: you've got the band and Peter, just storming it, and then you've got this audience. The energy that you get from the audience, just looking at their faces, is really powerful.

"When I'm filming, I'm just between those two things. I'm not part of either of them; I'm just standing in the middle, and I've got these two tidal waves either side of me. It's such an amazing feeling. I can see why musicians love that, why they become addicted to that, because your adrenaline is pumping…

"I didn't interview any fans, but I think there's a real passion and dedication amongst them. And I think what's so brilliant about them is there's no restraint. It's not a polite audience. They don't give a fuck – they're all there to be taken over by the music, and that is a really appealing thing.

"And I think that's where the energy comes from. That you've got this group of people who are all unrestrained – they're just giving over to it, they don't fight it. There are certain songs that are guaranteed to just pull their guts out – it's fucking great to watch it, it really is good… Imagine what it's like performing, knowing that you're generating that."

In the first week of the new year, the band announced a short UK tour that took in London's KoKo on 9th January, the Sheffield Plug on the 10th, and The Underground,

Stoke, on the 11th, while squeezing in a couple of intimate shows at Soho's Jazz After Dark on the 6th and 7th.

Patrick's absence from these dates meant that Peter replaced him on guitar – as had been the case since a Christmas show at the Rhythm Factory on December 22nd. A clutch of new songs, such as "Fixing Up To Go", "The Blinding" and "Sedative", were forming, and with the security of tour dates lying ahead, the future held promise, but Peter's impending court dates cast doubt on this fragile hope.

Fearing the worst, on 10th January 2006, a typically late Peter, who, as his solicitor, Eamonn Sherry later explained, had been held up by traffic and pursuit "by a number of other individuals," owing to the "press activity that there is in relation to this gentleman," appeared at Ealing Magistrates' Court. Pleading guilty to possession of cocaine and heroin – charges, dating back to his arrest on November 30th, that can carry a custodial sentence of up to seven years – Peter was released on unconditional bail, and told to reappear on 8th February. Leaving court in an upbeat mood, he was greeted by his mother, Jacqueline, sister Amy-Jo, Ronnie Flynn, Gerry O'Boyle of the Boogaloo, Drew and Adam, who were united in their determination not to allow him fall back into the welcoming arms of addiction.

Driving him to The Hilton, Shepherd's Bush, ready to put into operation a plan to find him somewhere safe to stay in the north of England – out of the glare of the paparazzi, away from temptation and free from the pressures of living in the capital – their hopes were quickly dashed when Peter expressed a desire to visit a friend whose company some considered detrimental to his chances of cleaning up; in other words, he was off to score again.

It was during this journey that Adam received a call enquiring about potential gigs for later that month and the next, an overzealous Peter, without the weight of the court case bearing down on him, agreeing instantly, even suggesting that Babyshambles stage a show each night for the rest of the year – an assertion he later denied, says Adam.

Adam — "We were all in the car, coming back from court and Matt [Bates] had given me a list of dates and called me to confirm. So I gave all those dates to Peter, and he was over the moon, saying: 'Yeah, let's do it.' There was an *NME* show, a few tour dates, a few TV shows – he was really gleefully wanting to do it.

"It was later that he declared that he'd never told me any such thing. I'm lucky I'm not in that position any more. I don't have to deal with the dates, but he was always doing that: agreeing to a show, then a week later he'd say he never agreed to it. He still does it, even now."

Opposite: Mik in shades at Laburnum Street.

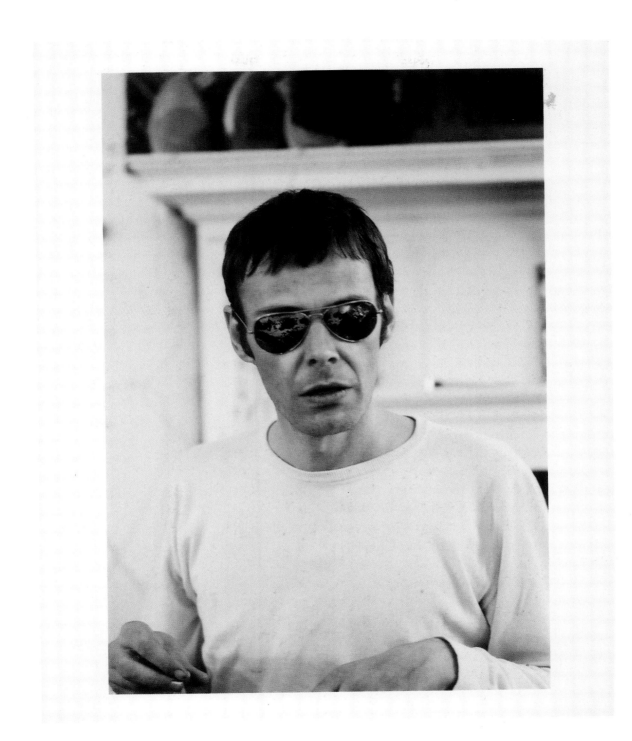

Peter failed to show at The Underground, Stoke, that night, leaving The General to lead the rest of Babyshambles, comprising Drew, Adam and Mik Whitnall who by this stage had started to put in occasional appearances with the band, in Patrick's absence.

The gig was nearly pulled by police anxious not to have another riot on their hands, Adam and Drew persuading owner-cum-Babyshambles tour promoter Matt Bates that Peter was on his way.

Peter repeatedly assured them via phone that he was a few minutes away, and though it became patently clear that he was most likely still in London or stuck on the motorway, they took to the stage in the fading hope that he'd join them at the eleventh hour.

He didn't, The General's improvised rapping unappreciated by a crowd that booed him off, Peter arriving in Stoke hours after the gig had finished and going back to a fan's flat to play an acoustic show with Purple. Not that the spontaneous performance made much of an impression on him: "Chev missed our junction on the M1 and no-one noticed, but I don't remember a gig?!"

After the gig, Mik's forgetfulness – he had left his guitar in the venue – meant that he had to stand completely still, in darkness, until The Underground's manager came to his rescue: "I went back in, and as I went in, the manager of the place shut the door behind me, didn't realise I was in there, and put the alarm on. All the lads went out. I was thinking: what the hell's going on here? The lads were shouting through the letter box: 'Don't move or you'll set the infra-red alarm off!', and the police were gonna turn up.

"I had some stuff in my pockets I shouldn't have had, so I had to stand totally still for, like, forty-five minutes solid. I was even blinking really slowly – if I'd moved an inch the alarm would've gone off and the police would've turned up, and I'd have got carted off. So I literally had to stand like a statue until the manager came back and let me out."

"It was really hard then: I was still part-managing the band, and part-tour managing the band, and playing guitar – all at the same time."

Another arrest, in Hackney on 14th January, on suspicion of possessing Class A drugs and driving under the influence, put paid to any chance of a full showing at Graz, Austria.

With Peter detained at around six in the morning, Drew, Adam and The General turned up at Peter's Laburnum Street flat a couple of hours later, heading for Stansted airport, where they met up with photographer Danny Clifford. But it soon became evident that Peter wouldn't be accompanying them on their flight, lawyer Sean Curran calling Mik to tell him of the arrest.

Danny Clifford remembers what felt like an eternity waiting at the airport while the quartet weighed up their next move: should they miss the flight to Graz and avoid wasting their time; or fly to Austria in the improbable likelihood of Peter joining them later on?

Literally standing at the departures gate, with minutes to spare until it closed, they decided that, on balance, it was worth taking a gamble: if Peter remained in custody, they would still have somewhere to stay in Austria, plus their flights had already been paid for; if he was released, they'd finance a private jet for him, despite the damage that such an extravagance would inflict upon the Babyshambles bank balance.

Arriving in Austria to swarms of press, Drew and Adam assumed their now-familiar role of explaining away Peter's absence, still unsure themselves at that stage whether he'd be joining them, phone calls to a friend of Danny's ascertaining that the chartering of a private plane was a possibility, were Peter able to make the gig on time.

Once at their hotel, countless calls were made in an effort to determine the seriousness of Peter's situation. When speaking to officers at Stoke Newington police station, the urgency of need for his release was withheld, such knowledge as good as guaranteeing his continued detainment.

By late afternoon, and still with no indication as to whether Peter would be able to make it, the show's promoters took Drew, Adam, Danny and The General out for dinner. It transpired that, far from the old, five-hundred-capacity pornographic cinema that the gig was supposed to have taken place in, the promoter's licence had been revoked, such had been the interest generated by the band.

A local radio station had taken over the promotion of the show and, able to reach more prospective punters, those keen to acquire a ticket proliferated so rapidly that an enormous aircraft hangar was booked instead.

But as the hours passed, the likelihood of Peter's presence diminished. It was fast becoming a logistical nightmare trying to figure out how the necessary connections could be made to fly him to Austria in time – and that was in the dying hope of his being released from custody within a matter of hours.

Danny's friend had a pilot and crew standing by, but as the clock counted down, and with Peter no closer to freedom, there was another decision to make: whether Drew and Adam, supplemented by The General, would perform.

The General, who had initially arranged the booking, was keen that it went ahead, while the promoter agreed to pay a percentage of the receipts as a sweetener. Adam and Drew reluctantly obliged, playing a couple of numbers – the second of which The General joined them for – but as soon as the track finished, they put their instruments down, walked off the stage, and returned to their hotel with the sense that they'd travelled to Austria under false pretences.

Drew —   "I've done it before, I've done it a few times, when we're supposed to be playing gigs, and I'd go out and explain that Peter's not gonna come, and play a couple of songs. It only really works overseas; if I do that in England I'll get a lighting rig thrown at my head.

"But, yeah, in Graz I came out with *Albion*, then General stormed on, grabbed the mic and started rapping over it all, and then we did "Pentonville Rough". And it later emerged that the reason why The General was so keen for us to go out and play a couple of songs was that way he'd still get paid."

Adam —   "I remember walking in, the kids going: 'Where's Pete, where's Pete?', Drew and I kind of knowing that he's not turning up. It's a horrible feeling – a horrible, dark, gut feeling. You know he's not coming, and you're sitting there waiting and stuff."

Sally
Anchassi —   "There's been a lot of no-shows where I've been sitting in the basement with Adam and Drew and Pat, or Adam and Drew and Mik, and they've gone: 'No, we're not going, they'll tear us apart.' But for some reason, that gig they decided to play.

"It was quite weird because Drew said: 'It was brilliant', and Adam said: 'It was awful.' 'No, it was really good, they were really nice, they responded really well, and it was brilliant, went down really well.' Adam was, like: 'Oh God, I was so embarrassed to get up on the stage... I was mortified.'"

Back at their hotel, Danny asked Drew and Adam whether they'd been paid. When they said that they hadn't, he arranged to be dropped off at the radio station's offices.

Demanding that Drew and Adam be given their fee, while issuing a warning that if that didn't happen the station's credibility would be publicly derided, and pointing out that fans would be entitled to pocket a refund in the event of non-payment to Babyshambles, he soon found himself in possession of a wad of notes. In return, Danny promised that the band would consider returning to Austria at a later date.

Back in London, during a three-night residency at the Rhythm Factory on the 17th, 18th and 19th January, Peter stumbled his way through three-hour mammoth shows, meandering from one song to another without performing them in anything like their entirety, and falling into Adam's drums as the audience stared on in disbelief, most leaving before the end.

More elongated jams than the usual medley of tunes, the disjointed songs lasted a good half-an-hour each. In between, Peter lurched across the stage and fell asleep standing up, blinking himself awake to pick up where he left off – if he could remember.

The edginess on stage transferred to the audience, who were divided as to their loyalty: one half were heartbroken and angry at the sight of an icon in freefall; the other rooting for him to turn it around.

Ashtar remembers a fight breaking out in the audience, a female fan defending Peter – the subject of vitriolic abuse – and herself against accusations that she'd "follow any stupid cunt," while suggesting that her antagonist "get up there when your head is in the same place as his."

Adam —

"He was out of his tree, with no coherency whatsoever. It got so bad that at one point people were scratching their heads in dismay, wondering what was going on, before sloping off home. In those situations I just grit my teeth, lock onto Drew, and hope for a swift conclusion."

Drew —

"He got it into his head that we were going to play every single song that we've ever recorded. I was so shattered, it was horrible. We played for so long that I think there were only about thirty people in the room when we finished playing.

"I remember looking at the floor, at the dance floor, and there were people falling asleep in the corner, near the bar. The bar staff had packed up the bar, wiped the tables down. Peter stayed around, played some half-finished song that he'd written a couple of days ago or something. That wasn't rehearsed – just played the whole thing from memory."

Ashtar Alkhirsan —

"I was really quite upset by that, because he looked so tortured, and I had never seen him quite so – he looked distressed to me, and I found that really upsetting… When it fell apart, the whole gig couldn't be brought back; once it fell apart, it couldn't be rescued. I found it really upsetting to watch.

"The most interesting thing for me was at the end of that gig. I went up to Peter, and I said to him: 'I'm off,' and he looked at me, and he could see the expression on my face, and I was upset, and he just said to me: 'You win some, you lose some.' And that was his approach: the gig was over, it had happened, and that was it.

"I think he's [got] a brilliant coping mechanism…that when things get bad, he actually seems to have an ability to let it go, whereas I would go home and brood on that…A lot of people will think that I'm just making excuses for him, but I don't think I am – it is all part of the way he is, and all the fans know this, and I tried to show this in the documentary…It's a banal thing to say it's a roller-coaster, but it really is great highs, and then suddenly it can take you right down to the bottom. But I've never seen him stay there for very long, in the time that I was with them.

"There is this incredible energy, despite all the problems he has with his addiction and everything. It's a miracle that he manages to do as much as he does, which is prodigious – there is a large output of work going on there."

Before the first date of another mini tour, on the 20th, Peter pleaded guilty to possession of heroin, crack cocaine, morphine and cannabis at Thames Magistrates' Court, pertaining to his arrest on 4th December, and was released on unconditional bail until 8th February, when he would face other drugs charges.

The mini-tour, organised to provide much-needed funds, kicked-off at The Underground, Stoke, that night, also taking in Liverpool's Carling Academy on the 21st, Nottingham's Rescue Rooms on the 22nd, the Cambridge Junction on the 23rd – a night that marked Patrick's reappearance on stage – and University of Essex, Colchester, on the 24th.

Returning to London after the Colchester show, Peter started to drive to Leeds for the following night's gig at The Cockpit, but, angry that nobody would join him, turned tail just as the venue had filled, leaving Drew and Adam wondering how best to exit the building in one piece, fearing another riot, as the crowd they were hoping to leave behind started baying for blood.

Adam — "I remember calling him and saying: 'Look, where are you?' He said he was en route, and then started making some excuse that he was going back to London for some reason, and then I think Drew spoke to him – and the venue's packed by now, loads of kids in there – and he turns round and decides he's not gonna come. Because no-one would get in the Jag with him from London, because he drives like a maniac, so the story goes.

"So, we were all in the venue – it's all locked-up, there's loads of kids outside… I gave Drew the nod, and my brother, and we just all legged it out of the venue to the bus, and got the fuck out of there… [that was] the only one time I've really feared for my life, because for some reason there were loads of kids outside.

"It was really hard to get out of the venue, and you could hear the kids getting really restless, word getting around that he might not be showing up. And you heard loads of stuff getting thrown, and I can remember just getting out of that door as I heard him announce it, loads of smashing…

"It all kicked off up there, and the guy said we can never play there again… So that was another good night for him. I just feel sorry for the kids in those situations. They turn up and he doesn't show up, and you just try and hide when that happens; you just try and get out of there as quickly as possible, keep your head down.

"It didn't ease matters that the tour bus we'd hired was an old converted transit with no heating that just kept breaking down. All in all, an awful tour."

Mik — "We were in London with Peter and he'd got the car at the time, and said: 'Who's going to drive down with me?' And I don't know how many people reading this book have been in the car with Peter, but, let's put it this way: it's not good for your health!

"And I said: 'No way,' and he got in a bit of a huff, I think because no-one would get in the car. So we were all on the bus to Leeds, and I had a feeling that because no-one would get in the car, he wouldn't turn up…

"We found out that Peter weren't coming, and me, Adam and Drew were, like: 'Oh shit!', so we made a few excuses, said: 'We're off to the chippy' – something like that – and ran round the corner, got on the tour bus, and waited in a multi-storey car park for the crew to turn up."

The next day, on the 26th, Peter was in trouble with the police again, arrested twice in the same day: first for erratic driving at 5.40am in Laburnum Street, E2, for which he was taken in and subsequently charged for alleged possession of Class A drugs; and then in Whitechapel, at 3.05pm, officers stopping him on suspicion of being under the influence, a search producing a Class A drug.

Mik and The General drove back to London, from Leeds, to find Peter and take him with them to Newcastle, in readiness for that night's gig.

Arriving at his place shortly before the second arrest, and finding that no-one was there, The General set off to a nearby dealer's to see if Peter was there, leaving Mik to attempt contact via phone: "I went to the phone box to phone Peter, and the next thing I heard was a screaming of car tyres and this Jaguar was coming really fast, skidding round the corner on its side. And it was Peter driving it, with two cop cars screaming round the corner, and it was a full-on police chase down the road. I was, like: 'Fuck's sake!' I came out of the phone box, Pete saw me, skidded round the corner, and sort of took off and left the cars in his wake."

Thinking that Peter had lost his pursuers, Mik caught up with The General, the pair tearing off in the hope of making up the ground between them. When the police pulled them over, they ran off, officers grabbing The General.

Mik, though, jogged all the way home, later discovering that Peter, too, had been collared, "while I was at home watching videos!"

That night's gig at Newcastle University was subsequently cancelled, as were dates at Glasgow's Barrowlands, Bristol Academy and the London Shepherd's Bush Empire, after Peter pleaded guilty to possession of drugs at Thames Magistrates' Court on 27th of January, his counsel's pleas for bail turned down – despite the procurement of a private jet to fly him to Glasgow for the Barrowlands gig and the promise of round-the-clock observation in the form of a minder.

Lawyer Sean Curran spoke of a witch-hunt against his client, who gave magistrate Stephen Dawson the middle finger as he was sent down, describing him as an easy target due to his notoriety, while a Rough Trade spokesman alluded to police harassment, saying that he'd been arrested "far too many times for it to be anything else."

Remanded in custody until sentencing on 8th February, Peter remained in Pentonville Prison, an administrative error making it impossible for him to attend his hearing at Thames Magistrates' Court on 30th January, for his arrest on 18th December, though the case was dropped due to insufficient evidence that he'd been at the wheel, the keys found on him not fitting the vehicle in question.

On 8th February, he was up before magistrates again, this time at Ealing, pleading guilty to charges of drug possession relating to his arrests on 30th November, 3rd December and 26th January.

Spared the immediate threat of another spell inside, Peter was instead ordered to complete a twelve-month drug rehabilitation programme stipulating monthly drug tests – failure to do so risked a sentence – and celebrated his release from Pentonville by hooking up with Drew and Adam for a freedom shindig at the Boogaloo Bar.

Advertised at short notice, the gig played to a genial atmosphere, with Kate serving drinks at the bar, save for the few minutes she took out to join the band for "La Belle Et La Bête".

After the show, however, once the venue had emptied, Mik's night soured when he was refused money for a cab home – despite having just played for nothing: "I saw Shane McGowan, so went over to Shane and said: 'Look, I can't get home, do you want to buy my guitar off me for a hundred quid?' And he said: 'Don't sell your guitar,' and gave me a hundred quid, said: 'Give it back next time you see me.' It was really cool, he's a nice fella. Next time I saw him, I went to give it him back, and he couldn't even remember giving it to me!"

With more court cases hanging over Peter, the feeling among some of his nearest and dearest was that the revelry was a little premature: "It was weird at that time", says Mik. "Because we didn't know one week to the next whether Pete would be in or out of the nick."

A couple of days later, a surprise gig at London's KoKo club, performed as a three-piece, produced what Adam referred to as a "triangle of concentration", he scrutinising Drew's playing, and Drew looking to Peter's guitar playing, to keep the sound as tight as possible – a tough job given Peter's tendency to swap songs midway through one another.

Adam — "Sometimes the three-piece shows are so spontaneous and fluid. The problems arise when we can't hear each other; if the monitors are weak, all you can do is take the visual cues, so I end up watching the rhythm of Drew's fingers, and Drew is glued to Peter's chord shapes – it's the only way we get through it.

"This, coupled with Peter's desire to play songs only just written, always makes for a challenging show. I think this particular KoKo show wasn't the best!"

The quartet of dates cancelled as a result of Peter's imprisonment were rescheduled for later that month, with fresh dates added – a tour that Patrick rejoined for dates at the Shepherd's Bush Empire on the 20th and, belatedly, on the 24th at Glasgow, his soon-to-be permanent replacement, Mik Whitnall, also making a few appearances along the way.

But before the month was out, on 27th February, Peter ran into trouble again, this time in Birmingham, where he'd driven to in order to watch Dirty Pretty Things, fronted by Carl Barât, the ex-Libertine with whom Peter had been publicly reunited with some ten months earlier in the Boogaloo Bar.

Pulled over on suspicion of stealing a car in London – a Jaguar that had been newly acquired from a showroom – along with two unnamed men, the trio were arrested for alleged possession of Class A drugs before being released on police bail, pending further enquiries.

On 8th March, a day after the band announced festival and European tour dates, he was back at Thames Magistrates' Court for the first review of his twelve-month community order, District Judge Jane McIvor praising his progress, despite Peter turning up thirty minutes late.

The following day, he made yet another late, unwelcome return to the court, standing trial for seven counts of drug possession, covering his arrests on 18th December and 14th January – a case that was adjourned for two weeks following a request by Sean Curran, on the basis that interview tapes and a series of statements relevant to the case were unavailable for use in court.

When the 23rd arrived, Peter pleaded guilty to seven counts of drug possession, Sean's appeal for sentencing to be adjourned until 20th April granted once he'd emphasised the progress his client had made in his drug rehabilitation order.

Outside the court, though, Peter kicked a microphone out of BBC Radio One reporter Trudi Barber's hand, having just cleared a wall to escape the bedlam engendered among the waiting paparazzi.

Mik — "At that time, there was no-one driving Peter around. Believe it or not, I drove Peter, [as] he was banned from driving. I had to drive the Jag from Peter's house – I can't drive, I haven't got a licence – I drove the Jag, had to wait outside for him.

"There were loads of bloody police everywhere, no tax on or anything in the window, and I was crapping it. Anyway, Peter came out, and they all swarmed round him as usual. So I stuck me hand in the air to let him know where I was, and he came running over and he was trying to get in the car, and they wouldn't let him and they were blocking his entrance.

"And he was, like: 'Let me in!', and as he got in the car, she rammed the microphone – there was one where he was stood on this plinth and he booted the microphone in the air, and there was another one where this microphone, as he was trying to shut the door, an arm just came flying into where the door was supposed to be shut, and he just booted it out the way. And, in fact, it's a good job he did, 'cos she'd have had her arm taken off."

The outburst meant that Peter would have to find time for yet another court appearance in a few months' time and, to top another miserable day, the band failed to show at the KoKo that night.

Still managerless, on 11th April, Adam and Drew set off for Waterloo station to catch the Eurostar to Paris, for the Le Bataclan show – another that was close to being pulled, on this occasion Peter and Mik going AWOL for five hours, Adam losing phone contact with them around midday.

Mik —   "I think Adam and Drew had enough of waiting for Peter to get his arse out of his flat. We'd sit waiting for him to come out for hours. So they decided to naff off to Paris on their own and wait for me and Pete to get there ourselves. But they didn't tell us they'd set off. So I rang them, saying: 'Where are you?', expecting them to say they were on their way to the flat, and they said: 'Oh, we're in Paris,' and I was, like: 'What? How did you get there? How are we getting there? Who's arranging this?' And at that time, I was still fucking tour managing and all that crap, so I was a bit pissed off, to be honest…

"But, anyway, me and Pete tried to arrange a helicopter to pick us up, but that fell through, so we bounced a lift off someone to the ferry port. And there were no foot passengers allowed on this boat, so we had to go on a vehicle, and we bumped into this poor, unfortunate Australian family, who, fortunately, didn't know who Pete was. They must have been the only people on the ferry who didn't…

"So we said: 'Do you mind if we jump on here to get on the boat?', and they were, like: 'No, man, jump on.'… Anyway, it pulls up to customs, and I'm sat there with my fingers crossed, and the customs man goes: 'Is that *the* Pete Doherty in there?' The family went: 'Who?', and they realised it was us. So you can imagine what happened – some poor Australian bloke squatted over a table having his arse looked at. Just 'cos he let us on his tour bus. I think his wife was abused as well. Just meeting me and Peter. I felt really bad for them…

"I just remember looking back, seeing all their belongings on the tarmac, rooting through everything. And then on the other side, me and Pete got off the ferry – understandably, the Aussie family didn't want to take us through. This guy came up to us – big old lump – and offered us a lift, and we were, like: 'Okay.' We got in his car with him. He was a great guy, but he had a very dark side to his nature. I kept

Opposite: Peter plays guitar.

asking what he did, and he wouldn't tell us, but it turned out he was a debt collector for a big gangster in London… I still see him around, he's a nice chap."

The show's promoter, anxiously awaiting their arrival outside the venue, crowded by a hive of paparazzi, ushered them, suitcases in hand, to what the boys supposed would be the dressing room.

Mik —   "We pushed through [the paparazzi] and had all our suitcases, said to the promoter: 'Which way to the dressing room?' He said: 'Oh yes, follow me.' So we followed him out to the dressing room, he opens the door, so we go through here and walk into the dressing room – except it wasn't the dressing room: we walked straight onto the fucking stage, with all our suitcases… and Adam and Drew just kicked in and started playing…

"That was horrific – literally put on the spot. You can imagine: travelling for hours and hours, and you're stressed and you just want to sit down and have a cigarette first, tune your guitar, then go on stage. But we were right on the fucking stage, guitars plonked into our hands. So, it was, like, ten minutes of me running around setting everything up while the crowd were going crazy – it was bedlam."

Adam —   "They [Peter and Mik] turned up, literally, as the promoter was on stage, ready to pull the show, and in they come… Me and Drew were on stage, [and] they're coming up the stairs… they run on stage with suitcases… like rabbits in the headlights, [and] don't realise there's a whole crowd there – it's like a comedy show…

"That's why we did a massive intro, [lasting] about ten minutes, before they sorted themselves out."

Unable to make it back in time from Paris, Peter failed to appear at Thames Magistrates' Court the following day, for the latest review of his community order – a case that was adjourned until 12th May.

He was also absent from a gig planned at Dublin's Temple Bar Music Centre on 13th April, missing two flights and arriving in Belfast the next day, offering no explanation for the no-show, for that night's show at the Spring and Airbrake, at which merchandise was stolen by kids too quick for a pursuing Johnny Headlock.

Adam —   "All day, you just get this horrible gut feeling that he's not gonna show up. And you think: it's alright, there's another two planes. And then you hear he's missed that one. [And you think:] alright, there's another plane. Then you run out of options.

"I remember being downstairs in that Dublin Temple Bar when he announced it, because we couldn't get out, and you could just hear the crowd go fucking mad, and it's the worst feeling in the world. Standing down there, thinking about all the people you've let down, you have that immediate, fucking horrible gut feeling, and then the fear of how the fuck you're gonna get to your bus without getting killed.

"But we got there in the end, and that night we ended up having dinner with Shane McGowan, I think, in Bono's place in Dublin. A good end to a shit night."

Next up came a gig at Derry's Nerve Centre on the 15th, Ireland in this instance offering a mixed reception, some fans' display of enthusiasm not quite what the band had been used to, and a death threat causing them to leave the venue sooner than they would have liked.

Mik — "D'you know what? It wasn't negative, just over-excited. The bus pulled in and there were bricks and everything bouncing off the bus as we pulled in. And then they were all kind of cheering. It was this weird kinda vibe – mental… You could feel the love at that gig… It was mental, just getting to and from the stage."

Adam — "We were on the tour bus – we pulled up outside this place in Derry – and right outside the tour bus, there was a bridge, and the roof of the tour bus was level with the bridge. I was opening it all up to get some air in there, poked my head out, and there was loads of kids there, cussing and that, and then something came flying over, so I thought: fuck this.

"And Peter's sitting right underneath me, by the lounge, and I said something to him like: 'It's wild out there, be careful.' And he goes: 'Oh yeah, whatever' – something to that effect – pokes his head out, and gets showered with bottles as well. Got called a plumbag and told to fuck off back to England."

Sally Anchassi — "It was so violent – they tore the windscreen wipers off; they were trying to rock the bus; they were bombing the bus with bottles and coins. Alizé (Meurisse, a friend of Peter's, whose photos appear in the book) was there, and she wanted to stay on the bus and stuff, and we got her out of the bus, because we were worried that we were gonna smash through and come through the side."

For Mik, another extended wander in search of drugs, prior to the gig, took him to a no-go area, and brought him face-to-face with a masked man who took exception to his placing of an order for only a small amount of heroin.

Bizarrely, Drew had a premonition about Mik's little adventure: the night before, he dreamt of a moustachioed IRA man with a thick Irish accent, who accompanied Mik on his drug-seeking mission and dropped him back at the tour bus. Which, some notable tweaks to the story aside, is pretty much what happened.

Drew —

"That kind of freaked me out, 'cos I'm not a particularly spiritual person. When people talk to me about clairvoyancy and all that kind of stuff, I'm the most cynical person in the world, but I do dream things a lot before they happen, and, I dunno, Stephen Hawkins could probably explain in some kind of time-relative thing.

"I think, in the same way you have memories from the past, I think sometimes you can have memories from the future, if that makes any sense; it doesn't mean you're clairvoyant. But I think if they happen, they can happen in dreams.

"And the night before that happened, I had a dream that some IRA guy with a moustache came back to the bus and took Mik away. And then came back later that night, and there was just this horrible, menacing, evil air coming off him. And that's exactly what happened the next day, and the guy had a moustache. That tends to happen a lot. I don't normally tell people about it, because they'll think I'm full of shit. But, yeah, that was worrying. Not the kind of people you wanna get into trouble with."

Expecting a ransom demand, Mik returned, some twelve hours after first setting off, to a hero's welcome, though the good mood didn't last long: a note was passed to the band's road crew after the gig, informing them that their presence was unwelcome, and that if they valued their lives then they should leave immediately.

Mik —

"I used to be known as The Bloodhound. The problem with being a heroin addict, [is that] you have to have it. A lot of people don't understand about it; they think you're getting it to get high every day. If you don't have it, you're very ill. So, every time we'd landed, I'd have to run off and find it. Y'know, cold – I didn't know anyone. We'd pull up into a town and I'd go and find a Big Issue seller or whatever.

"So anyway, we pulled into the Nerve Centre. I took off, ended up in Ballymena, which is, like, a hundred miles away from Derry. And it's rough as fuck. I got talking to these guys in a pub and they were, like: 'Look, you're talking to the right people here, but don't ask anyone else or you'll end up in a binbag.'

"And everywhere I went, people said: 'Don't say anything, you'll end up in a binbag.' Binbag, binbag, everywhere I asked – binbag. And I got talking to this guy in a bar, and he seemed pretty cool. Introduced me to these other fellas.

"Before I knew it I was in the back of this quite flash car with these two geezers sat next to me with suits on, and another guy driving into the middle of nowhere. And I'm thinking: what the fuck? I was carted off to this house in the middle of nowhere and asked how much I wanted. And I said: 'Oh, three or four.'

"And they thought I was talking about kilos. I was talking about ten-pound bags, d'you know what I mean? I was shitting it, thinking: fucking hell, what am I going to do? I actually had a grand on me, but that's nowhere near enough. But they decided that they didn't want to sell it to me, because they didn't want it leaving the country. And I was fucking well pleased, even though I was as sick as a dog."

Peter faced arrest again before the month was out, plain clothes officers in an unmarked police car apprehending him and another man in Roman Road, E2, on 20th April, taking them to an East London police station, where they were charged with possession of Class A drugs with intent to supply. Bailed until June, pending further inquiries, the arrests came just hours after Peter had been given a two-year supervised community order and eighteen-month drug rehabilitation order, on top of a six-month driving ban at Thames Magistrates' Court.

Away from Peter's legal headaches, Babyshambles' Wolverhampton Civic Hall show, on 25th April, was to be Patrick's penultimate appearance, his staggered exit complete after taking to the stage at the Bournemouth Comedy Club two days later.

Patrick — "It started off with charlie, and it was just, like: 'Yeah, fuck it, it was great.' But it soon became a nightmare, a fucking nightmare. We used to do pipes *on stage* – can you believe that? That's how bad crack addicts we were. Disgusting…

"I was fed-up of the drug abuse, I felt very ill, there was no management; I felt like Peter was testing me. At one point, we had a row and he asked me to leave. And I said: 'Yeah, alright.' Then he goes to the rest of the boys: 'I asked Pat to leave and he didn't even put up a fight!' I thought he might ring me to say: 'Yeah, I want you to stay in the band.' But I thought: no, I'm not going to. He's asked me to leave, I'm gonna leave. So it was three-quarters I left, and a quarter he asked me to leave."

For successor Mik Whitnall, a friend of Peter's for many years, his acceptance into the fold was the culmination of many years' worth of dedication working the circuit with a variety of bands, including Finley Quaye's, which rose to prominence with *Maverick A Strike* in 1997.

Reared on street, or Oi punk, his first band, Skin Deep, regularly exchanged blows with their right-wing counterparts: "We were skinheads at the time, but we hated the NF lot – we were dubbed as a big red threat. Our band was called communist by other bands."

Skin Deep had built up a large following by the time Mik packed it in to start afresh with 100 Men, a ska/reggae band. Staying with his new concern for a decade, touring in America and Japan, he then moved on to join Quaye's band.

When the pair fell out, Mik had a stint with Kill City, whose lead singer, Lisa Moorish, is the mother of Peter's son, Astile, before losing his way for a couple of years. In his mid-thirties, and with no direction for the first time in his life, he hadn't even been able to muster enough enthusiasm to pick a guitar up in six months. Then one day he bumped into Peter, who asked what he was up to.

Mik — "I told him: 'Basically nothing,' and he's, like: 'Why don't you come and work for us?' And I used to work with James Mullord, helping manage the band, guitar-checking…

"And then James disappeared, helped by one thing or another, and I started semi-managing, teching and playing the odd song with the band as well, which was a bit difficult for me. And then Pat left, and then I started covering for Pat.

"It was never intentionally a full-time thing. It just sort of happened, and me and Pete started writing loads of songs, and that was that, really."

With Drew, Adam, Mik and Johnny Headlock remaining in Bournemouth after the Comedy Club show, Peter returned to London to find himself at the centre of more controversy when, on 28th April, *The Sun* published a photo of him supposedly injecting an unconscious fan with drugs at his Hackney home, allegedly within the preceding five weeks.

As is so often the case with tabloids, the accusation was a false one, the girl in the photo a willing and compliant participant throughout.

Not everyone's idea of a pastime, Peter's fascination with blood has spawned a large number of paintings, and it was in producing this unique brand of art that the needle in the photo was required.

Of far greater concern – for Peter, if not the world at large – was the mole who leaked the shot to the press, but with an interchangeable cast of hangers-on flocking to him, the plethora of scandals fed to a ravenous media rarely surprise nowadays.

Peter, used to his possessions disappearing from his flat, initially failed to notice the missing photo, searching for more obviously sellable items – especially technical equipment – when trying to figure out what had been fleeced.

So when the photo surfaced, splashed across the pages of *The Sun*, it not only provoked alarm, but dismantled the progress Peter had been achieving in coming off drugs – he had been clean for four days, unaided, in readiness for an implant – as well as threatening the band's future, the interest an LA label had expressed ending abruptly upon publication of the shot.

Peter —

"I didn't even speak to the girl who was involved. And they just nicked me and said: 'Oh, you're going down for nine years for administrating a noxious substance…' When, actually, I was going to buy a pint of milk from the corner shop when they nicked me and took me to town, to Stoke Newington station, and I didn't know what the fuck was going on, either. I literally, at that point, had stopped reading those redtops, and they sat me in the interview room and they said: 'What the fuck are you playing at, can you explain yourself?' 'What do you mean, can I explain myself? What the fuck are you talking about?' 'What do you think is going on?'

"My whole flat got sealed-off by forensics. Every needle in the joint. And I'm talking about…over up to a thousand used needles were found in that large flat. Each one of them tested, and each one of them proven not to contain her blood…

that's the evidence that they needed, and they couldn't find it. And they couldn't get it, and they had to let me go.

"But then they actually bothered to take a statement from her, which made mincemeat of any allegations of administrating noxious substances."

Alizé Meurisse — "Peter was at home with some friends. He asked me to come over and take some photos. He also wanted to give me a couple of needles, filled up with blood, so I could do some blood paintings with him – that's how he suddenly got the idea of the set-up photo with the girl. It really was a set-up (I also took some photos of Purple pretending to punch him in the face etcetera). She was perfectly conscious, and I don't even think he really pricked her arm with the needle.

"That photo should never have ended up in the press. I have massive archives from the past three years, and nothing's ever been published (apart from the black and white photos in *The Blinding* EP, and some of the photos I stuck in Peter's diaries, *The Books of Albion*). The thing is, I used to get my photos printed for Peter as well as for myself; his copies were always scattered all over the place, and it was easy for anyone who had access to the flat to steal a couple of them… not to mention the fact that the place was broken into quite regularly (one night I was there on my own, and someone came in through a window!)."

Sally Anchassi — "He [Peter] was with Purple and a whole bunch of people and they were messing about, and then this photo came in. He wanted to hold a press conference – he was so angry and so upset – because he just thought: I'm gonna be the most hated guy in Britain, and he said: 'I want you to get a press conference together.'

"Anyway, I had such a negative view of the press that I thought it'd be a bad idea. Whatever positive reasons he had for putting it together, I knew that they would rip him apart, so I wouldn't let him do it.

"But, I dunno, maybe it would have been a better idea to do it at the time. But I thought: if you leave it, it'll die down, but if you do it they'll find some way of making things even worse… That was a really, really horrible time – so upsetting, because there was this American guy who was really keen to sign the band…

"The shows were being made, people were starting to listen to the music, and some record companies started to be interested in managing the band, but when that photo happened, there was then a point where nobody wanted to touch them… All I know is that he wasn't injecting her, and she obviously wasn't dying."

Nuha Razik — "I can't remember whether she wanted to do a painting with her blood or she wanted him to do a picture in her blood… but she was *completely* aware of what was

---

Next page: Babyshambles in action, Arena tour, 2007.

going on. In fact, she asked – she was laying on the floor with her eyes closed, perfectly set up for the shot.

"Obviously the picture was never intended to reach anyone. It was just a picture between us, messing around, and there was a clean needle, there was no heroin involved whatsoever…. She wasn't passed out, she wasn't fucked, she knew *exactly* what was happening. There wasn't anything immoral about what was going on in any way."

Adam —
"When that photo came out, I thought it was over for Peter and the band. I expected him to be devastated, but he took it all in his stride, really. He was upset at the betrayal, but didn't really see any harm in what he was doing.

"The thing is, so many people steal things from Peter, but he's such a forgiving, trusting guy, he just lets them back into the fold every time."

Tony
Linkin —
"I got a phone call at about ten-thirty at night, from someone at the *Daily Mirror*, saying to me: 'What have you got to say about this picture?' Obviously I didn't have a clue what he was talking about. Then he explained it to me, and I said: 'Well, I've got no idea, and I'll try and get hold of someone and find out', trying to say as little as I could, basically.

"The next day when I saw everything… it looked like it was staged, I must admit… but, even so, I was thinking: why would you want to stage something like that? Pete stays free about this sort of thing, but it's obviously going to cause him a lot of aggro, and… the people around him aren't exactly trustworthy. If it was done by someone who was supposed to be trustworthy, then they weren't…

"It's a hard one for me. It was hard for me to defend him on that one. Even now, with the blood paintings, I don't quite know why you would stage something like that, really. Unless it was with people you could totally one hundred per cent trust. For it to come out there was quite odd."

Mik —
"She asked him to do that, so that he could do a blood painting from her blood. There were a few burglaries from Pete's flat, and that photo went missing.

"He wasn't injecting her with heroin. He's never injected anyone with heroin – it's rubbish, and he nearly went to prison for that. And it's one of his so-called mates who sold that photo for ten thousand pounds."

Roger
Pomphrey —
"They [the tabloids] are ruthless, they are without conscience, they are without love, basically, and it's a shame that he's kind of allowed himself to be so exposed to them, because they'll only do one thing: they'll fucking hang him. Not only will they, they want to. And that, to me, is just a crime, but it's who they are and it's how they survive. It's what the tabloids do: they will love you and build you up as high as a

fucking mountain, and they will be the people to light the fuse of the dynamite to blow him out of the water. They can't wait, the evil fucks. Hate it, hate it. It's a shame. He needs protection from those people, more than anybody, really.

"He needs protection from a lot of people, but he needs as much protection from the British press as he does from bad influences in his life. It's not just Pete Doherty – they'll do it to anybody, as we know, whether you're a football player, a politician or a rock 'n' roll star. They want you to fuck up, because they'll put it on the front page and it'll sell newspapers. A bad indictment of the times in which we live.

"People will buy what they're fed, really. Sad. A sad indictment of our period. I'm not sure if it's ever been any different, it's just that a hundred years ago it was a public execution on the village green; now it's a public humiliation via the newsstand. But it is the same thing, without doubt. The morbidity of the human condition, really. A very dark place. It ain't my world, that's for sure.

"They will always do it. The problem is with it, if you're an artist and you're relatively new on the scene, I think initially it's quite flattering, because you've got your photo in the paper and you've got your name on the headline, and it's a very cynical form of seduction. They'll seduce you into it, but it's a fucking wolf in sheep's clothing, because once you're in, and once you've bought into it, you're their property and they'll hack you down.

"You have to be very strong, not without ego, but you have to withstand and protect yourself from that kind of press intrusion… I think most people wouldn't be able to cope with it.

"I was also quite impressed with the band. It didn't seem to affect them very much. They were very, very aware of what it was and the meaningless of it, but I think Pete, personally – certainly for Pete's family – it cannot be so pleasant. I know if I had to wake up and read that kind of stuff about my son it would break my heart. It would break any mother or father's heart if you had to read that or be exposed to that on a daily basis."

The Sun story destroyed the hard-won progress achieved in the preceding weeks. Peter's interest in blood had caused a considerable stir in his homeland, but it would soon spark outrage outside further afield – namely, in Germany and Spain – as attempts to raise the band's international profile ended in disappointment.

Choppy waters lay ahead, and it would be months before they settled.

9
Ladyshambles

Peter was arrested in accordance with *The Sun* story on 29th April, missing the Love Music Hate Racism rally in Trafalgar Square that day, after he was refused release in time to play.

Instead, he was held for questioning at Stoke Newington police station under Section 23 of the Offences Against the Person act, on suspicion of administering a noxious substance recklessly, though Drew was on hand to register support for the event, singing "Albion" in his absence.

Drew could have counted on support from Adam had there not been a breakdown in communications between the two; Adam, distraught at another letdown, left early and jumped aboard a London tour bus, whose guide swiftly launched a scathing attack on him and his bandmates.

Adam — "I was so gutted, I just wanted to get out of there. So I got on one of the tour buses. We were driving around Trafalgar Square, then the tour operator starts saying: 'And today, Pete Doherty and Babyshambles are meant to play,' and starts reeling loads of shit off about who Pete Doherty is.

"It was really negative, and I thought: do I stand up and defend him?, hoping he doesn't actually know who's in the band, because they've clocked me. I was all suited up anyway, looked really odd – a proper mod suit – and I was trying not to catch his eye. And then he was reeling all this stuff off about Babyshambles and what kind of people the band are – that they're drug addicts and stuff, and how he's let down the whole of the crowd."

Bailed the next morning until July, pending further enquiries, Peter used his website to protest his innocence, slamming *The Sun*'s "disturbing and ridiculously offensive 'story.'" Disclosing that the photo from which the piece was built around had been stolen, he confirmed that it was staged, declaring: "What a fucking liberty to suggest I'd bang up a sleeping lass. Darkness."

With *The Sun* story continuing to generate debate, Peter joined up with Drew, Adam and Mik for Babyshambles' foreign tour, playing at the Amsterdam Paradiso on 1st May, Brussels' Les Nuits Botanique Festival on the 2nd, the Arhus Train, Denmark, on the 5th and the Copenhagen Vega the following night.

The next date, at the Cologne Buergerhaus Stollwerck, on 10th May, had to be rescheduled for the 13th, Peter giving Sally, with whom he was supposed to have travelled, the slip, and missing a succession of flights, leaving Drew, Adam and Johnny Headlock stranded in Germany.

Then, at the Berlin Kesselhaus on the 11th, the threat of crowd trouble was averted when Peter eventually took to the stage five hours behind schedule.

Missing all of that day's available flights, a private jet was chartered to fly to Berlin but, missing that as well, arrangements were made for another that Peter managed to board – only to find that it wasn't deemed fit for service. On the brink of another pulled show to add to their burgeoning collection, a replacement for the crocked jet finally got Peter to his destination, where he received a frosty welcome from, among others, Adam.

"After a long wait and constant promises of being in various places, he finally shows up as if nothing's amiss. He does try my patience sometimes, but he got there and we played the show. I eventually forgave all his nonsense as he did sheepishly apologise during one of the songs, by coming up to the drum, looking upset, and mouthing 'sorry'."

After the show, with tensions rising in the band – Adam and Drew feeling let down by Peter's habitual no-shows, lateness when he showed up at all, and generally erratic behaviour – Peter further endeared himself to them by squirting a syringe of blood at the crew of MTV Germany, during an interview.

Initially refusing to participate, Peter was persuaded to go in front of the cameras by Sally, who reminded him that that was the least he could do, on account of the difficulties his late arrival had engendered. But with Peter not in the mood to oblige, the interview rapidly descended into farce.

Drew and Adam held the fort until he joined them, answering questions in a convivial atmosphere. When Peter sat down beside them a couple of minutes later, he wasted little time before producing a syringe with which he sprayed the crew and camera. A suspiciously dark red solution that was, he later told Adam, pomegranate juice, splattered across the camera, Peter hailing his effort as "a wicked shot" and predicting: "That's going to make a cracking link that is."

Drew immediately apologised to the crew, saying: "That's fucking fucked up," before storming off, leaving Adam sitting there, clueless as to his next move; seeing how agitated Peter was, and fearing an even more inflammatory situation, he quickly recovered his composure and did his best to salvage the interview once the camera lens had been sterilised.

Adam — "I remember seeing him fucking around with pomegranate juice in the room next door, so I thought he was gonna go out there and squirt them. And the fact that it was a syringe, I should have really known that he was gonna do something more sinister.

"As soon as he done it, I was kind of in shock. I didn't really know what to say. So I just sat there for a bit, thinking: what the fuck's just happened, what do we do now? It was all surreal. Everyone was knackered, anyway: hadn't slept for two nights, waiting for him. So it was a weird situation, and Drew got the real arse about it – rightly so. I think at the time I wasn't so shocked about it. It was only a couple of days after that I started thinking: fucking hell, what's just happened?

"It's a surreal Babyshambles environment; you start to, not lose your morals, but you start to be more accepting of things that you normally wouldn't. It's really odd. It really wears you down like that."

Peter —

"Oh, it was blood. It would have been no good wasting decent pomegranate juice on them. If they're gonna ask me lame questions…fuck-all to do with the album, fuck-all to do with the band – then I may as well respond in a befitting manner… And I'd just banged one in, and saved a bit of blood, and I thought: a lot of blood has been spilt. A lot of British blood has been spilt of foreign soil. They will always been some corner of a foreign field that is Forever England… So that was a reminder."

Drew —

"Basically, at that point I was coming to the end of my tether. The way I see it, we're a rock 'n' roll band and we make good music. And I was pretty fucking sick of any time I read anything, or there was any mention of the band, it was things to do with stuff that was not music-directed, and I thought for people to start taking us seriously as a band we need to turn that around.

"It needed to be: Babyshambles have played a triumphant show or the album's doing well, or they've got this great new song or whatever; other than: Peter's been nicked again, Patrick's in jail – you know, another gig where the drummer's jumped out from behind his kit and punched some kid in the audience.

"I was sick of that being the focus of the media attention and I'd just been speaking to the camera about how I don't like the no-shows thing. And Peter had just showed up late for the show that we had just played, and I was saying that that's not what we're about and I apologise to anyone who's ever had to wait for a show or turned up to a no-show… I don't like letting fans wait five minutes, let alone three hours – it doesn't sit comfortably with me or Adam – but we ended up doing that because of Peter's behaviour. And then I was defending him; I can't remember exactly what I was saying, but I was finding a way of trying to absolve him of any real culpability…

"And then Peter comes in and squirts blood at the lens of the camera. I felt that was quite undermining, really, and, like I say, my idea of stuff in the news stories about Babyshambles being about drugs and syringes and fights, and making it about music – it seemed that that gesture there seemed completely at odds with what I wanted to happen."

Mik —

"Me and Pete were stood in the doorway, and the MTV crew – one of 'em was Dutch, I think – were all talking in English, 'cos they were from different places.

"And they're slagging Pete to fuck: 'Junkie bastard, he's shit, I don't know how he's got this far,' blah, blah, blah. And Pete was gonna go storming in there, start slapping 'em about. And I was, like: 'Fuck that, man, you know?' [I] held him back a bit, and then Adam and Drew were sat there, and he just walked in with that syringe and squirted it on 'em just to piss 'em off, I think. Adam and Drew weren't pleased about that one, but they didn't know what had happened beforehand.

"There's always another side to it with Pete – he doesn't do anything for nothing, you know. He's not malicious or stupid just for the sake of it."

Sally Anchassi — "I said: 'You fucking come a day late, have you not seen the other room with all the food and everything else? They've asked us to do, like, five minutes for these people – is that so much to ask?'

"So he's, like: 'Okay, fine!', and went in there, and I think he was just, kind of: 'You fucking made me do something – I'll show you! If you make me do something, I will show you how I can do it, so that you never make me try and do anything again!'"

Anthony Thornton — "With the blood-squirting at MTV, there's a little hypocrisy going on. It was just some blood squirted at a camera. So what? Compared to the buckets of grand guignol of Alice Cooper in the '70s, it's little more than a thimble.

"Remember, Ozzy Osbourne bit the head off a bat on stage, and now he's been anointed as a national treasure. There's something a little bemusing about a media that revels in the glorifying of bad behaviour from the distance of a decade or so, but when there's a sniff – or, indeed, a squirt – they scream outrage.

"The speed that some media outlets can turn from advocates of unabashed rock hedonists to puritanical saviours of a nation's soul displays an ability to perform screaming u-turns that would leave even Jeremy Clarkson agog."

At the rescheduled Cologne date, the band took to the stage in drag, though Adam's embellishments were less convincing than his bandmates'.

By the time he came round to the idea, there was nothing left for him to wear, forcing him to make do with an old towel that doubled as a skirt, red lipstick, rosy cheeks, and – most bizarrely of all – residue from a crack pipe smeared over his upper lip to lend him the appearance of something loosely resembling a moustache. Their makeovers complete, the four-piece were announced as Ladyshambles.

Drew — "Peter and a few other people had been out shopping. And they bought a wig, and they were saying how funny it would be if we all went out in drag. And there were a few girls with us, so they lent us clothes. So we got coats and skirts and bras, [but] Adam wasn't warming to the whole drag thing. He was, like: 'I'm not fucking dressing up in drag.' But everyone else did, and then at the last minute he was, like: 'Hang on,

I'm going to look weird if I'm not wearing something', so someone gave him an impromptu moustache on his top lip. He should grow a moustache – it suited him… Mik in tights is not anything that anyone should ever have to see! Not a good look! He put a banana down his pants as well – it literally scared the girls; you could hear them screaming down the corridor and fleeing, fleeing for their lives!"

Mik — "That was a bit weird. We were waiting around, a bit bored, and Pete suggested we all get dressed up as women. There was some stuff on the internet about how well endowed I was, which was ridiculous because I had a banana stuffed down my tights – that's all it was. I remember the crowd screaming with horror; I forgot I didn't have any underpants on, and I turned around and bent down to adjust one of my distortion pedals, and heard this scream of horror from the audience. Sorry about that one, everyone."

Adam — "I'm, like: 'Well, I don't really want to dress up as a girl, but if you're gonna do it, get me a nice dress or something.' I had a pipe wiped on me to give me a moustache – there's photos of it somewhere, this ridiculousness – dirty old lipstick … and a towel round me. Great. [I was] neither here nor there: not really a man nor a woman – just, like, a geezer with a badly-drawn moustache in a towel, so it didn't really come off for me too much."

Peter — "I think we were just backstage larking about, Mik getting into tights. I think I insisted – like the thing with Pat knocking me out… I insisted that if Mik cared about the band, we go on stage with tights."

The tour moved to Italy for shows at the Bologna New Estragon on 26th May and the Rome Qube on the 27th – gigs that had been postponed from the end of the previous year and, in true Shambles style, were confirmed just a month in advance.

Italian tour promoter Eva Falomi, of Grinding Halt Ltd., was assigned to the band, and to ensure their safe arrival at the forthcoming shows. When first meeting them on the 26th, she saw a "healthy-looking" Adam, "skinny" Mik and "gaunt" Peter and Drew.

The boys had missed a number of flights and didn't play until around 1 am, missing a sound and monitor check. When climbing out of the cab that had ferried them to their hotel, Peter was mobbed by fans who he treated to an impromptu performance. A concerned hotel porter tried to tame the situation, but Peter extended the performance when Mik wheeled him around on a luggage trolley – up until the moment the hotel director arrived to put an end to the carry-on.

Determined not to call it a night, the festivities continued inside the hotel, the after-show excess proving too much for Peter and Drew, who drank so much they made themselves violently sick – so much so, in fact, that Drew was still honking up into sick bags on the train to Rome for the Qube gig.

Drew —   "Peter and I spent the whole night in a hotel room, and we were getting drunk. And Peter was talking about how he didn't want to go to rehab to get an implant. And the sadistic bastard that he is – there was two-thirds of a bottle of tequila left, it was quite a big bottle of tequila – he said: 'If you drink all that tequila, I swear on everyone's life that I'll get the implant.'

"So I downed it, and vomited pretty much constantly, from about six in the morning to including on stage at the gig. I vomited behind my amplifier while we were playing, and I came off stage and vomited some more…

"I woke up the next morning in the hotel room in a star shape on the bed, with Peter asleep on me in a star shape, too, his body totally covering mine, his head on my head. I woke up totally discombobulated – I couldn't move! I had to push him off – like: 'Aaaah, what are you doing?!' [He said:] 'I was just keeping you warm!,' and I leant over the bed, and it was just luminous yellow vomit…

"I have sort of snapshot memories of being on the train, holding my sick bag – it was the only plastic bag I could find, and it was a clear plastic bag! People were leaving us; there were suddenly empty seats around us on the train home. How embarrassing! But, you know, these things happen… To be fair, he kept his promise: he got the implant, so it was worth it, the bastard."

Adam —   "I remember going in in the morning to wake them up, and Peter had passed out on top of Drew, and there was sick everywhere in there – everywhere: in the sink, on the back of the seats… they were both fucking green. Cups of sick everywhere, where they'd been vomiting and stuff. It was nastiness."

Surprised that a band of Babyshambles' standing had decided against the far easier option of a flight, Eva recalls a "very pale" Peter and a "green" Drew, both of whom fell asleep in a pizzeria prior to the journey.

Upon arrival in Rome the pair perked up a little, but just 40 minutes before the show was due to begin, only Adam had showed, with Drew still sleeping off his hangover and Peter awaiting Mik's return. Twenty minutes later, everyone else had joined him – except Mik, who some 12 hours before embarked on a mission to score; only after an unintended excursion of the city's gypsy sites did he manage to procure the goods.

With Peter anxious for a hit, suffering withdrawal symptoms, Mik had been despatched to sniff some drugs out, though, as has so often been the case with Mik, calamity wasn't far away.

Mik —   "Again, I went off, found some homeless guys. Forty miles outside Rome, in the middle of nowhere, in the middle of this wood, with an ex-SAS-type geezer from Kosovo and this other big, strapping fella, and they knew I had a lot of money. And I was thinking: yet again, I'm gonna get fucked over here…I was in the middle of this wood, thinking: I'm gonna get fucking killed here…

"In the distance was this fire, and I kept walking, and it was, like, the biggest Romany gypsy camp I've ever seen… and this snaggle-toothed old hag came out and sold me loads of Chinese white heroin. Which was unexpected… I got what I needed to get, ran down the motorway, jumped in a cab, and got there about two minutes before we went on stage."

"All that bloodhounding stuff – I'm glad I don't have to do it anymore. Risky, risky business that."

The carelessness and naivety Peter has so often demonstrated vis-à-vis his drug use led to more trouble on the flight over to Barcelona for the Primavera Sound Festival on 1st June.

For all of the press intrusion, public denigration of his character and countless betrayals, Peter has had his fair share of luck along the way, and this was in evidence again on the 1st, when the very real possibility of a jail sentence was avoided due to the Spanish authorities' lack of knowledge regarding methadone.

Another predictably stressful day got off to a good start when Peter insisted upon taking an old, gargantuan monitor with him to Spain, this after stalling other members of the Babyshambles crew by repeatedly packing and unpacking his suitcase.

Mik —   "People say: 'Oh yeah, you've got everything but the kitchen sink', but he had fucking everything but the kitchen sink. He had this, like, 1980s monitor screen, the size of a cinema screen, animals – it was like Noah's Ark. We got to the airport and I was stood there laughing my head off, 'cos he's got this monitor – it must have been about two-to-three foot wide as well as two-to-three foot tall and deep.

"I remember seeing it wrapped in cellophane on the conveyor belt, thinking: what the hell is he doing with that?, and this monitor screen, wherever he went it came with us, for no apparent reason other than just being there… That monitor screen went all over the world for no reason – more places than most people see in their life, that fucking thing."

Heavy luggage invariably indicative of an uneasy Peter, his insistence on taking the monitor – a necessary measure, he'd argued, on the basis that the screen on his laptop was broken – gave cause for concern.

Opposite: Peter at the Ladyshambles gig.

Transporting this ancient, cumbersome piece of equipment to the airport by cab, it was painstakingly bubble-wrapped by check-in staff and carried on an EasyJet flight, booked for its cost-effectiveness.

The European shows, never the greatest payers, always held appeal, enabling the band to perform in front of fans of a different culture and holding the possibility of higher profile, more lucrative shows, as often the same promoters were involved.

But until the better-paid gigs came along, providing funds for a more comfortable journey, Sally had little choice but to fly with low-cost airlines such as EasyJet – unless, of course, in case of emergencies, when private planes were required to make sure Peter made it to shows at all, thus avoiding costly reimbursements to promoters.

Once the flight was underway, Peter disappeared to the toilet for an hour, having already smoked a few crafty pipes on board – achieved by draping a coat over his head – as part of a contest with Mik, who recalls: "We had competitions of who could smoke on the plane, shall we say, while sat in our seats. [We'd] put coats over us and would sit there having a smoke, hold it in for as long as possible. Blow the smoke into the seat, press your mouth against the seat, and blow the smoke into the seat [in front]."

Accounts of what happened next vary, though this much is certain: Peter felt unfairly victimised and, if people were foolish enough to buy into the tabloid version of his character, he'd gladly reinforce it.

Peter —

"These things were everyday events. Everywhere we went – and, to a certain extent, it continues to this day – I spray blood. Normally I write QPR in blood. It's standard behaviour. Normally, when I'm on the aeroplane, I blow smoke into a sleeping business man's face. It's just the done thing. Someone got wise to me, I went into the bog…

"I pulled off my shirt, I pulled down my kecks. Painting a scene for you. I pulled the lid of the toilet up; I left the other seat lid a bit down. Got sat on the toilet, and I've gone about my business, right? Next minute, someone's banging on the door. 'What are you doing in there?' I'm, like: 'Sorry, mate, I'm having a, you know – I'm having an Eartha Kitt. Give me five minutes, please.' 'No, we know what you're doing in there.' They're accusing me of doing something I'm not.

"Now, I would have taken it on the chin and chosen to ignore it. Instead of doing that, because they accused me of doing something I hadn't done, I rolled up my sleeve and tugged my tie around the top of my arm, and put a syringe behind my ear, and I walked up the aisle of the plane. Next minute, they've sealed off a part of the plane and have prepared for landing.

"I must admit they were quite reluctant to do anything. They were quite happy to see us in their country, and a few of the guards were going to the gig, so… they didn't probe too thoroughly; they sort of half did their job."

Sally
Anchassi —

"He went to the toilet and they started knocking on the door, pretty much as soon as he got in there. And I don't know if he was genuinely doing drugs or if he thought: fuck you, why are you knocking on the door as if I'm doing drugs? I'll show you!, which is a really big part of his psyche.

"So he came out of the toilet with a tourniquet round his arm – but I didn't notice that his arms were bleeding. I was sitting down reading, and he came back down, and he was, like: 'Shit, shit, shit!' And I was, like: 'What?' And I saw the thing on his arm, and I thought: what the fuck?

"And he was, like: 'Yeah, well they were knocking on the door and, anyway, there's a needle in the bin. Can you get it out? Because I'm in loads of trouble.' So I went up to try and get it out of the toilet, but they'd gone in there. I dunno what they'd seen, but they'd put a hazardous sign on the door and wouldn't let anyone in."

Forgoing the directives upon landing, cabin crew had to fend off passengers, frustrated at being held in the craft. Sally, meanwhile, had frustrations of her own: namely Peter, who wanted to smoke another pipe while they waited for the police to arrive.

Sally
Anchassi —

"We had a right row because we were still static on the ground, and he was, like: 'Give me back my pipe.' And I said: 'Your pipe?! You must be fucking insane! The police are gonna board this plane – you want me to take it out so you can fucking smoke a pipe in front of these people?' And he went into one. So I said: 'Fuck it, it's your funeral – you take it!' And he said: 'Well, no-one's gonna see me, because I'm gonna put my jacket on my head.' 'Yeah, because you're invisible – sure you are!'

"So he did it. He was piping on the plane while the plane was landed, and while we were waiting for the police to board. He had a couple of drags and he was, like: 'See, that wasn't so hard, was it?' And then the police boarded. And they said: 'Rows one-to-ten can go', and we were obviously at the back of the plane. Fuck that! I'm not gonna wait until they call me up, so I just got up… and walked off the plane."

When, a few minutes later, Peter, Drew, Adam and Mik attempted to join their fellow passengers in filing out of the plane, they were politely asked to step aside, along with an unsuspecting Spanish woman wrongly taken to be Sally, by now on her way towards clearing customs. Reluctant to immediately identify the innocent party among them, a boisterous stag party a few rows behind bought a little more time.

Mik, however, had something on him that he shouldn't have, and as a ploy to try and convince the police otherwise, he decried Peter's drug use, explaining how much of a hindrance it was to the band. "I was crapping myself, thinking: my God, they're gonna search me and I'll get fifteen years, so I was coming out with all this rubbish about how I hate drugs. And they searched everyone – even Adam and

Drew – and they looked at me and said: 'You're fine – go ahead, walk straight through.' I got away with that one by the skin of my teeth."

The only other person still to have anything on them was Peter – methadone, which, a multilingual Drew explained, was a heroin substitute for his friend, a recovering addict.

Ignorant to the fact that the administering of methadone via injection is painful enough to dissuade most users from attempting it, the authorities decided against testing the empty methadone bottle discovered in the toilet – down which, it transpired, Peter had flushed the needle.

And while carrying needles on flights is an offence, the matter wasn't raised by the police, who promptly released the foursome, the Spanish woman having already been allowed to go, once the band demonstrated that she had no connection to the Babyshambles camp.

Drew —

"The airhost guy who had called the police was being really annoying, and he was annoying the police there – it seemed like the police, from the outset, didn't see something serious to worry about. The whole time this little airhost guy was barking at them to throw the book at us in English, and I could hear them talking to each other, saying: 'This guy's a pain in the arse.'

"And when they went looking through things, they found a bottle – a methadone bottle – and I'm, like: 'My friend is a recovering addict and he needs to take his methadone.' And I also know for a fact that it's not illegal in Spain to have methadone about your person. I was, like: 'He just had to take his dose of methadone. And he did it, and this guy thought that he was doing something else.' And they were, like: 'Oh, for fuck's sake, well off you go, then'."

Adam —

"If he'd have just nipped in there, had a quick dig, [he wouldn't have got caught] but obviously with injections and needles you can't just stick it in – you've got to mix all the shit. That's what caused the problem.

"I was just sitting there, didn't even know he'd gone to the toilet, and got up. And there's this massive queue for the toilet, and you suddenly see them all sit down. And you're, like: the fucking doughnut's in there, isn't he?…

"Again, I thought: this is it, he's going down for this one, but, miraculously, he scraped through unscathed. I don't know whether there were any higher political interventions, but it seemed as though the customs guards really couldn't be bothered to go through the hassle of pressing charges or investigating further."

EasyJet announced that Babyshambles had been banned from its flights in future, a spokeswoman saying that crew discovered "a syringe hidden in a bin, covered in blood" in the craft's toilet, in which Peter had spent "an unusual amount of time."

She said that he had become "agitated and aggressive" when questioned by airline staff, and that he had failed to inform the airline in advance that he was carrying needles for medical use, for which he required permission.

Sally retaliated by calling the airline's top brass, reminding them that no needles had actually been found on their property, and that a tip-off from one of its staff stirred up the media circus awaiting them when stepping off the plane, the press having got hold of the fracas before police boarded the vessel. In fact, Ashtar Alkhirsan, who accompanied the band as part of her documentary, received a call from colleagues on the *Arena* team, back in London, as soon as she switched her mobile phone back on after the flight, enquiring about her welfare and wanting to know what had happened.

Once back at their Spanish hotel, meanwhile, Peter, despite having escaped what could have had serious repercussions, moaned at Sally for allowing him to leave his hat behind on the plane, taking his anger out on his room, which he promptly destroyed.

Later, she got taken to task for manhandling the monitor, which she had returned to Barcelona airport to collect, along with a guitar that had gone missing, struggling to carry them from the pick-up point to a waiting car, in the sweltering sun, to ensure that both were in her possession when the others showed up for a flight to Germany, the next port of call on the Babyshambles tour.

Ascribing Peter's agitation to an impending heroin implant, she was nonetheless in no mood for criticism. The pair had a blazing row in the airport, which Drew smoothed over, telling airport staff that they were a couple having a domestic. But an infuriated Sally, unable to find a flight to take her back to London, stayed in Barcelona for a holiday.

Before long, the band would return to Spanish soil for the Benicassim Festival. Before that, though, trouble lay ahead in Sweden; and for a friend back in London, who was to face temporary cessation of his freedom.

10

Chaos in Europe

On 5th June, Peter caught a flight to Portugal for his latest rehab attempt, where he was "kept under" to prevent his cravings getting the better of him. His detox led to him missing his second successive drug rehabilitation review at Thames Magistrates' Court – he was with the band on tour in Germany for his 12th May hearing – Sean Curran citing "valid reasons" for his client's absence and explaining that his treatment was said to be going well. District Judge Jane McIvor applauded his efforts, saying that, while Peter was "striving towards" negative drug tests, and that, despite it being a "tough struggle for him", he was "not going backwards".

Not for the first time, rehab failed to deliver Peter from addiction. Not ready to surrender his dependence on drugs, he hid a small quantity of cocaine in the head of a He-Man superhero figurine, purchased while in Portugal, before boarding a plane bound for Sweden on 16th June, when the band were to play the Hultsfred Festival.

Peter flew into the country with Johnny Headlock and was said to be so inebriated once the plane landed that Johnny had to push him into custody in a wheelchair after the pair were pulled over for exhibiting apparently suspicious behaviour – a sight welcomed by the scrum of press who gleefully captured the image, which rapidly proliferated across the globe.

Drew, Adam, Mik, Sally and a friend were already in Sweden, after surviving a scare triggered by Mik's stashing of drugs somewhere discreet, assuming responsibility from the supposed carrier, who panicked at the last minute. "The person who was carrying it for us went up to the customs desk and freaked out, saying: 'I can't do it, can't do it!', right in front of the customs people, and I had to say: 'Give it here,' and take it off him", Mik recalls. "And I walked up to these armed police, saying: 'Oh, you seen my mate?', trying to smooth it out, and I got away with it yet again. Walked through there with all this gear."

Peter and Johnny missed their original flight, and while they managed to make the next one, their detainment and subsequent fine of 30,000 kronor, for the discovery of cocaine traces in their urine and the contents of He-Man's head, delayed their release for around three hours.

Now running seriously behind schedule for the Hultsfred Festival, a private plane was hired to try to ensure that they made the show. A waiting car the other end sped them to the festival, but with Peter fresh out of rehab and vulnerable to relapse, the immediate appeal of a hit outweighed the longing for a life free from addiction.

Once at the venue, the band were given just a couple of minutes to compose themselves before their performance. Peter spent that time smoking a pipe – a mistake that had consequences after the gig.

Sweden's early sunrise lent the show an uplifting aura, the band making music as darkness gave way to light, despite originally being booked to perform the previous afternoon. But as soon as they finished playing, Peter was escorted off stage by armed police, who apparently noticed his intoxication on giant screens broadcast to the audience.

The rest of the band tried to wrestle him free but, after some pushing and shoving, Peter was bundled into the back of a police van. Told by Adam to lose whatever he had on him, a panicked Mik – who moments before inadvertently antagonised a security guard by clipping the back of his head as he hurled his guitar into the crowd – ran back on stage to launch himself into the audience, not reckoning on Johnny's presence.

Mik — "I've been arrested a lot throughout my life, but that was something special, man, I tell yer. We came off stage and, again, the promoters said: 'This way', sort of thing. And led us into this room. And the coppers were waiting there with these guns, put a gun to Pete's head, and carted him off…

"I had about two grands' worth of crack in one hand, and about the same of smack in the other… so I saw what was going on, shit myself, ran onto the stage, [and] jumped into the crowd. And you know what their festivals are like: fifty-thousand people there. So I ran to the back and I heard: 'Mik! Mik!', and it was fucking Headlock, right, shouting: 'Give us a line before you go, give us a line!' And I was, like: 'Shut up, man!' And eight coppers came swarming in, grabbed hold of me. Handcuffed me from wrist to ankle on both sides, picked me up upside down and fumbled me across the field on my head.

"Meanwhile, [I'm] still holding all this shit. They're walking behind me in case I drop anything, so I sort of crunched it up in my hands and let it drop as they were bouncing me across the field and got me behind this fence. And they booted the shit out of me.

"But there was this young lad there – he was about seventeen or eighteen – and he was screaming and shouting at 'em as they were pulling me across the field, trying to stop 'em, and they ended up doing the same to him. They shackled him up and he was behind the fence with me, getting a beating as well. And then they got me to the police station, the whole police station came out, and they made me and Pete strip in front of them.

"And just as we took our clothes off, he went: 'Right, put 'em back on.' And I was, like: 'Fuck this.' I went: 'No.' 'What do you mean?' 'No, you're strip-searching me aren't you? You've gotta look up my arsehole, mate.' I sort of walked over to them, and they were all sort of, like: 'Ooooh!' 'And behind my foreskin, have a look!' After that they kind of calmed down with us a bit.

"This guy kept coming in the cell with a gun and fucking wotnot, fucking about, and then they wanted us to piss into a jar so they could find out what was in our bloodstream. So I just kept saying I couldn't wee. They… didn't take any samples from me, so they couldn't charge me with anything. But I still got charged for possession of cocaine and had to pay seven thousand euros to get out that night otherwise I'd have been in there for months, and Pete had to do the same.

"We had to pay fourteen-thousand euros to get out that night, which, strangely enough, was exactly the fee we'd been paid."

Peter —   "[We were] beaten-up by the Swedish police and fined the exact amount we were supposed to get by the festival organisers. The fee that we were getting for the show…was very similar, maybe one or two euro dollars out… their justification being that I looked 'out of it on the big screen' – that's the reasoning they gave for arrest. And then finding no drugs on me, [they] made use of an old Swedish byelaw, which says that you're not allowed any drugs in your system. Which is a fucking joke, you know what I mean? They never did me for possession either – they found nothing on me illegal. They did me for having it in my blood. A world-renowned junkie who has traces of cocaine in his blood. In his blood. Not in his pocket. Not in his wallet. Not hidden up his arse. But in his bloodstream. Cost us forty-thousand. Junk. Forty-thousand euros.

"Johnny Headlock put up a good fight, though. He was taken in for questioning, and he stripped down there and then. I'd liked to have done the same, but I was handcuffed and I was facedown in the mud… but he just whipped his clothes off there and then and said: 'Come on, then – where's the drugs?' Mik tried to leg it, got rugby-tackled and severely pummelled by these hulking great, like – they were all massive. I remember, the Swedish policemen: I think – similar to Shrewsbury – they were gutted that they couldn't find anything, you know? It's, like, we cut it fine a few times. Too many times. We never learnt our lesson. Lesson being: you can't win 'em all."

Drew —   "The organisers had doubled-checked and checked and double-checked with the local authorities [to see] if there was gonna be any issue with us playing, and the police had said it was fine.

"So we played the gig, but before we finished, one of the crew guys came out, and brought it to our attention that by the side of the stage, at either side, the whole stage was lined with police. And so as soon as we finished we got swooped on by these police. And they demanded that Peter was gonna go to the police station with them.

"And when he started demanding an explanation, one of them radioed someone, and there was this meatwagon and about twelve *more* policeman – all in full bulletproof riot gear, truncheons and helmets – came pouring out. But there was already about ten policeman there, so in all there were about twenty-five policemen all manhandling Peter into this meatwagon, and the rest of them just stood there.

"And later they detained Mickey as well. And, again, we had to pay an enormous sum to get them out. And [they said] that: 'We've apprehended you because you're known drug users, and we don't like that kind of thing in our country.' That kind of stuff happened a lot."

Sally
Anchassi — "Mik, I don't think the police were interested in taking, but because he started to leg it the police suddenly became very interested in him. Not a lot goes on in Hultsfred, so they're on their full alert when it's festival time. They got Mik, he put up a struggle, and they're fucking massive – I've got some photos of the police there; Peter's a big guy, but he was dwarfed by the police there."

Peter was fined for having cocaine in his system, while Mik, despite losing the gear in his hands, unwittingly had some about his person: a small amount, in the pockets of the jacket he was wearing – Peter's.

This latest delay made the possibility of fulfilling the band's slot at the Swiss Festival, on the 17th, an increasingly unrealistic one. By the time they reached Stockholm airport, all available flights were taken, resulting in another cancellation for the country's fans.

And with no possibility of catching a plane back to London, Drew, Adam, Mik, Sally and Johnny had no choice but to spend the night in Sweden. With the band up for playing, an impromptu gig was staged at the Debaser club, Stockholm, after Adam struck up conversation with its owner while sitting outside the premises enjoying a drink with Johnny.

Another chaotic night, Peter scrapped with the stage manager. He also set about trashing the venue when its owner tried bringing the gig to a premature close just a few songs in, concerned that the edginess of Babyshambles' act was in danger of triggering a riot. When the stage manager closed the electricity down, his fears were very nearly realised, Peter launching himself at him and having to be dragged off stage as fans added to the bedlam by throwing punches at Debaser staff.

To cap another splendid show, Adam received warning that the police were on their way, on reports that Babyshambles were carrying knives. When he found the culprits, he was met by the sight of a girl running around a wrecked dressing room with her hair on fire, Johnny hosing her down when the blaze started to get out of control.

Peter — "You didn't need to bring up the fire extinguishers. Not so proud of that, or the fight with the promoter – that was quite embarrassing. It was three songs in, and he decided the atmosphere was getting a bit lairy. The crowd were starting to turn on security, and he asked me if we could take a ten-minute break. I told him to fuck off, and he said not to be so rude. I sized him up, thought: you speccy cunt, told him to fuck off again. He took his glasses off and gave me a good hiding. And then turned off all the amps, so that was that…

"This girl is going on and on. I think she was determined to wind me up or upset me. You know: 'What it is: not just that you can't sing anymore. It's not just that your standards have really, really slipped. But, you know, I think you've changed for the worse as a person,' and all that. Coming out with all this. Really severe and really personal. Really upsetting stuff for me. Some really touchy areas. And Johnny could sense my discomfort, and did what he thought the right thing to do as a friend and compatriot, and set fire to her hair. And she was last seen quite visibly running down the street in Stockholm, screaming for all she was worth."

Adam —

"Debaser was another typically shambolic experience. For some reason, both Headlock and Peter managed to get hold of some old army knives that they'd brandished to each other whilst dancing and running around the club.

"The promoter pulled me aside to tell me that the police had been called, due to reports that Babyshambles were carrying knives and starting fights, so I went to the dressing room to warn them. Inside, I found all of the furniture ruined by a fire extinguisher, a girl with her hair on fire, and Peter and Headlock having a knife fight – time to go, I thought."

Drew —

"We came with an American punk band, '60s psyche punk – can't remember what they were called. They seemed really normal guys, but then they got on stage and started in the middle of songs – they were really good, really loud and heavy – snogging each other. Like dirty, toothless, filthy-looking, scabby ghetto punks… just snogging each other in the middle of wailing guitar solos. So confusing…

"There was this little promoter guy – quite small and skinny, wore glasses – and two songs in Peter smashed the in-house guitar amp and pulled one of the light fittings from the ceiling in an attempt to stop himself falling. And the guy was, like: 'Okay, this is not happening – you're too fucked to play.' And Peter squared up to him, lamped him, and the guy just took off his glasses and beat the shit out of Peter – fucking properly!"

Mik —

"There were loads of people hanging around in the dressing room for no apparent reason. One of these girls was getting a bit much, grabbing hold of Peter all the time, and one thing led to another and she was set on fire.

Opposite: Mik recording on a laptop, Laburnum Street, London.

"It was pretty bad, really – her arm looked like a fucking roman candle; [we were] rolling her around, trying to put her out. When we got on stage, the crowd were a bit weird and there was a fight. Peter tripped up and fell backwards and smashed all the equipment by accident. He fell on it and all the amps fell down, collapsed. We'd only done a song and a half and that was it, we'd finished. Got thrown off the stage. Crap gig."

The Swedish trip over and done with, Peter, Drew, Adam, Mik, Sally and Johnny returned to London the following day.

On 24th June, a day spent waiting at Waterloo station left Adam considering quitting the band, he and Drew expecting a call, at the very least, from a missing Peter and Mik: "We waited until about eleven o'clock until the last Eurostar went, and they didn't turn up, and we went home", says Drew laconically.

The latter pair's failure to show made it impossible to play at the French Festival that evening. Not that they didn't try to reach Paris; more that they set off, in a cab from London, at around the time they were supposed to be playing.

A thousand pounds lighter from the journey to Paris, Peter and Mik stayed in the French capital. A disinclined Drew and Adam joined them for a gig at La Cigale the following night, after which Peter went missing again, bringing about the cancellation of another show the next day.

Drew —   "We were headlining a festival – which is kind of a big deal – and they decided to drive. Or they hitched or something… and turned up in France at, like, four in the morning, miles from the festival. And Peter calls up: 'Where were you, we've got a gig, haven't we?' [I said:] 'We had a gig. Last night.'

"And so somehow, somebody organised us a gig back in France the next night. Which was really rude, really. Imagine you booked Babyshambles for a festival. They don't turn up and then they do a gig in Paris the next night – d'you know what I mean? It's really bad form. But that's what happened."

When Peter rejoined his bandmates, they set about laying down tracks for sessions that came to be known as the *French Dog Blues*.

The material garnered formed the template of Babyshambles' second album, *Shotters Nation*, released in October the following year; and while great inroads were made, it didn't quite match the prodigious amount of work Peter intended to bank.

Drew —   "Peter had decided we were going to record the entire album in one night. By six in the morning, we'd got, like, three songs done. He was saying: 'Come on, hurry up.' We were supposed to get on the plane at, like, nine in the morning. He was, like: 'Quick, we've only got another eight songs before we leave.'"

Adam — "The whole French debacle actually ended up being positive in the end. Initially, the missing of our show really upset me and Drew, so I felt that without a valid excuse I might have to call it a day – I mean, they had missed six Eurostars.

"The next day we got a call apologising and asking us to come to Paris. Reluctantly we agreed, and ended up playing a small French club, which went some way to redeeming our friendship. We also managed to blag some studio time, which is where we recorded the initial album demos."

Back in England, Peter told Thames Magistrates' Court, at a review of his drug treatment programme, that he was to have another implant fitted, following complications upon his return from England, from Portugal: "Customs had cracked opened the box of very, very delicate Naltrexone tubes in glass test tubes. God knows why – it was all medically-approved for export. I think because they'd never heard of the fucking stuff, and they completed unsterilised it, made it completely unsafe to administer.

"And so my trip to Portugal was in vain, and I couldn't receive an implant, which kinda threw me…what happened in Portugal, in my time there, it was not good for everyone in the band, who continued to see me on a downward spiral."

Judge Jane McIvor nevertheless noted his progress and recommended that his drugs tests be reduced from twice to once a week.

On the 21st of July, the band flew out to Spain for the Benicassim Festival, where they were joined on stage by Shane McGowan for the Pogues' classic, "Dirty Old Town". In London, meanwhile, Ronnie Flynn, who had agreed to look after Peter's Laburnum Street flat in his absence, feared for his life when a pair of chancers, who only an hour before tried to pester him into buying drugs, forced their way in and set upon him, later kidnapping him in their desperation to find money and some gear.

Ronnie Flynn — "He was asking me to lend him some money, and I wasn't gonna lend him any money. And he went away. And then about an hour later I went outside to the shops and these two guys rushed in and started battering me with a hammer, and then went upstairs, smashed the place to pieces. One of them started saying: 'I've left some drugs here. It's under the carpet in Pete's bedroom.' And I said: 'Pete doesn't have any carpet in his bedroom.'

"They basically thought there was gonna be piles of cash and mountains of cocaine and heroin lying about the place, none of which there were. But then they started battering me to tell them where the money and the drugs were; of course, there wasn't any. It was really quite nasty. I mean, we had a balcony, and the door was open, and I was ready to jump off, but the neighbours were having a barbecue on theirs, and I thought: surely they're gonna call the police…

"I had to call someone to send some money round, because I thought they were gonna kill me. And then they smashed the lampstand. I've got all scars on my head… they cut me to pieces. And it got really quite scary when this one guy kicked in this glass cabinet and then started slashing himself really deep on his arm. And I thought: I'm next.

"And one guy went to the toilet, came running out, then he pissed himself… And then they drove me to Hammersmith. They tried to hit me on the side of the head with a hammer, and I stuck my hand up – kind of reflex. I punched him in the eye – not intentionally – and he reeled back. And I thought: right, they're just gonna kill me now. So I just ran out, got out of there, and then came back.

"They'd fucked off. I stood round the corner and then went and got all of Pete's diaries – anything that I could carry of any value – chucked it in a cab and fucked off up to The Boogaloo."

Peter — "Anyone who would have known me at the time would have known that there was no drugs or money in that flat, and sticking a screwdriver up Ronnie's nose was going to serve no purpose. Ronnie getting a screwdriver shoved up his nose, and then having to escape over the balcony… the German neighbours were a very straight lot, anyway – very straight; always saying things like: 'You wouldn't want the police to know about last night's activities.' 'Well, what happened last night, then? What was going on, then – gun-running? Slave trade? Fucking white slave trade?'

"I'm not sure this is true, though. This is what we must ask ourselves. The place got a bit of a battering, and Ronnie got a screwdriver up his nose. It was undisputable that a screwdriver went up Ronnie's nose… Unless you're a bookworm or a trinket fiend, there's not much for you in my gaff. Records, books and trinkets."

Mik — "That was bizarre. Peter had people round his flat – he's a very trusting guy. People came round and saw everything in there, and thought there must be a big stash of money. While we were away; broke in expecting no-one to be there, but poor Ronnie was sat there. So they tied him to a chair, slapped him around a bit."

Ronnie and The Boogaloo's Gerry O'Boyle returned to Peter's flat the next day to find a trashed, blood-spattered flat, from which they removed anything of personal or sentimental value, in case Ronnie's assailants returned.

They didn't, but while Ronnie nursed his wounds, Babyshambles' mounting reputation for trouble was breeding suspicion among promoters. There was never any question, the occasional ropey performance aside, about the quality of music or the ability to lure the punters in; of greater concern, was whether they – or, more specifically, Peter – would turn up, whatever the circumstances behind any delay or no-show.

The list of promoters unwilling to chance their arm was getting longer. Thankfully, Danny Newman wasn't one of them.

II

The Blinding

An event that had been in the making since May came to fruition on 27th August 2006, as a long, stressful summer drew to an end

Turnmills owner Danny Newman had been searching for an act to headline that summer's Get Loaded In The Park festival – the third of its kind – and with the Reading/Leeds festival falling on the same weekend, he was under pressure to deliver.

Beginning life as a weekly Thursday night event held at Turnmills, a friend suggested taking the Get Loaded concept to a bigger stage – namely, Clapham Common, which could hold up to 20,000 people.

In earlier years, the event brought bands such as The Happy Mondays, The Farm and Flowered Up back together to perform, but, not wanting to be pigeonholed as a promoter of nostalgia gigs, Danny needed an emerging force that would appeal to a new generation of festival-goers; and a band capable of shifting tickets – quickly.

His friend, club manager Andy Peyton, suggested that they book Babyshambles, at a time when the band was without a manager, their infamy dissuading all but the bravest of agents to chance their arm.

Danny had experienced at close quarters Babyshambles' riotous stage act, the band playing Turnmills in August 2004 – a night he described as "mad, shambolic fucking madness", with pints thrown and property smashed.

Thankfully, the experience wasn't enough to deter him from taking a high-risk punt, figuring that each party could do the other some good: Danny needed a fresh, edgy headline act, at a stage where tickets for Get Loaded should already have been on sale; Babyshambles needed focus, unity, and a major platform on which to prove that they had what it took to jostle for prominence at the forefront of the British music scene.

An inauspicious start, *The Sun*'s feature about Peter supposedly injecting a fan was published the day after a booking had been made with Matt Bates. Things didn't get much better – at least not consistently so – in the obstacle-littered weeks ahead, some of which seemed at first appeared insurmountable, only the resolve and determination of key players Danny, Adam and Drew preventing a disaster of gross proportions.

Granted unlimited access to the band in the absence of a manager, Danny offered a safe environment to rehearse and record in, a place free of hangers-on; a refuge of sorts from an increasingly judgemental, hostile outside world.

Danny Newman — "It was a case of us taking them under our wing and saying: 'Right, you've got the club, you've got food – you can come and live here, basically – you've got the club downstairs.' I think everyone stopped associating Babyshambles and Pete with music, and we were a music event, so that was always gonna be a tricky part."

To push the festival, Danny worked to raise the band's profile in the music press and beyond, starting with the "Beg, Steal Or Borrow" single, recorded in Turnmills' downstairs studio and given away with *Metro*, London's free weekday newspaper.

In addition, the *NME* gave the band pride of place on its front cover, but while the exposure gave Get Loaded some much needed publicity, it took a couple of interviews to garner the material from which it was generated.

The first was conducted in Turnmills after an extended photo shoot that lasted almost four hours, a bored Peter taking exception to one of Anthony Thornton's questions, cutting the interview short.

A couple of days later, Peter redeemed himself by ringing Anthony at work, talking him through some of the band's latest tracks and demos, while claiming that he was contemplating a place in the country with a pond, some ducks, and his guitar.

The Babyshambles cause, meanwhile, was strengthened when Andy Boyd and Adrian Hunter came on board to steady the good ship Albion.

Babyshambles had been without a manager since James Mullord's departure the previous autumn, and though Adam – and, at crucial stages, Drew and Mik – had filled in admirably, it was time for somebody to come in and take responsibility for the day-to-day running of the band.

Adrian had known Peter from his time with The Libertines, staging a show on which they shared a bill with I Am Kloot, a band he'd been looking after together with press officer Andy Fraser. Every so often their paths would cross and they would exchange a few words, but there was never any mention of management from Adrian, who already had Scott 4 under his stewardship.

A former employee of the Silvertone record label, Adrian came close to signing the band Andy was in at the time, The Shave, on a singles deal for "Catwalk Queen", though they had yet to meet personally. Adrian drifted out of management, but fancied a new challenge, and, after a chance meeting with Andy one night, they agreed to work together.

They came to nominally manage a band called the Phoenix Drive, a side project of Drew's, but it took more than three years before Adrian actually realised who Drew was, his remarkably short memory seeing to it that he forgot their daily encounters.

Drew — "I used to live in Parkway in Camden, and Adrian was always in the Good Mixer pub in Camden. And I was always there at some point during the day, probably 'cos it's a good place to meet someone or have a quick game of pool or something. And he was always there with a Guinness, doing the crossword. And for three years I met him every day, and every day he didn't recognise me.

"It was unbelievable – like *Groundhog Day*! 'Alright, Adrian, how you doing?' 'Who are you?' 'It's me, mate: Drew. Adrian, we have met. We were out all night, and ended up in the kebab shop – don't you remember? Eight man's pool?' 'No.' 'Three years of seeing me every day?' 'No, fuck off.' 'Right! You cunt, Adrian!' 'Don't call me a cunt, you don't know me.'"

Adrian Hunter — "Apparently, I used to be introduced to Drew on an almost daily basis in the Good Mixer, but never remembered him the next day. Suffice to say, my memory has improved slightly since then."

When somebody handed Adrian a Phoenix Drive demo, he liked it so much he called the man behind the music – Drew. They arranged to meet and, once Adrian overcame his initial embarrassment, he expressed an interest in managing the band – interest cemented once he and Andy went along to a few Phoenix Drive gigs.

But with Drew fully committed to Babyshambles, there wasn't an awful lot for them to do. Phoenix Drive had made an album, but they weren't gigging and there were no plans to take any material to a record company.

Not that Adrian ever expected Drew to sacrifice his dedication to Babyshambles for the sake of his side project: "I fully appreciated that, because he was in, perhaps not the biggest band in the country, but they were certainly the most exciting band in the country at that time."

He and Andy went to watch Babyshambles at Brixton Academy in February 2005, the former recalling: "I remember just standing with Andy… seeing where Drew's head was at, and then just seeing the excitement and the fervour of the fans, and the quality of the songs, and just being overtaken by the whole vivid, live performance. And just being fucking blown away by it, and nudging Andy and saying: 'This is what we've gotta fucking do, this is the kind of band that we need, you know? We need a band that's doing something that are fucking great.'"

Adrian left London shortly afterwards, sick and tired of his job at the time, to return to his home town of Gourock in Scotland. He and Andy agreed that they would continue to collaborate; when something of worth came along, he would return to The Smoke.

About six months later he received a text from Mik, a friend for over a decade, who suggested they have a chat, with a view to possibly managing Babyshambles, who, with "The Blinding" EP coming along nicely, needed to find a home for it and future material. In addition, Drew was instrumental in trying to organise a meeting, aware that, long-term, the band could use some managerial expertise.

Not that Adrian's initial contact with Peter ran as smoothly as he might have hoped: "I was in Leeds, on tour with Sam Sallon, supporting Rodrigo Gabriella, and I immediately called Peter, who, as usual, didn't pick up. I left a message and then called Mik. I asked Mik if Peter knew I was going to call, and he said no!

"So I felt a bit of a tool, imagining Peter getting this random call from me, discussing management. I don't imagine he ever got the message, anyway, in retrospect, as it's not often he checks his messages – and, even more rarely, replies."

The foundations for change were, in fact, laid a few months earlier, in Edinburgh, for a Babyshambles gig that Adrian's friends, Odeon Beat Club, were supporting: "I was hanging out in the dressing room area, and Peter came out of the production office and looked a little startled, said hello, and that he thought we should have a little chat at some point. That chat took quite some time to transpire but, luckily, it eventually did. One of the main things I remember about this was a large wad of cash hanging precariously out of his back pocket and thinking: this band need a proper tour manager."

After a get-together at Turnmills, at which Andy met Peter, Adam and Mik for the first time, it was agreed in principle, albeit very loosely, that they might all work together.

With Get Loaded drawing ever closer, and Peter's caricature making the news more often than the man behind it, his more human side was demonstrated on *Friday Night With Jonathan Ross* on 7th July, the illusion of a useless drug addict hell-bent on self-destruction shattered by a calm, placid persona that won many of his doubters round.

The fascination with his personal life was stealing attention away from the Get Loaded festival and, with tickets not moving, the Jonathan Ross interview, together with a flawless rendition of "Beg, Steal Or Borrow" – unrecognisable from the clumsy attempts made during rehearsals – provided a much-needed fillip.

But on the day of the show, Danny, who described Peter as the "Scarlet Pimpernel" – coined as a result of "having to hunt him down all the time" – had his patience tested to breaking point when Peter went missing, pairing up with Johnny Headlock to try and track him down.

After hours of fruitlessly driving around crack dens and dealers' abodes, they eventually found him, wasted, at home, whisking him away and effecting a plan that would see him suited and booted, and armed with a present, in readiness for his date with the Beeb.

Danny's wife, Holly, a fashion fitter and make-up artist, helped spruce Peter up in tandem with his sister-in-law, Heidi, a hairdresser, bringing a selection of suits, shirts and ties for him to try on, and pruning his light mop of hair. Madness reigned, Danny remembering a "mad little crew – one was delivering this, another was drawing him, Ashtar's filming… something was always getting drawn."

Knowing that artist Alizé Meurisse had produced sketches of Peter, he asked whether she'd be willing to part with one to give Jonathan as a gift. Reluctant, Alizé offered instead to sketch a new picture that Danny filled in with watercolours and got Peter to write the lyrics to "Beg, Steal or Borrow" over.

To add the personal touch, the picture was addressed to Jonathan, his wife and children, the names of whom had been sourced in advance. The picture was framed, wrapped, and given to Peter just before the interview, to present to Jonathan, the gesture moving Ross and modifying a largely negative public perception of Peter.

Suddenly, record companies started expressing an interest in seeing what the band were up to, putting to one side their fears that their frontman was a liability not worth the hassle that committing to a deal entailed.

Danny Newman — "He was smashed out of his head on the show, before he went on… [but] he was honest, and I think geezers wanted to be his mate and birds wanted to mother him. And you get those two things right and you're laughing, and that's what he did.

"And everyone was, like: 'Oh, I saw that Pete Doherty thing, he's actually alright, him, isn't he?' And I'm thinking: wicked, these are normal people, I know that… and then you see those perceptions start to change, and all the girls are, like: 'Aaaah, isn't he lovely?'… And I think the present thing endeared him to everyone in the audience. It just worked, you know? And we created that, so that was quite nice to see."

Mik — "I think it did help, because people saw him for what he is – he's a nice, gentle bloke; well mannered, clever. Not just some idiot who wants to get off his head all the time, because that's what rock stars do or whatever. He's not like that. He's always been the same since I've known him, since before he was famous."

Adrian Hunter — "Sitting at home with my mother, who thought I was mad for pursuing this job, on that Friday night in smalltown Gourock, I remember her saying what a sweet boy he seemed – little did she know!

"After coming to a few shows and both her and my father meeting Peter, they're two of his most ardent fans. I remember the first time my tiny Scottish mother met Peter – she gave him a belt and told him he was a 'daft wee boy', albeit he's about two feet taller. They come backstage at some point every time he's in Scotland to say hello, and he's always lovely to them. It's quite a sight to see your mum dancing at the side of the stage with Babyshambles, in front of a crazed audience of Glaswegians!"

The Jonathan Ross gamble paid off. Tickets started selling again and people were lining up to interview Peter, but, behind the scenes, his drug use was causing headaches.

In one interview, for example, he curled up in a ball and fell asleep after one pipe too many, his interviewer, who had already been made to wait several hours, told to return when Peter was in a more coherent state.

"It was a bit strange", Mik recalls. "They were asking weird stuff and I don't think he was too up for doing it, anyway. And mid-session, we just heard this snoring noise, and that was it – it was all over."

A twenty-four-hour concern, Danny regarded that year's Get Loaded operation as a "day-by-day-by-day thing". At no stage did he dare look too far ahead, the precariousness of his situation exacerbated when shouldering much of the weight Adam in particular had been lumbered with in previous months.

Danny had been wary of pushing Peter too far and risk damaging the trust that had built up between them; and yet realised that, if Peter was left to his own devices, he could be staring disaster in the face come late August.

With media interest in Peter mushrooming by the day and the police knocking on Turnmills' door in search of an easy tug, Danny spent much of the summer on tenterhooks. He would give the paparazzi the slip when driving Peter to and from Turnmills, repel the countless negative influences more interested in persuading Peter to bankroll drugs binges than allow him time to recover and recuperate, and try to ease the concerns of the doubters – his corporate backers among them. And now that he had assumed Adam's responsibilities, he would handle the largely fraught task of overseeing the organisational side of things.

It was decided that another single, "The Blinding", would be recorded at Turnmills, and given away with Get Loaded sponsor, *The Big Issue* – another publication that put the band on its front cover – to encourage sales.

Former Happy Mondays keyboardist Dave Parkinson – a friend of Danny's – landed the job of producing the track, having been sitting in the studio when Adam walked in to discuss it with Danny. The trio chatted a while, whereupon Dave was asked whether he fancied the job. He gladly accepted, but, racked with nerves and eager to impress, he drank so readily that he can barely remember the first time he met the rest of the band.

In possession of a patchy, at best, memory of the encounter, Dave did recall Peter saying that he wouldn't last "two seconds", which hardly filled him with optimism for the task ahead.

Despite having worked with another musical heavyweight in Happy Mondays' frontman Shaun Ryder, Dave experienced a level of trepidation when meeting Peter for the first time. He had been expecting some semblance of the untamed, boisterous ruffian so often portrayed; instead he found "a really, really softly-spoken … easygoing… soft-natured guy."

Nursing a punishing hangover, Dave returned to the studio the next day. Before he knew it, he was marooned in a crack and heroin haze that blurred most of what occurred during the following weeks into a shapeless mass of time.

His immersion in this fug was so extreme that his girlfriend, Maria, chucked his bags out onto the street, for failing to see her or return her calls for three weeks. For a couple of those weeks, Dave barely slept at all, so absorbed was he in his alternative reality. When he finally resolved to get his shit together and return home, he somehow ended up in Watford, rather than his intended destination: Brixton.

Other than snapshots of being on a train at some point, he has no recollection of what followed, until waking, cocooned amongst bin liners' full of trash, to find a badger having just pissed on his leg: "I didn't sleep for weeks, so I must have crashed out for three days. I was in a back alley, behind houses next to some fields. And my leg was really hot, and there was a badger walking off. I was, like: 'What the fuck's going on?!' I had a serious hangover, thinking: what the fuck am I doing here?"

Bewildered and feeling bloody awful, Dave caught a train back to south London, discovering to his horror, when picking up a newspaper, that he'd lost three days; and that, when eventually making it back home, he no longer had one – for a while at least – a friend taking pity on him and letting him doss down on a floor for a month or so, until Maria was ready to have him back.

Dave
Parkinson — "I didn't go home for literally three weeks. I was just off my head for three weeks. Just stayed there… I was just constantly high; I didn't come down. I lost my relationship over it, [but] I crawled back, she took me back…

"On the recording side of things, it was quite a haze, looking back now. It genuinely was a haze – I can hardly remember. I dunno if that's how it was for the rest of the lads… I was constantly on drugs, so my reasoning had disappeared. I didn't think about what I was doing. That was the darkest moment for me: coming home and finding my bags outside the house and that, and having to sleep on a floor."

Evenings at Turnmills would routinely involve a continuation of the frenetic drug-taking that filled the afternoons – to the disapproval of Danny, who, with a responsibility to keep the premises free of narcotics, had to repeatedly remind the culprits that he couldn't risk having any on his property. But with addictions to feed, he found himself having to rid Turnmills of a ceaseless supply of Class As – a chore that added to his growing list of worries.

There would also be nightly feasts for Peter, Mik and Dave, who raided the club's kitchens when everyone else had gone home. As far as Dave remembers, all three wore nothing but chefs' hats, with he and Peter cooking three-course meals. They would tidy up after themselves, leaving no trace of their having been there, and disappear again, no-one any the wiser – until, a couple of months later, Dave revealed all to Danny, at which point he found himself on the receiving end of a severe bollocking.

Dave
Parkinson — "It was quite tempting, because you'd get to midnight and everyone's starting to think: well, there's a bloody restaurant and there's no-one there – we're the only people in the building, we might as well go and use it. As long as we tidied up afterwards no-one'd know we'd been there, so we made ourselves a three-course meal every night."

Mik — "Danny would go home and Dave would have the run of the place. In the kitchen they had loads of really nice grub. We'd have Turnmills food in the daytime – it was really good – so Dave would go in there, ask us what we wanted, and he'd start cooking up loads of elaborate meals and wotnot. We'd just eat and drink all night whilst recording. It was a good vibe…

"Dave got naked! That was him getting naked! 'Cos Dave got right into recording with us; me and him were almost living there. He used to sleep on the studio floor."

Peter — "He did it very rarely, but when Mik mixes valium with alcohol, he can't get his clothes off quick enough. It was never a sexual thing, I assure you, but it was always a case of: he starts banging on about the Yorkshire Moors and ancient Britain, and how clothes represented the Tory government's means of controlling the people; and how the working class had been destroyed, and how nakedness was the new working class and it proved we were all equal in equality. You know, the fact that he had a big knob – he used to tell me that I didn't admit we were equal in God's eyes, and we should wrestle. It was all absolutely insane…

"We'd reach a point of equilibrium, where Dave would stop gibbering about his girlfriend and not being happy that he lived in the studio twenty-five hours a day…Mik would have done enough drugs, you know, to have made him vaguely fucking satiated…I was in a space where I felt I could explore ideas that I had musically, and felt confident enough to play them to other people – basically, Mik and Dave – and we'd be away.

"And then we'd need a bit of sustenance as well. We were together, we were united, we were on adventure, and we needed to eat. So, er, I don't know where he gets this thing about three of us dining with chefs' hats, because, basically, I was the fucking kingpin when it came to the cooking. My Chinese omelette, man, has yet to be beaten."

On another occasion, Dave and Peter shared a bag of Ecstasy pills that had been stashed beyond the gaze of Turnmills' security. Crashing out hours later, Danny's brother, Paul Newman, otherwise known as Tall Paul, was met with an unusual sight the following morning, clocking the pair holding hands, on the back of watching Mik fumbling about on the floor, half-naked.

To add to Paul's dismay and exasperation, he had expected Dave to be ready to work on a tune, later disclosing that he'd been concerned that heroin had played a part in his state that morning. As it turned out, Dave's inebriation didn't prevent them from cutting a great track, though he had to put a few whiskies away before he was able to get going.

Dave Parkinson — "I don't know whose they were, but there was a bag of pills in the studio and, obviously, it's in a nightclub, so someone had probably left them there from the club or something. We decided to just do them all. I was on the floor and I woke next to Pete… That was a bit strange, that was. We just lay on the floor, holding each other. I woke up, thinking: what the hell's going on? I think the pills must have been really strong and we must have just been loved-up or something…

"He walked in and saw a load of bodies on the floor with their tops off, and me curled up in the corner with Pete. He thought I'd been on the heroin all night; he was worried about me... There was a reason for him to say that. I knew I hadn't been on the heroin, but he thought I had. But it's his studio – his and Danny's – so I have to show a bit of respect. But I was meant to be working with him; I was, like: 'I'm here, aren't I? At least I turned up. I just stayed over the night!'"

Mik — "They were both asleep, both holding hands in their sleep. Dave woke up, all '*Eh?*', and Tall Pall walked in, and God knows what he thought… [There was] loads of paraphernalia everywhere. It was a right fucking mess, and they had a massive argument, 'cos Dave was working for Tall Pall at the time, producing his new album, and I think he lost the job because of it. Dave lost a lot because of recording with us!"

Peter — "We'd fallen asleep in a position that, from a certain angle, if you squinted and had a twisted mind, you might think that something was going on and was a bit iffy. But, in actual fact, we were just curled up like dogs."

But while there were plenty of amusing shenanigans punctuating the recording period, they were blemished by occasionally sinister incidents, including the time Peter administered a trio of heroin shots in quick succession – a practice that can result in imminent death.

Previously, when Peter had been injecting in the studio, others had been present, but in this instance, left alone with him, Dave was suddenly, and very

---

Opposite: Peter and Mik at Turnmills.

uncomfortably, conscious of the precarious position he found himself in – especially as there didn't appear to be any life in Peter.

Dave
Parkinson — "I know you're not meant to do three in a row… It was just me and him in the studio, and he'd injected one, and I thought he's doing what he does. And then he did another one straight after it. And he did a third one, and I know it's dangerous to do that, and I looked at him and he collapsed, and I thought he was dead.

"Seriously, I just sat there and thought: shit, I hope he hasn't just died in front of me here, because it was just me and him in the room. And so I started tapping him and he came about… I've gotta admit, I did shit myself. I honestly thought he was dead."

Amid the fun, frolics and darkness, Dave had a job to do. Deliberately avoiding the band's material, not wishing to be influenced by their or Peter's body of material, he set about stamping his own distinctive mark on the record. Together, he and the band laid down enough tracks for an album.

Dave found his new workmates supportive and unquestioning of his directions, which, as it happened, were minimal: "Recording, the best thing to do with the lads is just let them play – don't butt in too much – and if I wanted them to do something, they'd just stop straight away and do it. They wouldn't question it, they'd do it straight away, so they were quite professional like that. I do remember that part of it."

He noticed that, often, Peter's voice sounded better when practising, the comparatively dull recording environment unable to excite him – and, indeed, the rest of the band – in quite the same way that a stage does; later, he would regret not setting a microphone up inside the main control room, in order to capture these takes.

Dave
Parkinson — "He was much better when he was warming up…I think it's more to do with him being a performer – he likes being on stage, he comes alive when he's on stage, Pete.

"Sometimes you get that when you're working in the studio with a band: they're not the same; I guess they buzz off the crowd. When you're in the studio, it's all very technical. It's a very serious place to be, a studio, because you know that whatever you record, that's it – that's gonna be there forever."

A potentially major bar to the recording process came in the form of the army of hangers-on trailing Peter.

Initially tolerated, Dave found them to be so disruptive that he had to throw them out of the studio: "You concentrate on your job, and every two seconds someone would turn up, and it would get on your tits after a while." Often, their exchanges would be heated, as Danny found when ensuring "the right people were here [Turnmills], and the wrong people were out the door."

Danny
Newman — "I fucked 'em all off, I wouldn't have it for a second, because I just didn't want 'em [there]. I was quite aggressive with some people – just, like: 'Who are you, what d'you want? No, mate, sorry, he's not here.' Bang, and shut the door, you know? A lot of that."

At night, when the club was open, the studio's close proximity to the dance floor caused more problems, revellers recurrently walking in and disrupting recordings, Dave remembers: "You got people wandering in, going: 'Fucking hell, that's Pete Doherty!' It used to happen all the time – especially girls. Loads of girls coming in all the time. Pissed me right off."

Peter would also draw double-takes from punters when casually wandering around the club during breaks in recording, and when sinking the occasional bevvie at the bar. But when focused and lucid, Dave found Peter a quietly conscientious character with a remarkable talent: "It takes a lot for him to push his button. He was really easygoing. He'd just sit there and sort of wouldn't do anything; he'd just be interested in recording his music, and he was almost totally oblivious to everyone around him… If there was an earthquake, he'd carry on writing… He's just a natural-born songwriter, [he] can just churn them out…"

Dave also saw in Peter a number of personality traits that he shares with another man renowned for his devil-may-care take on life, Shaun Ryder.

Other than a mutual fondness for drugs, both possess a stage presence that sets them apart from their peers, as well as an unwillingness to be pressured into doing anything that they don't want to.

Dave
Parkinson — "That's another thing him and Shaun have in common: they'll turn up when they're ready. With Shaun, we'd all be ready to go on, thinking: where the fuck's Shaun? And he'd just be sat on the tour bus having a fag or having a smoke. And we'd go: 'Shaun, we're on now', and he'd go: 'I'll come on when I'm ready.'"

With Get Loaded just weeks away, a dire appearance on Channel 4's *Transmission* threatened to damage the band's rising, hard-fought credibility.

Joined on stage by Purple and The General, the band gave perhaps their sloppiest performance yet, stumbling their way through "Killamangiro", during which Mik fell into the audience; "Pipe Down", at the end of which the stage was trashed; and "Sedative", as Peter slurred and forgot his words, looking disorientated.

It could have been far, far worse had Peter been caught smoking a pipe on stage – a sight spotted by Danny, watching in the production room, backstage. Had it not been for Danny knowing a stage manager at the *Transmission*, the band might have been thrown off the premises, and the media tossed another gratefully-banked headline. "He was just taking the blatant piss", says Adam. "I've seen him do it at airport queues before… He couldn't give a monkey's."

Danny Newman — "He used a pipe on stage… Smoke was coming out [of the corner of his mouth], but he didn't have a fag in his hand. But no-one twigged, thank God, because that would have been a fucking terrible thing – Pete Doherty live on television. That would've been the nail in the coffin."

Mik — "[I] don't even remember playing; [I] fell off stage twice. Apparently – I don't remember this, as I say – they talked me into going on stage with no top on, no socks. I looked like a fucking condom stretched over a bird cage. I was awful, really out of my nut. That's the first time I've ever done that in all the time I've been playing guitar – the first time I've ever gone on that hammered that I couldn't play as well as I wanted to. I was so embarrassed about it… it set us back a bit…

"I'd just like to take the opportunity to apologise to the rest of the band and the fans for that."

Sally Anchassi — "Mik was off his face. He was so pissed, because he'd given up the other, and started drinking so much, and he had, like, one shoe on and one shoe off. He didn't know where anyone was or where anything was, and we had to carry him around."

Adam — "Possibly the worst performance I've ever, ever been involved in. Mik was out of his nut from the word go. He started drinking and wotnot, and by the time we got on stage, The General and Purple had showed up, and decided to join us.

"It was a total mess. Mik was plastered, Peter was on another planet, General didn't know the song, so just blopped here and there, and Purple hadn't really ever been on stage before. So the result was quite expected, really.

"I came off stage and just left. Drew came with me. It was there that I decided that the following week I would talk to Peter about how I felt, ultimately resigning. We had so much potential and talent, and here we were destroying everything.

"The following week I went to see him, pulled him away from his crowd, and set about explaining myself. Before I could start, he looked me square in the eye and said: 'I know it's been messy, but it'll get better. Just hang in there', which kind of stumped me. So I took that as a positive on his part, hoping that he realised how out of control the band were spiralling. So all seemed well, temporarily."

Drew — "We had Purple and General rapping all over every song that we did, and Peter grabbed a scaffolding unit thing and pulled it down – almost killed half the audience… I think someone had a pint glass, or there was a lot of water, and all of a sudden there was a lot of fluid on the floor and lives cables spitting sparks everywhere, 'cos he'd just pulled down a big lighting rig. And they had to evacuate the building, 'cos they thought people were going to get electrocuted."

Peter— "Proper fucking night – that was a proper Shambles night. You know when Adam comes out fuming, you know that it's been a good night. It was just scandalous from the word go. Mik was rotten, though. Mik had never looked so fucking, like, amazing. All he had on was a pair of red pants and some tight jeans, and he was walking around the studio, scaring the living daylights out of all these boy bands and girl bands…all there, like, lah-di-dahing it and hobnobbing it, and then: Mik wondering through the throng on the wonderful Hammersmith Studio's balcony, shouting like that: 'The rock's here. The rocks are alright, but the brown's fucking shit. Let's have an armful before I gotta go on and do the show' – you know, at the top of his voice…

"Purple made his on stage début. Don't think Adam was too happy with the outcome of that. Purple himself still talks about his role in *Transmission* and what a success it was, and how great he was so…you know, mixed feelings, I think, all round."

Adrian Hunter — "I remember *Transmission* all too well. I was in Scotland, and was calling up to see how things were going for the preparations. I managed to get Danny on the phone, and asked how things were. I could hear all sorts of shenanigans kicking off in the background. Danny, not altogether convincingly, told me that all was fine and it'd all be cool. Throughout the day I heard more and more reports about just how 'unfine' things were. In the end, I couldn't bring myself to watch the show.

"To hear that Peter had asked Purple, who I actually like, and The General to, not only join the band on stage, but join the fucking band! I thought: you know what, right – do I really want to do this? It was months before I could even bring myself to YouTube the performance after the descriptions I heard, and my worst fears were all true – it was a disgrace. They shamed themselves, or, more accurately, certain people shamed the name of the band and their reputation. A fucking childish, self-indulgent, fucked-up disgrace. That wasn't music, and music was supposed to be what it was all about. Another chance wasted to prove how good the band could be to a cynical public."

The shoddy performance discouraged Danny from booking any more interviews in its immediate aftermath, wary of what could have been an avalanche of negative publicity in the run-up to Get Loaded, potentially destroying all of the previous months' hard work.

Neither he nor the band could afford any negative publicity, any derailments. Get Loaded was drawing ever closer.

Pretty soon, it looked like it might not happen at all.

12

Get Loaded

With Get Loaded just weeks away, the scrutiny on Peter was ramped up. Countless interview requests were made but, with Peter rarely in the mood or together enough to comply, Danny put a number of questions to him in advance. Figuring that the questions requiring answers via faxback would be similar in nature to his own, Danny was able to relieve Peter of a large part of his media burden.

On the 14th of August, Babyshambles' scheduled appearance at Bar M, San Antonio, for the Ibiza Rocks show, had to be cancelled for the second time. Peter's Portuguese rehab forced the cancellation of the first scheduled date, and on this occasion Peter was told that Mancunian gangsters wanted to do unpleasant things to him, and that it'd be in his best interests not to fly out to Spain. "At that point there was too many drugs being consumed and everyone was paranoid", says Adam, though Peter's cause wasn't helped by his passport having expired, efforts to obtain a temporary one foundering after his mugshot fell short of regulations.

A few days later, on the 17th, disaster struck when Peter was arrested re-signing bail, his confinement further endearing him to his Swiss fans, their hopes of seeing the band dashed when the slot at Rock Oz Arene was axed, along with Belgium's Pukelpop on the 19th.

Ignoring Adam's advice, Peter walked into an East London police station with a can of Tennents Super and a guitar, playing to perhaps his most ungrateful audience yet, officers taking him in, saying he was unfit to re-sign bail. He was told he would have to be held in custody until an appearance at Thames Magistrates' Court the following day. Charged with seven counts of drug possession pertaining to his arrests on 20th and 29th April and 7th August, this latest brush with the law was catastrophic timing.

It was proposed by the court that Peter be jailed until his next court appearance on 4th of September, making the band's appearance at Get Loaded, which had another three thousand tickets to shift, an impossibility.

Danny, who was only in court by chance, curious to observe the legal process for himself, realised that he had to act quickly if he was to rescue Get Loaded and preserve Peter's liberty: "I dread to think what would have happened [if I hadn't attended court]... And thank God I did, otherwise it would have been over...

"I think one of the boys said he [Peter] was like a drowning man, but he wasn't drowning – the geezer's hand was sticking out of the water. He'd drowned; it was just [a question of] pulling him back up."

With just five minutes' break until court resumed, Danny asked a friend who had accompanied him that day to try and book a room in The Priory. The first site he tried was fully booked, but the group's Southgate clinic had one room available. The problem: Peter had to sign himself in in person, but, as he was in court, on the brink of getting sent down, this was a physical impossibility.

It was suggested to The Priory that Peter sign an admittance form, faxed over by the clinic, in the presence of his solicitor, Sean, who was in court defending his client. The Priory agreed. Now it was up to Sean to persuade the court that Peter should be sent to rehab, while underscoring the importance of fulfilling his Get Loaded obligations.

Danny Newman — "Sean's gone back in and said: 'Right, your honour, if Pete doesn't do this big show in Clapham, then he's not gonna get this money. If he doesn't get this money, he can't pay his rent… he's got to do this gig or he's fucked, because… all the record companies are gonna be down there, they wanna sign him; if he doesn't, you're ruining this boy's life – that's it.

"So, she accepted it. Fucking thank God. I said a little prayer in there."

The proposal was accepted on condition that Peter lived and slept at The Priory, and complied with a daily curfew between 10pm and 8am. He would be allowed out only for Get Loaded In The Park on the 27th.

It was only out of having no choice in the matter, Danny believes, that Peter entered rehab. And, indeed, he was very nearly ejected, deliveries of drugs invoking the wrath of Priory staff, including the nurse charged with looking after Peter.

Peter — "The rest of the band weren't too happy with her. She was quite amazing, really, in some ways, because she was so beautiful, she really was… She was tall – I think she'd been a model, a dancer, and she knew me from day one, from the first hour's conversation we had together; she had me sussed. What she knew – most certainly, most surely – was that if I was to give up alcohol and drugs – and all these things that are forbidden by the twelve-step programme – she knew that, for that to happen, I could not be in the environment I was in. I couldn't be associated with people that I was associating with. I couldn't go on tour. I couldn't be in a band. I could not expose myself to temptations for at least a year, a year-and-a-half.

"And Adam and Drew and Mik and Sally and Adrian and Andy, they all turned up for this meeting, and she was, like: 'If you care about this boy – because he will die, you know – he's to do nothing for a year-and-a-half.' And none of them could get their heads round it; they…just saw her as the enemy. She was talking absolute sense. It's a disease, addiction; it's not something you can trifle with, you know? And you need help.

"And I had so much help from the people around me, fortunately, because the people I was closest to at the time – Sally, Adam, Drew, to a certain extent Adrian, Andy. It wasn't a danger for me to be in their company. The nurse knew danger came from being around anybody, you know, anyone who drank – that was just as bad, 'cos it would always lead me back to the needle. And that's in my make-up, really."

Danny, who had heard stories comparing Peter's latest spell in rehab to Kesey's classic tale of life inside a mental hospital, had to drive to Southgate, together with Sean, to convince the clinic that bad influences would be kept at bay.

Desperate that events not take another turn for the worst at this late stage, they went to great lengths to reassure staff of Peter's safety on the day of the festival – an outing that The Priory disagreed with and had protested against – while guaranteeing his return by the ten o'clock curfew insisted upon by the courts, Danny promising that his team of security would escort him there and back.

To aid Peter's recovery, Drew, Adam, Mik and Sally, together with the provisional new management team of Andy Boyd and Adrian Hunter, were allowed in to air any grievances they harboured regarding his behaviour – "We'd go in and all sit in a circle and chat with Peter, and he'd sit there like a naughty schoolboy, looking down. To his credit, we knew he was totally straight, and it was a chance for us to tell him what we thought", Adam recalls. "And it was good. It was generally me and Sally that spoke up about different people and different situations that made us feel a certain way, and he apologised."

With Andy based in London, a skint Adrian travelled hundreds of miles up and down the motorway each week, working a few days in a record shop back in Scotland to earn enough to keep him going, and then catching the Megabus to London to continue building a relationship with the band, occasionally dropping in at Turnmills for meetings with Andy.

During one trip back to Glasgow, the morning after Peter had been kept in when re-signing bail, the bus broke down. By coincidence, he received a call from Adam, who explained the circumstances behind Peter's arrest and offered to pick him up in a slip road near Brent Cross, where the bus had broken down.

Adrian Hunter —

"I often think what would have happened if that bus hadn't broken down and, more to the point, if I'd got on the replacement, which arrived before Adam did. The driver thought I was mad when I just walked off in the middle of the motorway and, in retrospect, perhaps I was – look what I got myself into! Joyful insanity!"

Ending up in a pub close to The Priory, it was decided that it was high time new management were brought in to solidify operations – a decision that came as welcome relief for Mik, who had grown disenchanted at, he feels, being put-on, his mounting responsibilities far outweighing the recognition he received and the pay he'd been trousering.

Mik — "I was taking all of the equipment – and I mean *all* of the equipment – into every gig. Arranging for the tour bus to take us to the gig, and then actually playing on stage. And so if Peter snapped a string, I'd have to stop playing my guitar, change the string. And it got to the point where it wasn't professional enough – you know, you can't have a guitar player stopping mid-set… it was ridiculous.

"I said to Adam: 'Look, we need to get roadies on board at least, or some guitar techs.' And Adam said: 'Why do we need a guitar tech for the guitar tech?' And that really pissed me off – I was more than a fucking guitar tech by then, you know. I said to him: 'Fuck it, I'm going, I can't do this any more.'…

"Something had to give, I couldn't do it any more. Could physically not do any more. And I was getting nowhere near enough for what I was doing. It was outrageous – there were people just hanging around who were getting more money than I was and, me being the way I was, I wouldn't say anything about it. But, eventually, it just got to the point where I didn't care any more; I had to say: 'This is it.' And Pete accepted to get management on board, which I was more than glad about. About time!"

Adam — "Andy and Adrian had been trying for some time to help manage the band. Drew knew them initially, but I soon got to know them and thought that it was the only way forward. I knew they weren't the biggest management company in the world, but I thought at that point we needed a personal touch.

"The band was at rock bottom. Danny had given us a leg-up, but we were now sinking once more. Also, I was exhausted with all the running around and just holding the band together. I couldn't do it any longer, so for me it was a welcome relief."

Drew — "Pretty much as soon as James left they let me know that they wanted to manage it, and I suggested it to Peter, who just looked at me blankly and changed the subject. And I tried and tried loads of times to suggest it, but he wasn't having it.

"And, all of a sudden, he seemed to register that I was saying that I knew people who thought they could manage us. And they've done a good job, man, they've done alright."

Over the next couple of weeks, Andy and Adrian began tentatively looking after the band's interests, as both sides sussed each other out. But with Get Loaded creeping up on them, more important matters demanded attention – namely, ensuring that the band didn't notch up a potentially catastrophic no-show.

Taking no chances on the day of the festival, Peter was ring-fenced by Danny's security, who made sure that no disruptive influences got anywhere near him.

Adrian remembers what he describes as "embarrassingly heavy security" when collecting Peter from The Priory: "It was like a presidential fucking parade! There were about thirty big geezers around this car… and this car's doing about two miles an hour, and me and Peter are just looking at each other, going: 'What the fuck's going on here?!'"

Mik — "There was only us that could speak to him, and management. He wasn't allowed to do interviews and he had to have a chaperone with him, so [in] our dressing room – we had this little hut behind the stage – there were sixteen security guards placed round it… and then ten feet away from them there was another ring of security guards, and then another ring. And it was ridiculous – like, bloody hell, I could see people trying to come and talk to us and getting ushered away, and it was absolutely bonkers."

The sheer scale of the wall of security for a while prevented even Peter's bandmates from joining him, Adam in particular bristling at the snub, as Drew recalls: "One of the security guards twatted Adam in the chest. Adam said: 'I'm in Babyshambles – I'm the drummer, we're gonna go see him.' 'No, you're not.' 'Why not?' 'No-one's going in there.'

"Adam's got a bit of a temper on him, and it almost kicked off. Before it did, this guy came up and said: 'What are you doing? These boys are in the band'… Adam's going: 'Wanker! Hahahaha, wanker – you going to stop me now? Wanker!' You could see this guy's face going from white to puce."

Adrian Hunter — "Sally did a sterling job in the face of death threats from some of Peter's 'friends', who were livid that they couldn't get near him, either, annoy everyone around, or just generally act like arseholes.

"We were there to play a show – do a good fucking show. It was a statement of intent, a manifesto – it was a statement to the effect that Babyshambles needed to make: 'Yes, we are this good. Yes, we can headline a show this big. And, YES!, to the doubters, tabloid demonisers, and generally ignorant haters… there are people out there who are fucking loving this band! Stick that in your pipe and smoke it,' to coin a well-worn phrase."

Peter arrived around half-an-hour before their slot, joining Drew, Adam and Mik to close the event with a blistering performance that silenced their many critics, Adrian Hunter, whose other memories of the day included "Peter vomiting copiously over Goldie's trainers, which, I imagine, were brand new and quite expensive," recalling "the vicarious buzz of watching an amazing live show that you feel in some way you have been part of making happen."

Peter —

"It was a return. Not a turning point – a returning point, to the four of us actually being able to spend some time together on the stage. And making some noise, you know? We made a right fucking racket that night. And, to all intents and purposes, it sounded alright."

Danny
Newman —

"I was with people that'd been following him for fucking years, and they said that was the best one they'd ever see him do. He was sick at the end of it, in the car – I think it was the adrenaline and everything else; he really gave it his all.

"I said: 'Please, don't smash any of the equipment up.' Obviously, he smashed a guitar, and he threw it out into the crowd, and I thought: 'Oh, fuck it, if that's the worst that's gonna happen, who gives a fuck?'...

"It was a case of us taking a massive punt on it – a massive chance on it – thinking: fuck it, let's do it – let's headline these people, let's just do it and see what happens. We knew it was gonna be a rough ride, up and down. Looking back now through everything, I wouldn't have changed it for the world, because it was an amazing experience, and I think we got a lot of credibility for the campaign that we did around Pete... A lot of people along the way could have helped us and believed in us, but didn't, so fuck those people...

"Just when we thought it was off the rails, we pulled it back on, and that's what it was like the whole campaign; just when you thought it was fucking-up and it was off, we just got it back on track."

Drew —

"Get Loaded In The Park was a good one. There were a whole couple of months where, in the lead-up to it, we were in Turnmills and Peter was on probation. And we got through that, Portugal and the implants, and it seemed like this headline festival at the end of all this was punching above our weight.

"And it was during the period where the ratio of shows to no-shows had got ridiculous, so it seemed like a really brave move for Danny to book us as the headline act. And Peter had been in The Priory for a week before the gig, and it was touch-and-go whether, up to even, like, a day before the gig, they were going to let him out to do it.

"And they did, and we played a storming set, and it was kind of vindication, and: 'We're capable of doing this, we can play shows this size.' We proved the naysayers wrong and proved ourselves right."

Dave
Parkinson —

"I thought it was absolutely brilliant. They absolutely rocked it. I've gone to see them quite a few times now, and that was definitely their best performance I've seen. I think they play better to the bigger crowds. I know they do a lot of little gigs and that, but it always seems quite tense when they do these tiny little gigs. I've noticed: put them in front of a big audience and the whole band just come to life. I think they really perform better. They like to put a great show on, basically, all of them do."

Anthony Thornton —— "Get Loaded was important – in fact, crucial – for the band. They were without a deal, they had an admittedly well-earned reputation for no-shows, and yet somehow they'd been booked to headline a festival. It was a tremendous act of faith on the behalf of both the organisers and the fans. The show itself proved they could hold their own in front of a large crowd. It proved they could be reliable: I'm convinced it was key in Parlophone's decision to sign them… I think it really made a difference. They proved a lot of doubters wrong, absolutely. They'd been working so hard in the run-up to that, and they did it, and it was great."

As soon as Peter finished performing, at five-to-nine, he was bundled into a car and rushed back to The Priory in time for his curfew – with just five minutes to spare.

Months of hard work and perseverance had paid off, though for Danny there was a sense of mild anti-climax: "It felt quite numb actually, because after a big party like that, often you have a drink, you stay behind. But we'd gone straight away, we got there, dropped him off.

"And I remember being at home, about half-past-ten, on my own, after all that, and it was just a mad fucking experience, y'know what I mean? I just sat there and reflected on that time, from start to finish, and I didn't know whether to laugh or cry. I just felt numb, not empty, but just quite fucking exhausted… But it was amazing. I'd do it all again."

Mik —— "I hadn't seen him for a month – we hadn't rehearsed or played together for a month – so it was quite weird going onto the stage, in front of twenty thousand, and having to play. I was crapping myself.

"We had half an hour together before the gig, just sat there talking. Did the gig, walked off stage, had ten minutes at most, and then Peter had to leave. And it was quite upsetting, really. It was very strange. Yeah, it was surreal."

Opposite: Adam at the piano.

13

Shotter's Nation

Peter's post-Get Loaded return to The Priory also meant that shows in Milan and Germany, had to be cancelled. And with his September court date looming, the new management team of Andy and Adrian worked with Adam on a framework to assist his recovery, pursuing a tour and record deal.

At Thames Magistrates' Court on the 4th, Peter's sentencing on seven counts of drug possession was deferred for a couple of months, though he was asked to return to court in October for a review of his drug treatment order. Judge Jane McIvor, who confessed a fondness for new song "The Blinding", said that a jail sentence "would be counter-productive... and would undo the hard work that a lot of professionals have put in." If Peter remained drug-free, she said, he would avoid being locked up.

In the second week of September, Babyshambles announced a short-term record deal with Parlophone division, Regal, for *The Blinding* EP, along with a UK tour that was to begin on 25th September at the Music Factory, Carlow, and finish at the Newcastle Academy on 10th October.

Leaving The Priory on the morning of the first date, Peter immediately made for Heathrow, to catch a flight to Ireland for that night's gig, where Kate joined the band on stage for "La Belle Et La Bête".

Adrian
Hunter —

"The country's most notorious singer, the world's biggest supermodel, and little old me being whisked through Heathrow special services, being pursued by paparazzi, flying off to the first show of my first tour with the band, most likely to be arrested at any given point by any copper bored enough. I also remember the looks on Nigel and Keith, the newly employed techs', faces when the chaos began to unfold. I had to take them downstairs on the bus that night and tell them that this job would never be normal, but that, if we worked together, it may move in that direction – but there was no chance in a fucking million that it would be anything like what they were used to.

"It was quite a speech, because it was the first time I'd actually witnessed the true bedlam that unfolded. Even I was unused to it, though I managed, I hope, to drum up a bit of Dunkirk spirit."

The following day, on the tour's second date at the Dublin Ambassador, Kate made another appearance, as did Shane MacGowan, the Pogues man helping belt out "Dirty Old Town", as he had done at Spain's Benicassim festival that summer.

For Mik, there was relief at being unburdened of the multi-faceted role he'd undertaken up to that point: "It was a good laugh. It was the first tour we'd had where I was the proper guitarist. I could relax a bit more and enjoy it, because on previous tours, before the gig, I'd be running around, guitar tuning, setting up everything, and having the stress of playing as well. So just to be able to walk to the dressing room, knowing that I could sit and relax before the gig, was really good for me."

The tour took in another eight dates, before shows at the Liverpool Academy, Glasgow Academy, Nottingham Rock City, Manchester Academy and Newcastle Academy were axed, a spokesman for EMI, Parlophone's parent company, saying: "It has become clear that Peter embarked on this high profile tour too soon after his discharge and still needs time to recover from his extensive rehab treatment."

Upon learning that Peter was considering pulling the dates, a meeting was held at Kate's. Sitting around a huge table in a darkened room, Peter told his bandmates that, in light of his recent treatment, he needed time out. The tour's opening dates had taken more out of him than he had expected, and he simply didn't have the reserves required for such energy-sapping shows – something Mik found no difficulty getting his head around: "Part of The Priory's programme is that, basically, you have eight hours, every day, of counselling – people talking to you about drugs. That would drive me round the twist; I mean, he did that for a month solid, non-stop.

"And then, for it to just stop, must have been quite strange for him. Can you imagine: all that time you go to work, he was sat there and talked to by someone about why he shouldn't be taking drugs, trying to get to the bottom of why he does take them. It's exhausting. It might sound easy enough but, believe me, it ain't. And for that to just suddenly, totally stop, and go into this situation, is surreal."

On the 18th, at a review of his drug treatment programme, defence counsel Bruce Clark told Thames Magistrates' Court that Peter was living outside London as part of his efforts to stay clean. Judge Jane McIvor said that the order's weekly appointments "had not been as successful as expected", and ordered him to return in January for another review.

Halfway through the month, the band re-entered the studio to lend a hand on a cover of The Clash's "Janie Jones", released on 30th October in aid of Strummerville, the charity in memory of inspirational vocalist Joe Strummer.

His daughter, Lola, came up with the idea for the single, and discussed with Statik and Drew, who had been friends for years after meeting through photographer James Medina, about which track to plump for.

Statik has produced and remixed work for, among others, Lethal Bizzle and the Arctic Monkeys, and collaborated with Drew on various projects, dating as far back as his pre-Shambles days. The pair agreed to produce the track, with Drew directing the video, though Peter's confinement in The Priory at the time of the shoot prevented him from appearing on film.

Recorded in a tiny studio off Holloway Road, twenty-one guest vocalists contributed to the track, including We Are Scientists, The Kooks, Jack Peñate, Jamie T and Carl Barât, though he and Peter recorded their parts independently of each other.

In agreeing to do the single, Babyshambles were, primarily, supporting a charity close to their hearts, though on a more pragmatic note, Adam says: "It was great for us because at that time we had nothing [on the agenda], we were just grabbing at anything, trying to get a bit of a profile for the band, trying to get it back on its wheels… I think it helped stabilise our relationship with EMI, the fact that we went and recorded it and got it out like that."

Towards the end of the month, Peter felt ready to hit the road again and, fancying a European jaunt, Babyshambles flew to Italy for a five-day mini tour, all but Peter wearing crew cuts – a trend unwittingly instigated by Mik, who, fag clamped firmly in the corner of his mouth, made a mess of Adam's crowning glory.

Adam — "Mik cut my hair at Kate's, said: 'I'm just going to give you a trim', and it ended up like a prisoner-of-war cut. So they just got the clippers out because it was all lumpy. Cheers, Mik."

Mik — "I think everyone got drunk and decided to get number four haircuts. I didn't balls Adam's up – it's just he wouldn't sit still enough. He wouldn't let me finish the bloody thing – it's his own bloody fault!"

Once in Italy, a walk along a deserted beach in Rimini, the tour's third stop, offered indications as to how that night's show would unfold. "I just had this sense that Peter wasn't very happy", explains Adam. "And I remember speaking to Adrian about it. We were, like: 'Shit, we better be careful for this gig tonight', 'cos normally something like that is the calm before the storm, and that sadness is followed by anger and rage. It was a really big show and it had undersold. And it was just a bad vibe there; in the dressing room, beforehand, I could see in his eyes that he was going to flare up."

Adrian Hunter — "There certainly was a lot of anger and rage that night. Jesus Christ. I had never seen the like. We arrived at the hotel and I went to see Peter in his room, because I could sense something really bad might be in the offing. We were having a chat, and then – wham! A big old glass ashtray flew into the dressing table mirror, and I nearly got twatted by the rebounding ashtray and my arse lacerated by flying shards of glass. Perhaps a foresight of what was to come that evening. Jesus, if only it had been a couple of broken mirrors. This was before we even got to the show."

Held in a massive bunker, Peter forgot his words and smashed the stage lights in, assisted by Mik, their inebriation fuelling the assault. Italian tour promoter Eva Falomi clearly remembers the darkness that descended upon the Velvet Roc Club that night: "As frequently happens, the show mirrored the leader's mood: it was angry, mean, pure energy, two destroyed lights, one microphone thrown into the dancing crowd."

Suspecting that the first pangs of withdrawal were beginning to bite, Adam, about eight songs in, signalled to Drew that they should end the gig prematurely. The negative energy demonstrated on stage was merely transferred to the dressing room, which felt the brunt of a good kicking; before seeing its way back to the band's hotel.

Inflicting thousands of euros' worth of damage, that evening's massacre encompassed the destruction of a couple of rooms and the letting off of a fire extinguisher that, in turn, set off the fire alarms and damaged the air conditioning system, which spewed lime powder into other residents' rooms.

When the full extent of the carnage was realised by staff, threats of arrest were made. And while a charge of criminal damage wouldn't have caused insurmountable problems, anything more serious had the potential to undermine Peter's chances of avoiding any more interruptions to his freedom.

Not that that seemed to bother him or Mik, who pelted the hotel's area manager with handfuls of pizza when he had his back to them, on the verge of calling the police. Had it not been for Adrian's success in persuading them against continuing their fast food assault, they may have been back behind bars sooner than anyone imagined.

Mik — "He [the area manager] made things worse, that guy... In the middle of the night there was a knock on my door. I opened the door and Peter just came marching in with an army of people I'd never met before. Okay, there was a lot of people in there, but there wasn't that much damage to my room.

"The bed was turned upside down and the lamp was smashed, and they tried charging three grand. So I went up to the room and put the bed straight, and said: 'I'll pay for the lamp.' I don't know what kind of lamp it was, but it wasn't worth three thousand pounds... he was just going overboard about it all."

Drew — "It looked like a huge giant had picked up the room, turned it upside down, shaken it, and put it back. It just looked fucked. Things that were supposed to be on the floor were on the ceiling... I just don't know how the fuck you make a room look like that – it takes real effort to destroy something that entirely. So, understandably, the rather conservative hotel staff were a little perturbed. And demanded a ten grand deposit...

"Mik was so fucked he had proper Orville voice in effect: when he gets fucked he sounds more and more like Orville – he sounds more like Orville than Orville does. He was covered in blood and broken glass, and he was walking around with his arse hanging out. He was holding a spliff in one hand and an almost finished bottle of rum in the other, going [in Orville voice]: 'Can I go to the pub please?'"

Adam —

"In the morning, there's all this commotion downstairs. It was something like fifteen thousand euros' worth of damage initially, but we managed to talk them down.

"The curtain rail was off, the bed was, like – I don't know how – but in the corner of the room, and the wardrobe was on its back somewhere."

Adrian Hunter —

"Mik is incredible. You got to love him. I remember trying to explain to him that the damage to his room was of an extent that we were looking at a night – at least – in the cells. He's trying to claim minor damage. Fuck me! It was like a couple of dinosaurs had had a fight in a doll's house. Then, somewhat inadvisedly, he starts chucking food at the area manager of the hotel group, while I'm trying to calm him down. He was livid, and the few words I could make out from his rant were 'animales' and 'carabinieri'.

"Now, at that point I knew we were in trouble, and 'dumb and dumber' outside weren't making it any better. I managed via Ginsberg [Italian promoter, Emiliano] to cut a deal for the damages, which involved us paying nothing upfront, and for repair invoices to be sent to us in the UK, thus avoiding Italian prison food. I distinctly remember at the time, Mik being completely battered and Orvilleing: 'Fookin' best three thousand euros I've ever spent'… Then he sobered up!"

A couple of nights later, at Rome's Piper Club, a bottle, thrown from the audience, struck Adam full-on in the face, knocking him out.

Halfway through *Sedative*, he glanced down at his drumkit for a few moments. The bottle, which popped his nose open and split his lip, didn't immediately affect him but, after delivering another couple of strokes, he slumped over his drumkit, unconscious, having to be helped off stage by Eva and Drew.

His bruised face swelling up like a football, Adam was then taken to the dressing room, while the band took a ten-minute break to see if he could continue playing.

Adam —

"It was an experience, 'cos if you get hit, normally it's in a fight and you know it's coming but, with that, I just didn't know what the fuck had happened. Bewildered…

"Drew asked me if I wanted to go on. I didn't really want to, but I thought: fuck it, and went back on. Did "Albion" and "Fuck Forever", and don't know how I got through it. It was very odd. I saw the footage on YouTube after and saw Peter get the mic and attack random people with it."

Peter —

"Battle of Rome… He got a full-on bottle in the face. It's nasty business as well…We walked straight into the crowd with the mic stand swinging out and [said]: 'Who's done that, who's done that? A thousand euros to the person who can tell us who did it!' And of course, me being a mug, saw one hand go like that, and fucking went for the fella who was being accused. And he was just going like that – obviously went for the thousand euros, instead of justice done… It came from somewhere towards the back. It was a helluva shot – it was a Machiavellian sort of a stretch…I watched that gig time and time again, and it was actually quite a good gig."

Mik — "Adam got knocked out while he was sat on his drums – a fucking full bottle of wine just missed my head and smacked Adam full-on in the face. I remember seeing it spinning through the air and whack Adam square on the head. It was horrible… It totally knocked him out.

"The geezer from EMI Publishing, Kenny McGoff, was there. There was, like, two fights in one night, because everyone dove into the crowd to try and get the geezer who did it. And I saw him [later on] at the hotel, after the photography incident, as well. I was, like: 'Oh my God. Look, mate, I'm really sorry about all this.'… And he went: 'Don't be fucking stupid! As soon as I saw that cunt throw that bottle I was straight in!' He'd waded in and started beating everyone up! I didn't realise! He's brilliant, he is."

Adrian Hunter — "That night, I remember being particularly hot and sweaty inside the club. There wasn't so much a feeling of violence in the air, but something rum was afoot. The bottle incident was the match that lit the flame. I remember it almost as in slow motion. It seemed to take an age to fly in, hit Adam square in the face, and he just seemed to slow down. He was still drumming as he sparked out, getting slower and slower, and lower and lower.

"As soon as we got to him he was taken downstairs, and all I remember is a blur of me and Peter, possibly others, trying to get over the barriers to find the culprit, and some massive Italian security screaming: 'Tranquilo! Tranquilo!' We were far from fucking tranquil, and whoever threw that bottle can consider himself somewhat lucky he was enough of a coward to hide away. How do you say arsehole in Italian?!"

Drew — "I remember thinking: good fucking shot! I always miss! Nah, that was fucking bang out of order… I saw this bottle of wine sailing through the sky, [thinking:] that's obviously going to go over his head. But, nope: it landed – clonk! – on Adam's head.

"We'd all stopped for requests, and – clunk! 'Adam, are you still conscious?' 'Yeah.' And then he passed out, so I picked his ass up and dragged him backstage, mopping his blood off his face. And he was looking at me with blood streaming down his face. 'What happened?' 'Man, someone caught you a good 'un with a bottle of wine.' '… a bottle of wine?' 'Yeah, you could die.'

"And – ah, God – I was trying to make Adam look a bit decent, and check he still knew what year it was. And Peter and Mik went out, and I think Peter tried to clump someone in the audience. And, eventually, we came back out. Fair play to Adam – he's a soldier. He got back on the kit and finished the set…

"It just descended into bedlam for the rest of the set. Peter smashed a bottle and cut his arm, and Adam and I just completely destroyed the drums."

Luca C —

"I've got loads of friends who went to that gig, and I can't really work it out, because they give completely opposite versions of the facts. Some of them said: 'Oh, Babyshambles were really struggling and the gig was pretty shit, and the tension was building-up to the point that someone just lost it and threw a bottle on stage.' And another version I heard was that, because of the whole Kate Moss thing – which I think is the most likely version – Peter had become the public sensation and the one who was referred to as Kate Moss' boyfriend.

"And a lot of, like, what would be Chavs in England, but the Italian version, started going to the gigs – people who wouldn't buy the album, those sort of people. They go to the gigs, and were shouting for the duration of the gig, and someone probably got too pissed and decided it was a good idea to throw a fucking bottle of wine at Adam, who passed-out."

So often the recipient of underspent aggression, the dressing room was again the victim of a thorough trashing when sets of brand new trainers, brought along by an Italian sportswear firm in the hope of a patronage, were bounced against the walls, sending anything not anchored to the spot soaring through the airwaves.

Adam —

"It was like a mix of trainers, blood, pasta and glass – that's what I remember seeing in the dressing room at the end of it."

Adrian Hunter —

"The dressing room was full of trainers that some company had gifted the band. They were vile! I remember someone saying: 'You British do the rock and roll, we Italians do the style.' Oh dear, oh dear, oh dear!

"We were barricaded in the venue at the end – the crowds were too much for us to leave safely. Well, that's just like a red rag to a bull for Mowgli. He led me a merry dance that night. Up walls, over gates. Crazy. Back indoors, I escorted Mik to another room, as he was feeling a bit poorly at one point. Some geezer came up, claiming to be Dario Argento, and wanted to 'rap' – his words, not mine – with the band. I had Mik in a bucket in one room, and Peter going doolally in another, so I politely declined. Christ, he was persistent. It was a classic case of: 'what part of no don't you understand?' Eventually, he scuttled off and fell backwards down some stairs, clutching his drink."

At one point amid the chaos, Peter took a seat as somebody drove a large, unsterilised hoop, complete with dangling elephant statuette, through his ear, before hopping on

---

Opposite: Drew and Adam in the studio.

the back of a friend's scooter for a lift back to the hotel. In next to no time they were being chased by had the paparazzil, who, in turn, were closely trailed by the tour bus. First back, Peter found himself facing a scrum of paparazzi. Jumping onto the tour bus, he re-emerged to find himself jostled by paps with even less regard for his welfare than those back home, one tossing a camera at his head.

Blood slaloming down his face, Peter launched himself at his antagonist, aided by his bandmates, who seized the opportunity to vent some more of the tension that had built up over the course of the evening.

Peter —   "He'd have been alright if he'd just stayed toe-to-toe with me, but Mik jumped in and bit his neck, and hospitalised him, actually, poor fella. He wouldn't get out of the way. He'd taken quite a few snaps and was, like: 'Alright, it's time to go.' I was on a bit of a buzz, anyway, 'cos it had been a fucking strange, crazy, adrenaline-fuelled night. I'd just had a fucking scooter maniac taking me on a whiz-bang tour of Rome…

"He just takes the camera off and says: 'Come on, then,' and he's obviously been going down the gym and wotnot – he's bulging all over the place, and I'm in full junkie mode, you know? But I stood my ground. Took a couple slaps, gave him a few back, but, before too long, Adam grabbed an ashtray and Mik had drawn his teeth and drew his winkle-pickers, and the bloke didn't stand a chance…we had him in the bushes, giving him the kicking of his life."

Mik —   "We got into our van, got to the hotel, and the photographers were waiting there… I think they thought we were going somewhere else, but they slashed out the van tyres and then really proceeded to manhandle us. The photographers here aren't allowed to touch you, but over there they grab hold of you, and when you try and walk somewhere they won't move.

"And so Pete was walking, and there were thirty photographers in front of him, not moving anywhere, so he couldn't move. So he tried to push past them, and this one photographer smacked Peter on the top of the head with one of his cameras. I saw his arm go back, and he hit Peter in the face with his camera lens, and then just started smacking Peter.

"And I was, like, fifty metres away on top of some mound, so I could see it. I thought: what the hell?, and Peter's getting done over by this guy. In the newspaper pictures of me, it looks like I'm kicking this bloke while he's laying on the floor, but I ran over, and he was a big old lump. And I hit him, but I was very lucky, 'cos he was standing in front of this giant plant pot, and when I hit him he fell backwards and tripped over this plant pot, and I dove on him and started biting his ear.

"And Drew came running over – and Drew's never hit anyone in his life – and kicked him square in the face. I couldn't believe it! So much for Drew being a pacifist! You know what I mean?! Not a bad blow for your first one!

"And it all kicked off, and Adam came running out with this giant brass ashtray he was chucking at the paps, and there was a full-on pitched battle in front of the hotel. Next day in the papers it said: 'Bloodbath.' But they deserved everything they got, those folks. And more… All that kind of shit happens far too often, and we get done for it."

Drew — "We were going to the hotel, and the paparazzi in Italy look like bodybuilders. And so we were trying to get to the hotel, and there was this one guy – a man mountain of a pap – he was stood right in front of us. It was, like: 'Come on, man, can you let us pass? You're in front of the door, stopping us from getting in.' [He] whacked his camera on Peter's head, and then Peter's head starts pissing blood. And all three of us just sorted him out, fucking laying into him…

"And the paps were big – they were big dudes – and so Adam's decided to become the controlling adjudicator and chaperone everyone in, calm the paps down. And got Mik, Peter and myself into the hotel, and made sure everyone was inside.

"And as we were walking off to the lobby, I could see him looking around. And he just grabbed a big black ashtray – you know, those stand-alone ashtrays you get in hotels – and went out on his own and started swinging at the paps on his own. I was, like: 'Fucking hell!', so I ran out, and it all kicked off again."

Adrian Hunter — "Andy and I got back to the hotel to witness the aftermath of the battle. We'd been sorting out the settlement with the venue, and gathering discarded instruments after getting the band safely – so we thought – off to the hotel. When we got back, the hotel lobby looked like a triage unit. Peter was bleeding like a stuck pig. Head wounds often bleed more and look more serious than they are, so I had a squint, and this was a proper skulling!

"The little guy from this hotel who looks like Supermario – every Italian hotel has one, trust me: check – was in slight shock; I don't think he was too enamoured with the pools of blood in his lobby. Tell you something: those Italian paparazzi are fierce. The UK boys are just monkeys with quick fire cameras, but these guys are fucking gorillas! Shanked our bloody tyres during the night, too, and poor old Ginsberg had to change them and sit in the van all night, guarding it."

Comically, there was, after the event, talk of an official complaint on behalf of the pap responsible for sparking the row – a charge met with derision by a spokesman for Peter, who said that such talk "will certainly interest Pete's lawyers, who clearly saw Pete being hit with a camera outside his hotel."

Their Italian adventure over, the band flew back to England.

On 8th November, at Thames Magistrates' Court, Peter was handed a £750 fine and ordered to pay £250 compensation for inadvertently hitting Radio One Newsbeat's Trudi Barber's hand, when striking out at reporters outside the same court for his 23rd March hearing, his evaluation of the press as "harassing scum", he was told by magistrate Helen Skinner, not in anyone's best interests.

Previously pleading not guilty to an assault charge, Peter reneged after watching coverage of the incident, and apologised for any harm caused. He would pay the fine and compensation at a later date, he said, as he had just twenty-seven pence on him.

Adrian Hunter — "I'm sitting in the court room when the sentence was passed, thinking: thank fuck it's not custodial. Then comes the matter of means testing, and Peter says he's got twenty-seven pence on him. I'm a thinking: she's going to think he's taking the piss and do him for contempt or something, but she was fine about it. The inevitable stories arise – 'Doherty Skint Shocker' – but, to be honest, he did only have twenty-seven pence in his pocket. One of the few occasions when I've heard Peter give a straight answer to a straight question."

On the 18th, nearly a week after Ashtar's *Arena* documentary was aired on BBC2, Peter was arrested on suspicion of possessing crack cocaine.

Another tug for erratic driving led to his latest arrest, along with two others. Held overnight, for "substances recovered", the three were released on bail from Bethnal Green police station, pending analysis of the find, until December – another month of controversy and touring.

Three days into the month, actor Mark Blanco appeared to accidentally fall to his death from the second floor balcony at Paul Roundhill's Whitechapel flat, the setting for a party. Less respectable sections of the media went in for the kill, implying that there had been an altercation between Blanco and Peter before the incident, though the allegations were without foundation, Peter later cleared of any involvement.

Peter — "The ultimate tragedy is the family losing their son. It's deeply saddening…so much talent, and life. And, obviously, he was in a play at the time, before he accidentally died. He was in the *Accidental Death of an Anarchist*. It was quite a cool underground production of it. And that was that. A young actor and writer cut-off in his prime."

Adrian Hunter — "I'd been babysitting my good friend Magoo's little daughter, Kitty, on the Saturday night and, inadvertently, my phone had run out of charge in the early hours. I woke up on the Sunday morning to an endless stream of text notifications from Andy, telling me of missed calls all through the night. I called him back immediately, to an answer of: 'WHERE THE FUCK HAVE YOU FUCKING BEEN?' I could tell from his voice that something had gone heartily amiss. It was one of those: 'Do you want the bad news first, or the bad news first?' moments. I opted for the bad news, and was told of Marc Blanco's death, which was a dreadful shock.

"Andy then proceeded to tell me about the hotel trashing and, more worryingly, that Mik had been stabbed. As soon as I found out he was okay, I asked Andy where he'd been wounded – i.e. belly, back, neck? Andy simply said: 'Once in Homerton and once in Farringdon.' Dark humour, indeed… We then proceeded to the hotel, to be greeted by a stony-faced concierge, who, on the whole, treated us better than I would, given the devastation we were to encounter in the room. He kindly supplied us with industrial-strength bin-bags, and we set to work. My abiding memory of those hours is of Harvey Keitel's character in *Pulp Fiction*. I won't say any more on the matter of hotel room trashing, as I find it clichéd and ungentlemanly.

"Next task was to find Peter and get him somewhere to get his head down. We found him in a pub in Belsize Park again, surrounded by cronies and a smattering of proper friends. He had a bit of a tantrum, and then a bit of a cry, and then a good Samaritan tucked him up for the night. Nice way to spend your Sunday. The day before a court appearance which would govern whether the UK tour would start the following day or be cancelled forthwith. Stress?… Naaaah!"

On the 4th, the day *The Blinding* was released, Peter paid Thames Magistrates' Court another visit, leaving £770 lighter because of a fine for five counts of possessing drugs. On top of that, he was disqualified from driving for four months.

That evening, The Blinding tour, which included rescheduled dates axed in October and extra shows, commenced at Newcastle Academy. As well as playing tracks from the EP itself and the usual medley of older material, an assortment of new tunes were booted about. "Delivery", "Unstookie Titled", "UnBiloTitled" and "Carry On Up the Morning" were perhaps the most impressive of these new creations and, indeed, the quartet made it onto the following year's successor to *Down In Albion*, *Shotters Nation*.

There was also an appearance in the seventh floor car park of Selfridges, London, on 7th December, in support of fashion label Gio-Goi, for which Peter had been recruited to design a range for co-founder Anthony Donnelly.

Placed in a plush hotel close to the retailer's Oxford Street base, such a surfeit of booze was consumed that the next day's gig was performed while half the band were still shaken by its after-effects.

Well intentioned plans to see Peter holed-up in his hotel room the night before, with a mini bar for company, were never likely to come to anything. By 5am, bored and sick of being confined to one room, he took off, heading for an all-night Russian bar in Shoreditch.

When Drew, Adam and Mik awoke shortly before the show was due to start, Adam was nursing a stinking hangover, having been out with Mik, who has a remarkable ability to withstand the most brutal drinking sessions without adverse effects. As for Peter, there was still no sign of him – until, with just five minutes to spare before the gig was to be cancelled, he showed up, looking considerably worse for wear.

Adrian Hunter — "I dragged myself out of the tour bus and made my way to Selfridges, hoping Peter would be there – more fool me. We were guided to the personal shopping area, where 'ladies who lunch' have someone buy their Christmas presents for their friends and family – don't you love the personal touch?!

"The tension was building, and Peter remained uncontactable. After a few days on the road, I decided it best to avail myself of the luxury private showers and de-stress a touch. Two minutes under the water, and the door's being battered by Anthony's brother, Christopher, telling me that my phone was ringing and Peter's name was showing. I streaked across the personal shopping area – much to the horror of some very genteel ladies.

"Peter offered one of his usual esoteric excuses and even more useless descriptions of his location. I got through half of 'Get your fucking arse over here now!' before he hung up, and the waiting began again. An anxious Anthony heard I'd spoken to Peter, and demanded to know where he was and when he was coming. At that time, I didn't know Anthony quite as well as I do now, so I was very careful with my answers."

Adam — "We all turned up and I scraped through this challenging four-song set in the car park. It was a corporate, media affair to launch their clothing range, and the photos they took of it say it all. I felt so fucking sick, I got out and vomited, and they'd invited all the world press, all the news."

Mik — "We wouldn't have done that gig for anyone else, to be honest. Peter, we didn't know whether he was going to turn up or not, but he eventually got there – thank God – and we did it. We all stayed in the hotel, and there was a party in the hotel all night… We didn't get much rest – even Adam and Drew were in the photos looking worse for wear. It was a good laugh, but playing in Selfridges was bizarre."

A hectic, trying and emotional 2006 drew to a close amongst talk that Peter risked breaking the community order restricting him to short-haul travel, if, as had been speculated in the papers, he followed Kate to Thailand to see the New Year in.

Such warnings – hardly a deterrent to somebody as neglectful of authority as Peter – were ignored when he joined Kate on the island of Ko Samui for what many believed was the setting for a wedding ceremony.

The story was enough to reawaken the nation from its New Year hangover, photos of Peter and Kate appearing as apparent evidence of a spiritual union. A spokesman for Kate quickly refuted the claim, insisting instead that they were merely enjoying some time away together; though not for long, Peter finding himself back in Blighty following a bust-up with a taxi driver.

Peter —

"I really ruined that; it really was a special time. But I went…right off the Richter Scale in terms of valium over there, which is dirt cheap over the counter. And I can't explain it, I mixed it with alcohol… It's worse than crack, it's worse than anything. It is. It is, absolutely. You wouldn't remember what you done, and you'd be glad. You wouldn't remember what you'd done, but they'll tell you. Apparently, I was so obnoxious to this taxi driver, I'm ashamed to tell ya. He's had enough – he'd had it out with me – but also, what I done – the combination of shit I'd taken – plus the Thai moonshine that they make, it gave me superhuman strength.

"So I was taking on this taxi driver, and he was starting to cry, and I had him. And all the other taxi drivers, they sort of ganged-up on me and joined in. And I'm out of my nut – it wasn't really a fight, you know? I had them all, and the police, in admiration, they gave me a bed for the night, 'cos I didn't know where I was.

"Next thing you know, I'm waking up in Heathrow with a Thai policeman's jacket on. It's kind of indicative, really, in many ways, of the great Babyshambles contradictions of that latent talent and potential, combined with that self-destructive insanity, which leads to these awful, awful, regrettable situations. Turns us into monsters."

To exacerbate matters, he faced "further tabloid infamy," as he put it in his diaries, when "some Australian arseholes have me on camera phone banging up and apparently slagging Kate off…to be fair I was in a hell of a state at the time and we had fallen out."

This deplorable situation served to emphasise to Peter the potent impact his lifestyle has on his relationships: "It happens time and time again. People'll say: 'Oi, bet I get a few quid of you smoking crack. I bet I get a few of you shooting-up.' And I'm, like: 'You know what? Lend us twenty dollars, so I can get a bag, so I can fix it up. And then you can sell the pictures for as much as you fucking like – I couldn't give a flying fuck.' And that's been a very foolish and quite a sad attitude, really, and it's just led to a breakdown, really, in the most beautiful relationship I was ever involved in; which is, I think, the one with my father. He's a man I admire. He's a man, I think, who I've done a lot to impress him, to make him proud, as a son – so proud. And, maybe, one day I will, again, be able to."

While the media continued to speculate as to the authenticity of the marriage claims, Babyshambles welcomed 2007 in with a series of intimate gigs, the first of which was held at the Dublin Castle, Camden, on 11th January – at which Mik was knocked out and a fight broke out on stage.

Drew —

"I remember before the gig started, seeing what looked like a kind of Frankenstein lurch, hobbling his way across the stage. I remember thinking: who's that old geezer?, and looked up, and it was Mik. 'What the fuck's up with your foot?' And he did his typical tooth-sucking thing: 'I'm alright'. He didn't tell me what happened. Just shook his head ruefully… He could barely take the weight of himself, let alone Eggnog."

Mik —　"I got knocked out at that gig. Pete jumped on my back. I broke my foot seven days earlier… but he forgot about my foot and dove on me. I couldn't hold him – he's a big old lump – I was playing my guitar and I was, like: 'Wooooah!', and swerved into the crowd, and they all moved and my forehead smacked onto the floor. And I got carried off into the Dublin Castle sea.

"And I didn't have any shoes or socks on, 'cos I was pretty worse for wear that night. Got carried off, and Pete said he could just see two feet and two red socks sailing away from him in the crowd. I still had my guitar round my neck – I was out cold, apparently; they said I was sailing around there for a good couple of minutes.

"They dragged me back on stage and my guitar was still on me, but all the buttons had been shaved off. My guitar was in a right state. I remember coming round: my mate was slapping me round the face… I lost everything that was in my pockets. It was horrible. My head was fizzing. Good gig, though. Brilliant gig."

Adrian Hunter —　"Bedlam – simply fucking bedlam! Amazing, punk rock, soul mayhem, and the promoters paid the band a hundred quid. We'd obviously have got considerably more if Peter hadn't broken that pesky lightbulb. I loved that show. I wasn't pleased when the local paper had pictures of the promoters in it, saying they'd pulled off a coup in getting 'Doherty', because Adrian Hunter, a 'Camden Character', was one of their DJs."

The Dublin Castle gig was also the first live Shambles gig that Amy Winehouse attended. An old friend of Mik's, the two had started hanging out again after briefly losing touch while concentrating on their careers.

Mik —　"She'd come specifically to see me play, 'cos she'd never seen me play with the band before. She didn't know what to make of it. And that's the first time her and Pete were in a photo together. 'Cos she wasn't in the paper at all at that point; "Rehab" wasn't out or anything, no-one knew who she was…

"She said: 'You're more famous than I am.' She actually said that – can you imagine it? There's lots of photos of her outside with Pete, and that night me, Amy, Peter, Hannah, my girlfriend, my brother, Tom, and Alex, Amy's boyfriend at the time, all went to a hotel to write a song together. That's the first time we tried to write a song together: me, Pete and Amy."

Before heading for said hotel, Peter went for a pap outside the venue, narrowly missing his target, though, typically, the photos that appeared in the press the following day overplayed the altercation, as Mik explains: "He didn't attack him, he just went towards him and did a kick – sort of a karate kick – and it looks more dramatic in the paper than it actually was… Amy was photographed with us by the paparazzi, and it was weird: after that, 'cos of the association with Peter, they took an interest in her then."

On 12th January, Peter scotched rumours of a spiritual union with Kate by telling fans at Catch 22, Shoreditch, that he didn't believe in marriage. A day later, he faced another arrest, this time on suspicion of car theft, along with two others – a charge that was subsequently dropped – while at the Boogaloo Bar, Highgate, on 15th January, the band played to an audience that had snapped up tickets within fifteen minutes of their going on sale.

On the 17th, at a review of his drug treatment order, Judge Jane McIvor praised the progress Peter had made, despite reminding him that "it's a long process and there is another nine months to go."

Defence counsel Bruce Clark said that: "Most people would have failed by now", and, after the hearing, Peter said that he was for the first time "actually turning up for appointments in a coherent state."

That evening he put on a solo show at the Rhythm Factory as part of a three-night residency, and on the 18th and 19th Babyshambles played in celebration of a new record deal, agreed with EMI subsidiary Parlophone, the agreement – penned on 16th January – ending months of speculation about which label Babyshambles would sign to.

Various record companies had expressed an interest in the band but, scared off by the financial outlay and shenanigans involved in the making of *Down In Albion*, were unwilling to commit to a deal, telling Andy and Adrian to come back to them once an album had been made; whereas Parlophone gained the upper hand on its rivals by demonstrating the commitment to drive Babyshambles forward, to take the four-piece where they deserved to be.

Adrian Hunter —

"Parlophone were a label that stuck to their guns, came to the shows. They put their money where their mouth was with *The Blinding* EP, because there was no commitment to do anything with them after that, but they wanted to show willing from their part.

"They were never in the band's face, they conducted themselves like gentlemen, on most occasions – on every occasion! – and it just came to quite a long period of negotiation, which as a manager is frustrating, but as a member of a band it's doubly frustrating, to basically getting a fucking good record deal – a really, really good record deal – and I think that the band are definitely with the right label."

Andy, perhaps a little too honestly, couldn't guarantee that he'd be able to exert a great deal of control over this quartet of free spirits – "You don't manage Babyshambles; you just advise them and sort of push them in the right direction" – and at that stage had no idea himself whether he'd even be in the job six months down the line.

He put it to Parlophone's Nigel Coxon, head of A&R, and Miles Leonard, the group's managing director, that they give it six months to afford both sides enough time to see whether they liked one another. They did, and as Andy and Adrian built a relationship with the band, any fears on the label's part, that Babyshambles might not be able to deliver, were vanquished – especially so once *The Blinding* was released, the EP proving the key to unlock the deal eventually struck.

More, and larger, offers soon landed on the table, but in the end just two rivals fought it out to secure the band's signature. And given Parlophone's dedication to the cause, coupled with its impressive stable of artists – Coldplay, Blur, Gorillaz, The Beatles and, until recently, Radiohead, among them – the label won the day.

Mik —   "I had such faith in our music that I knew if it weren't Parlophone it'd be someone else. I mean, it was nice that it was Parlophone, 'cos of the history of all the bands that had been signed and stuff, but, you know, Warner Brothers were after us, a lot of bloody major labels wanted to sign us at the time.

"We were offered more money by the [other] labels, but we went with Parlophone at the time because there was artistic license, and the people at Parlophone, like Nigel [Coxon] etcetera – all the people that run it – are all wicked, really nice people; we got on with them really well, we were accepted for what we are. We couldn't have asked for anything better, so we went with them… Warner Brothers… want things more their own way, and we're not like that. We want to do what the band wants to do; we'd rather be small and independent… We wouldn't be the band we are if we pandered to what the record company wanted us to do."

With a new record deal in the bag, Peter had entered a treatment centre, on 18th of January, as a day patient, enabling him to play the Rhythm Factory that and the next night, prior to another rehab attempt at the end of the month, in the Capio Nightingale clinic, north London.

At the beginning of February he was charged with four driving offences relating to his 18th of November arrest – failing to produce driving documents, driving with no insurance, driving with no MOT and failing to comply with driving licence regulations – and bailed until the 13th.

On that day, he was fined £300 and disqualified from driving for two months. Lawyer Sean Curran explained that while Peter accepted driving with no licence and insurance – the two other charges against him were dropped – "He had left the task of getting an insurance policy in the hands of one of his managers, who hadn't done

---

Opposite: Drew and Peter learning new songs before stage time, Aberdeen, 2006.

so. He has passed a driving test but has never applied for a licence. But he is entitled to have one."

Refocusing on the music, the band embarked on a European jaunt that took them to Germany between 15th and 18th January. Then, back in the UK, the band played shows at the Manchester Apollo on 17th February, followed, the night after, by the *NME* Awards Show, held at the Brixton Academy, and, on the 19th and 20th, at the Barrowlands Ballroom, Glasgow.

But as the month drew to a close, it was Mik's turn to have his name blackened in the press, falling victim to betrayal at the hands of a former friend who sold pictures of him to *The Sun* posing with an antique gun.

Mik only posed for the snaps in the first place because he'd been given the shotgun – incidentally, an 1850s model rendered impotent, owing to the fact that it had been welded up, with no cartridges to fit even if it was serviceable – as a birthday gift, not thinking for a moment that they would fall into the wrong hands.

Rumours circulated that the band's tour bus carried guns and a safe containing £75,000. But while the stories were without merit, some were unwilling to take their chances on the bus, among them Adam, who booked a hotel room, suspecting that, sooner or later, the police or, worse, gangsters would come calling: "I remember thinking: oh shit – we're sleeping with guns; people must think we're crazed maniacs!"

Drew was among those with no suspicion pertaining to an impending robbery or assault on their lives, knowing nothing of Adam's strive for self-preservation: "Oh, cheers for giving me a head's up, Adam! 'You off, Adam?' 'Yeah, just fancy a night in a hotel, mate.' 'Fair enough – anything in particular?' 'Nah, just a bit of a sauna and that.' Hehehehe! What a cunt! It's outrageous! I didn't know Adam had done that – that's the first I've heard. Cheers, Adam!"

In fact, the only gun ever to grace the tour bus, on which the shots were taken, was a plastic Luger imitation – which, as Mik points out, "was brought on the bus by the twat who sold the story anyway!"

Adrian Hunter —

"I remember opening the paper and just thinking: oh great, here we go. I can understand Mik's rage. He was shafted. All Mik has ever wanted from this is an admission and an apology… He's never got it, and I think he deserves it. Me and Mik have our falling-outs, but I like to think that he knows I'd never cold-bloodedly fuck him over, and vice versa. We've been mates too long. That's why I find this sort of thing so abhorrent. Someone was taken in, shown hospitality, and then stitched Mik right up – just wrong."

Babyshambles' growing popularity was reaffirmed in mid-March, when an arena tour, taking in Manchester, Newcastle, Brighton, Bournemouth, Wembley, Birmingham, Nottingham and Glasgow, was announced for November.

Behind the scenes, however, there was uncertainty as to whether the band would still be together by then; or, in fact, for very much longer.

Nearly two years after the last scare of its sort, it was thought that Peter sacked Drew and Adam; and while Mik wasn't part of the cull, his mounting personal problems, which included his brother's temporary confinement to a coma – the result of a car crash – deprived him of the close contact he and Peter share: "I hadn't seen Peter for a month, and that's the longest I haven't seen him unless he's been inside or whatever. He was getting nervous, wondering why I hadn't been down… And he got paranoid about Adam and Drew… Drew started doing his own thing with his band and, again, Peter was paranoid, thinking that Drew wasn't putting all his efforts into our band… He gets the wrong end of the stick sometimes."

Drew —   "I remember at the time, Andy saying that at one point in his cracked-up, paranoid ramblings, he picked up a magazine, and there's a picture of me doing something else. 'Cos, you know, I play for Phoenix and Mongrel, and play for Helsinki, and have other projects going on, and am heavily involved in Love Music Hate Racism. And I get called a lot for quotes whenever there's some kind of politically relevant thing happening in the media.

"I think at some point he started to claim that he thought I was doing too many things, that I was seen in the newspapers too much, on account of Drew McConnell doing something or other. And he didn't like that. And, fucking hell, man – if we're going on column inches… !"

Talk also alluded to whisperings in Peter's ear, from a long-standing associate, that it was time for a new challenge away from Babyshambles; to exacerbate an already uneasy atmosphere, a night after performing a solo gig at the Hackney Empire on 11th April, he was joined at the same venue by Carl Barât.

It was the first time the duo had played together publicly since The Libertines' second and final split back in 2004 and, unsurprisingly, rumours of a reunion littered the press in the show's aftermath. Carl's spokesman, Tony Linkin, quickly dispelled such talk, however, insisting: "They just got together for the night. There are no plans for anything more than that. Babyshambles are doing their own thing and Dirty Pretty Things are doing what they are doing."

An emotional night all round, Carl felt that, while "it was very odd… it was like slipping into another suit, really – the old suit; it would be odd to go back into that old bedsit on Camden Road, but it would still feel natural, because we were where we were for a reason."

The seeds of the onstage reunion were sewn at the Shockwaves NME Awards in March, though it was co-manager Andy Boyd who suggested Hackney as a venue after seeing a Steven Berkoff play there – "I thought it'd be a great idea for Peter to come and just play his guitar in there." Only after the venue was booked was booked did it occur to Andy that, as he had yet to inform Drew, Adam or Mik about the shows, he could be seen to be orchestrating a solo career for Peter; and, in the wake of the second night, a Libertines reunion.

Andy had, in fact, been asked by Peter to put to Carl the possibility of playing together again for a night. When Carl agreed, Andy even offered to drive him to Hackney, such was his conviction that the pair wouldn't drop their respective bands in favour of resurrecting their partnership on a permanent basis.

The seeds of the onstage reunion were sewn at the Shockwaves *NME* Awards in March, though is was co-manager Andy Boyd who suggested Hackney as a venue after seeing a Steven Berkoff play there – "I thought it'd be a great idea for Peter to come and just play his guitar in there."

Peter eagerly agreed to the proposal and a couple of dates were booked. Only then did it dawn on Andy that, as he had yet to inform Drew, Adam or Mik about the shows, he could be seen to be orchestrating a solo career for Peter; and, in the wake of the second night, a Libertines reunion.

Andy had been asked by Peter to put to Carl the possibility of playing together again for a night. When Carl agreed, Andy even offered to drive him to Hackney, such was his conviction that the pair wouldn't drop their respective bands in favour of resurrecting their partnership on a permanent basis.

Andy Boyd — "I just do things spontaneously and instinctively. From then on, I sort of just had to accept the consequences of that. When the press started reporting on The Libertines, then I realised: oh shit, I have opened a can of worms here, maybe… But the good thing is, I knew there was no chance of a Libertines reunion, right from the start. It was never discussed, it was never on the cards; otherwise, to be honest, I wouldn't have said to Carl: 'Do it.' I'm the last person who wants a Libertines reunion. We'd just signed this deal with Parlophone, with Babyshambles – all four members had signed a deal. I did it, I negotiated it… To be honest, it's a bit naïve from the rest of the band to think I would push him in that direction, because it's the band's deal."

Adrian Hunter — "I don't think at any point Andy ever in a month of Sundays imagined a Libertines reunion, or to cause tension within the band. It's a simple fact that Peter was always going to want to do something solo – it's in the record deal, for goodness sakes.

"However, in retrospect, it did cause a lot of tension, undeniably. We got through it, though. It's a case of: damned if you do and damned if you don't. I remember these shows being rather wonderful, but with an underlying vibe which, though not unpleasant, was not what it should have been."

Adam — "That was very odd for us, 'cos we didn't know whether we'd been sacked or not. So we went to see him and he was fine with us, but there was a bit of an atmosphere there. I think he realised what had been said and he felt quite bad for it…

"I thought it was maybe the wrong thing to do for the band, for the union of the band. I think it's good for Pete to do solo stuff, but it didn't help the camaraderie and unity of the band."

When rumours of a split persisted, Adam took his concerns to Andy and Adrian, who suggested that they let it blow over. When he confronted Peter about it, he looked oblivious, wondering what all the fuss was about.

"It kind of taught me", Adam begins. "When those things happen, not to panic anymore – it's, like: we'll see if it's still like this in a month, and then bring it on. These things happen all the time.

"I think what it is: he's in a really bad place drugs-wise, paranoia with crack and the smack, and things just seem very odd to him. People suggest stuff and he just goes along with it, without even knowing what he's going along with. So he takes the wrong type of people in his ear and everything goes to pot."

At Thames Magistrates' Court on the 18th, Peter told his latest drug treatment order review that those closest to him had "had enough" of his addiction, giving him an ultimatum: either he choose the drugs, or them.

With harmony within the band seemingly restored, they used their Babyshambles site to announce a couple of intimate gigs as part of the Camden Crawl Festival at Studio 88, Chalk Farm Road, on 19th April.

On the first of the two shows, Peter threw the drum kit and amps into the audience when, a couple of songs in, he made a mistake halfway through "The Blinding". "I remember him looking round", says Adam. "Probably trying to find someone to blame, or realising: fuck, I've messed this one up… I just smiled at the fact the snare drum's gone – it wasn't my drum so I wasn't bothered."

Drew — "The tagline at the end of the chorus, he often gets it wrong. One is: 'Crossing the roads without you, out you', and the other one is: 'Things to be getting on with, on with, on with, on with'. And he got it wrong.

"Adam and I had completely recovered – he messed it up, and then Adam and I, as we so often do, brought it back – but that was it: he was too embarrassed. And when he does something like that, he often feels like he has to make it a show some other way. So he just picked up the drum kit and threw it in the crowd."

The feeling among the fans seemed to point to a typically edgy but scintillating Shambles turn, though Mik simply couldn't see it: "I think it was more out of embarrassment that he did that than anything else. It did my head in – it's weird that every time me and Peter, we'll do a gig, we'll look at each other when we come off stage, and we'll all comment about: 'What did you think about that?', and me and him agree that it was shit. You can bet your bottom dollar that everyone else will say it was a brilliant gig. Every time we say it was horrible, everyone says it was great…

"I thought that was a terrible gig, and everyone was, like: 'Ah, that was brilliant, there was energy', and all this crap, but I thought it was an awful gig. And everyone seemed to think it was brilliant. You can't win – or you can't lose, actually!"

Adrian Hunter — "Me and Adam did a site visit of our own, and it looked like a nice wee place to play. However, when we turned up on the day, someone hadn't quite worked out that you somewhat lessen the capacity of an already small room when you put in a stage, a PA, a lighting rig, a sound desk and a film crew.

"It was the hottest day of the year in a room with no air conditioning and a lot of heat-generating lights and equipment – not to mention a crowd three times the size of the capacity you have. An oven, basically. Amps started failing, people started fainting… Very poorly thought-out and executed by whatever production team were in charge."

At the end of the month, it was announced that Stephen Street would produce the second Babyshambles album, the template for which had already been laid down. The deal was struck when Peter, Mik and Andy paid a visit to Stephen's HQ, Olympic Studios, in Barnes, west London, armed with a number of demos, including some that, in their fuller form, ended up on *Shotters Nation*.

Andy convinced Stephen that Peter was in a good place mentally, stressing how eager he was to clean his act up. Stephen, a Libertines fan with a particular fondness for *Up The Bracket*, harboured doubts about Peter's ability to stay off the gear but, with the strength of material at his disposal, he chose to put his concerns to one side and take Andy's word for it. It would be a challenge, he thought to himself. And it certainly proved to be that.

Stephen Street — "I could tell Pete wasn't completely kind of, um, compus mentis, as it were, but I was prepared to take it on because I was told by both the label and by Michael [Mik] that he was very keen and very excited to work with me on the album, and was prepared to get his act together. And I didn't really fully understand much about that side of things. But I was told he was going to have an implant that would suppress his desire for drugs."

The recording started off on a bright note with "Delivery", but by the second day things were already on the slide, Peter and Mik's poor timekeeping and drug habits swiftly negating the opening day's success. And, when Stephen banned the use of heroin in the studio, the toilets soon wore splashes of blood from the administering of the drug, sparking a series of complaints from staff at the site.

Adam —

"There were needles everywhere. Going to the toilets, there'd be blood everywhere – it was fucking horrible. And it's quite a high-end studio – it's not a dingy shithole – so I was trying my best to keep prodding them to stop that, leaving their shit about."

A combination of nerves and the inability to stay clean were, Stephen believes, responsible for Peter's disappointing vocals during the first few days of recording: "He was coming in in a pretty hammered state most days. Even Drew and Adam didn't understand why he was doing it."

One of the earliest songs recorded, "Carry On Up The Morning", found Peter in fine form when delivering his idiosyncratic guitar licks. Vocally, however, his verses were, for the most part, what Stephen refers to as "pretty much gibberish… The problem with Pete [is] it comes in fits and starts. You'd have a great bit of guitar and the next verse would be absolutely unusable."

Stephen Street —

"There were some songs where Pete was singing a different lyric every time. And a lot of them it was just psycobabble, it wasn't really great. And I took him to one side and I said: 'Look, Pete, you're known for being a wordsmith. You're a great songwriter, people look up to you. These lyrics just aren't good enough, you know?' There were a couple of days I said to him: 'There's no point you singing this to me now, because you don't know what it is you're singing and you're changing every other line.' I said: 'Go home, sort it out, sit there with a pen and paper and write the lyric, and get it sorted in your head… People look up to you, Pete, for being a great songwriter – pay them back by being one.'

"Look, if I haven't got a good vocal performance from Pete, it's not going to come to anything. You can have the best backing track in the world, but what people want to hear is his singing on top, his poetry, and they want to hear it performed in a coherent state. If you listen to his first Libertines album, his lyrics are sharp. Bang bang bang – they're sharp, they've got clarity. That's what I pointed out to him: 'That's what's disappearing, Pete, you can't let that go. Everyone looks up to people like Morrissey, where the strength of the lyric is strong, and you can be like that, too, Peter. You've got to make sure you can nail it – none of this 'that'll do' vibe.'"

Peter made reference to the episode in *French Dog Blues* – "I model lacklustre panicky in vain, search for the remedy. No words, only melody come, so I take the day off", and, later: "I still model lacklustre panicky in vain, search for the remedy. No words, only melody came – ah, take another day off."

On occasions, Stephen's strict stance prickled Peter, but, as he put it: "Sometimes I did upset him. But, then again, I wasn't there to be his best buddy. I mean, I grew to like the guy very much, but I still didn't want to be one of those 'hanger-on, yes' people around him. We had to get the job done. I felt that, if he didn't deserve it, at least the band deserved it."

Adam — "From day one I knew it wasn't going to be easy, 'cos Stephen's a really straight guy, but fair – if it's not straight, he won't listen. Personality-wise, he's a top, really nice guy. I thought: it's either going to work with Peter or it's not, but he was quite strict with him.

"He was, like: 'I want you in by eleven and we'll work till eight, nine.' He was slightly flexible on that, but obviously Pete and Mik roll in around five, six, seven, eight or nine. Some days where fuck all got done, me and Drew just sat there twiddling our thumbs."

Peter's arrest on 5th May, in High Street Kensington on suspicion of possessing Class A drugs, hardly helped matters, but it failed to shock him into anything resembling sobriety. Rather, he continued to show up in the studio worse for wear, testing his producer's patience to the limit – and that of his fellow musicians: "The first time Stephen pulled me and Drew aside and said: 'Look, the guy needs help, some serious help, he's gonna die.' And he was really upset about it, saying: 'I don't want to be around it, can't be around it'", says Adam.

Peter often remained at the studio into the early hours of the morning. When unable to persuade Drew or Adam to keep him company, or when they failed to convince him to jump in a cab to go home, an engineer at the studio, Mo Hausler – christened Snickledorf – would find himself listening to Peter's predominantly disjointed ramblings.

"A few times, when Peter was mashed-up, we were all trying to get him into a car", Drew recalls. "And he wasn't having it. I think, about one in the morning, Adam and I were just, like: 'Alright, mate, this is our taxi, we've got to get in.' 'Oh, I want Snickledorf', etcetera. Poor lad, he just sat there."

On other occasions, Peter would wander into the control room – "You'd come back in the morning and they'd be loads of leads out, like a gremlin has been in there", remembers Adam – forcing staff to lock the door to the room once Stephen had finished for the day.

Flagging spirits were further antagonised by days where Peter and Mik failed to turn up at all, wasting the thousands it cost to hire the studio each day. Frustrated and vexed at being held back by persistent patterns of behaviour that

---

Opposite: Peter and Adam writing a set list before a gig.

were seriously constraining the band's potential, Adam, still sore from talk of sackings the month before, toyed again with the notion of calling it a day, ultimately resolving to stay put.

He almost had an immediate change of heart the day Bert Jansch was due in to record "Lost Art of Murder", finding Peter "all over the place, throwing up", despite Stephen forewarning him that he expected him to be on the ball.

"Again, Pete that day was completely off his head", Stephen remembers. "And I just felt it was disrespectful to Bert, to myself, to everyone involved in the record, to behave like that."

Stephen's frustration was such that he told Peter to leave the studio, stating, in no uncertain terms, that he couldn't work with him in such a state. Peter stormed out but, within the hour, rang Stephen asking for another chance. If he promised to try and nail the track, Stephen said, he could return. Which he did, a touch contrite.

A series of heart-to-hearts followed, Stephen firing a couple of warning shots across Peter's bow. He made it clear how impossible it was to make a record in such chaotic circumstances, and felt occasionally that he pierced Peter's armour, sharing moments of clarity.

He even thought at times that he was succeeding in drumming the message home, that he was getting through to him, but his optimism was swiftly shattered, and he had to be persuaded by Drew and Adam to work on a couple of backing tracks until – or if – they managed to get a hold on the situation.

Drew's efforts in trying to prevent the recording of the album disintegrating were all the more remarkable given that he was in constant pain, and couldn't sit down, owing to a broken back.

The injury – specifically, a broken sacrum bone, just above his coccyx – was sustained when lunging to catch a double bass that, as it turned out, smashed into smithereens: "I was in a lot of pain… I had this brace round my lower back. There were quite a few times [when] I had to talk Stephen out of leaving. Actually, that guy had me at his shirt as he'd been walking out the door, saying: 'Please, just come and talk for a minute.'"

Stephen Street —

"We'd kind of managed to clean the slate and start again, and then in a day or two we'd be back to the situation where, again, he was completely out of it… It was frustrating for everyone in the band, especially for Drew and Adam – they couldn't work out why he was being so wasted. They felt that he would be fine. Thank God, they were very together.

"There were a couple of times I had to say: 'That's it, I've had enough – I'm off, this is no way to work', and I was doing it, really, to shock Peter into shape, because I didn't feel I could walk out on the rest of the band, because they were so keen to keep the ball rolling. But I had to, a couple of times, threaten to say enough, and walk out, because if it carried on as it was going we were never going to get the record finished."

Andy Boyd — "Stephen just came up to me quite a few times and said: 'Andy, I just can't do this.' And I said: 'Please, stick in there.' And he did, luckily. Actually, it was down to Peter as well. Peter went into the control room a few times…

"He knew Stephen didn't wanna do it anymore. He was at his lowest ebb and he went in there and said: 'Look, I do wanna do this, just stick it out. I do wanna do it.'"

Adrian Hunter — "The first two weeks of that session were best described as traumatic. I think Peter felt the pressure, and it manifested itself in ways which were sometimes heartbreaking.

"I will always have the utmost respect and gratitude for Stephen Street. He stayed when he should have gone, thanks to some sterling diplomacy by Andy. Tom and Mo are equally deserving."

The various warnings dished-out to Peter were, however, not enough to bring about the corrections to his lifestyle that were necessary to get the record made. He would often disappear with Mik, returning in no condition to work, leaving the rhythm section to carry the recording process forward. As Stephen opines: "Dynamically, if it hadn't been for Adam and Drew really driving it on, I don't think we would have got it done. At least they were together – I could turn to them and say: 'Look, Pete's not really up to this, let's try and nail this backing track as best we can, even if Pete's a bit wayward.' And they would be great – keep hammering on; even if Pete'd gone half a beat out, they'd get it done."

Stephen assumed that Mik's own struggles with drugs made him Peter's perfect confidante, but, concurrently, he was growing anxious that their bond represented a major obstacle to getting the album made.

Convinced that, for the good of the record, they were better off apart, he told Mik to take a couple of days off. His decision rattled Mik, and Stephen felt that there was a wall between them for a while as a result, but knew that, for Peter to perform without distractions, he had been justified in his actions.

Mik — "The way Stephen works, he's a no messing type of guy and, as it turned out, it was good that he was like that. 'Cos if he'd been the kind of guy who'd allowed us to do what we want in the studio, maybe nothing would have got done. Or the guitar takes wouldn't have been like they were; the vocal takes wouldn't have been like they were. And he kept me and Peter apart towards the end of it…

"But they preferred it if Peter was in the studio when I wasn't there, and vice-versa, to stop us messing about. It's like two kids at school who weren't allowed to sit together 'cos they were arsing about – that kinda thing, maybe."

Stephen tried getting it through to Peter that the fog of addiction was overwhelming him, clouding his judgement; becoming the greater part of him, rather than a crutch for his creativity. He spoke to him about his younger brother, who took his own life after developing paranoid schizophrenia, a condition that arose out of the use of recreational drugs.

"I told Pete about that, trying to point out that not everyone's got a safety net around him like Pete's got. He's got management, he's got people that care about him, and he's worth money, so they look after him", says Stephen. "There's a lot of kids [who] look up to him and do the same kind of thing, but haven't got that safety net and end up like my brother, dying. I think that touched a nerve with him.

"I remember sitting there talking about that with him. He was in tears and, you know, that's the thing with him: underneath it all… he's a young man who's got that emotion and depth of character that people look for in a decent human being, but it's just sometimes hidden under this fug of drug addiction."

Peter — "I think I had it in my mind that we were going to go in as a band and record this album come hell or high water, as and when we needed to – you know: press record and get on with it. Not: come in at eleven, leaving at ten, come in at eleven, leaving at ten, not working weekends. It just, like, didn't occur to me so…as I was wont to do in this situation, at that time, sitting in the disabled toilet, you know, and banging-up all day. It was just a lot easier for me than facing the fucking rather uncomfortable experience, you know, that was being offered to me in the studio next door…Adam saying about how we needed to do this and structure this song like that, and Drew doing the same."

"And that's how it was for two weeks. And then something changed. Something dramatically changed. Stephen sat me down and…told me about his brother, who had substance-related problems. He told me that he'd thrown himself off a railway bridge. Now, if I was gonna continue living my life like that, I was quite happy to do it, but if I wanted to record an album my way, I was free to do it – this is Stephen saying this – but I'm not gonna be a part of it, he said.

"'I'm not gonna sit and watch you fall apart, the band fall apart, this whole thing fall apart. I don't wanna be involved in it. It's not positive. I'm not getting any enjoyment from it. It's breaking my fucking heart. So, like, change everything now, or I'm fucking off.' And it really made me think, you know? I thought, what does he mean: 'Do it your way? I thought we'd been doing it your way.' But I hadn't really been doing it his way. I hadn't really been listening to him."

Stephen felt that he had to adopt a consistently rigid form of discipline to underscore the fact that he wasn't one of the yes-men who pussyfooted around, stroking Peter's ego.

His methodology was, Andy Boyd remembers, at times quite dictatorial; while some producers favour a more organic process, devoid of a tight framework, Stephen adheres to a regimented system with little room for manoeuvre: "But that's what they needed, that's what Peter needed, and as much as I know that at times Mik didn't find it that enjoyable, found it too regimented – he said it was like being back at school – it's, like: when all said and done, making an album is work… A lot of bands, I suppose, do it in that ramshackle way – they go all through the night. Stephen won't do that…

"Imagine having someone that's as rebellious as him [Peter] – you'd get nowhere. He needed that kind of antithesis – Stephen is the antithesis of Peter, and they met in the middle somewhere."

And, despite occasional resistance to his pragmatic approach to laying the record down, Stephen demonstrated that, by anchoring the project with his steady discipline, he was able to bring structure to Babyshambles' typically skiffly, anarchic sound. As Andy says: "We knew we were with a professional with Stephen. We knew that if we got our heads down and did the job, that he would do his. You don't have to question that with Stephen – he's a fucking master, he's Premier League."

A thought echoed by Mik, in spite of his and Stephen's disagreements: "He's such a nice fellow, Steve. I've got a lot of time for him, I really like Steve Street – he's a good bloke. It was the first time that I've been in the studio and let the producer do his job without trying to stick my oar in. It's, like, in the past we'd had producers and stuff, and I've been, like: 'I don't like that, can we have it like this, etcetera?'

"Like on the first day we got there, Pete had this guitar sound that I didn't like – I thought it was too distorted, sounded like a heavy metal guitar or something – and I said to Steve: 'That's horrible, it sounds rubbish', and he said: 'Well, don't worry about it, in the mix it'll sound fine.' And I thought: well, sure, he knows better than I do. And in the end he was right – it sounded fantastic. So I kind of put my trust in him – that's his job, he knows what he's doing."

Peter, not one to be told what to do and when to do it, continued to verbally spar with Stephen until fully committing himself to the record – "to the point", Stephen explains. "Where I was: 'I'm not prepared to put up with this, so you either get your act together or I'm going to fuck off, or you can fuck off until you're better again'… I had nothing to lose, because I knew if it failed, EMI wouldn't have blamed me for it."

Curiously, the trigger for a renewed, unswerving assault on the album was the Celebrity Soccer Six tournament, staged at Upton Park on 20th of May. An unlikely saviour, the event brought a unity that had been lacking in that first two weeks, helped by Stephen's inclusion among the Shambles squad that day.

Managed by former QPR great Stan Bowles – somewhat of a result for Rangers fanatic Peter. Former West Ham striker Frank McAvennie was among the ex-pros playing in the tournament, which Babyshambles won, Peter netting the winner in the final.

Peter —
"It was a certain inside of a right foot – that fucking sweet crack to the inside bar. The stanchion, the – what do they call it? – the angle between the post and the crossbar. And it went straight in. It was that moment that everything changed. And as I waved one finger in the air, Stan Bowles-style, to the roars of about four-hundred prepubescent West Ham fans, I knew that this was what I wanted to do. I mean, usually people think: if we can do this, if we can win this, we can do fucking anything…

"To be honest with you, no-one got on. No-one really knew each other. No-one spent time socially with each other. I don't think anyone particularly liked each other. After doing that, after feeling so proud, having won, as Babyshambles, we were all suddenly: right, we consider ourselves Babyshambles. We're Babyshambles. We are contenders. We are reigning champions. Let's make a fucking record, like, worthy of champions. And we had it there on the mixing desk."

Adam —
"That was the main week we got most of the work done, after winning the Soccer Six, 'cos I think maybe he realised he could achieve stuff without being on gear, and he had the confidence."

Stephen
Street —
"I think the game was a bit more of a team thing, getting it together again. And obviously he couldn't play football completely smacked out of his head, so that was good… It was really great to see Pete that day. It was a high – not a chemical high, just playing football and winning the tournament. And he came in the following day and was so invigorated, and I got more out of him in the two or three days after that weekend than I had in the previous two weeks. It was fantastic."

Andy
Boyd —
"There was a work ethic after that. Everyone got in and fucking did their job. It couldn't have been more different from those two weeks to the next two weeks. It was a complete antithesis of one another. It was quite weird, actually. In that way it was quite surreal as well, going in the day after, going: 'Is this the same fucking band?' But there you go. Thank fuck for that football tournament."

The morale of those involved in the making of *Shotters Nation* was immediately and dramatically lifted in the aftermath of the tournament, breaking the tension that had threatened to derail the album and promoting a sense of unity that had been lacking beforehand. "Peter was on a natural high for a few weeks after that", says Drew. "He took a lot less drugs for a long time after that."

Stephen was at last able to get stuck into making the kind of record he had originally envisaged – one showcasing sonic diversity: "I just wanted to show

Babyshambles are not a shambles, [that] they can do anything they put their minds to."

Once he had all of the tracks recorded, Cenzo Townshend, who also worked on *The Blinding*, was charged with the job of mixing them. A straightforward process, Stephen had already thought through in meticulous detail how he wanted the album to sound, deciding as he went along how to shape individual tracks, and painstakingly fishing out the best cuts for Cenzo to work with.

In contrast, *The Blinding*, a more experimental release, was a far tougher job, according to Cenzo, who, with the EP, had to wade through Peter's numerous vocal takes himself: "They were trying to do lots of things, putting lots of ideas down, so it was just a case of reading through what they'd done and putting together a cohesive set of instrumentation for their songs… With *The Blinding* EP, I don't think he ever really reached a point where he'd decided exactly how he wanted to sing it. Lots of different vocal takes on there."

Adrian — "The songs have a broader appeal to the general public, but without for a second losing what is essential about Babyshambles – which is not losing the grit, not losing the soul; not losing the sort of organised chaos, you know? A tramp wearing designer clothes. A designer tramp. Musically."

Mik — "If you go into a studio to record your album or you record whatever, by the time you've finished recording it you'll hate it, 'cos you've heard it that many times over and over, and every single facet of the song and every little nook and cranny of it you know. So it's not that you hate it, as such, but you don't want to hear it again, 'cos you're bored of it.

"I don't know why, but I play the album constantly. Pete was the same, all the band members were the same. We all said the same thing. It's quite bizarre – I've never had that before. I've never been as proud of some music I made as I am of that album. The next one's going to be even better."

14

Delivery

Peter's diaries, *The Books of Albion: The Collected Writings of Peter Doherty*, were published on 21st June by Orion Publishing Group. Three months behind schedule, this weighty tome covered Peter's life from his time with The Libertines, before the band broke through, until January of that year.

Two years after first playing Glastonbury, Babyshambles returned to the festival to perform on the Other Stage on 23rd June, with Peter playing solo the next day, on the Park Stage.

He returned to court on the 26th, for charges relating to his 5th May arrest, when he was stopped in Kensington, and was ordered to appear again on the 3rd of August, when he would be sentenced for more drugs and motoring offences.

Another appearance on Jonathan Ross' Friday night chat show followed on the 29th of June, Peter's frankness, coupled with a touching rendition of "Lost Art Of Murder" – a song that would appear on *Shotters Nation* – offering, as he did the year before, an alternative to the tabloid-generated caricature doubtless accepted as truth by some of the audience. But as soon as a couple of days later, he was at the centre of more negative press activity, when stories broke that he had been seen with a model he met in a London nightclub, prior to appearing on *Friday Night With Jonathan Ross*.

Thrown out by Kate, Peter took the unusual step of using the *Daily Mirror* – the very paper that stitched her up in September 2005 – to express his love for her and to let it be known how he longed to win her back, saying: "I can't get hold of her any other way. I need Kate to know that I still love her. She has broken my heart."

On 3rd July, still reeling from the breakdown of his relationship, he arrived over two hours late at West London Magistrates' Court, confessing to drugs possession and driving with no insurance or MOT. Given an ultimatum he'd encountered before – either go back into rehab, or go to jail – he, unsurprisingly, opted for the former.

He was instructed to enter a clinic in Harrogate, North Yorkshire, on 16th July, first appearing with Drew, Adam and Mik at T in the Park, Kinross, Scotland, on the 7th, and at the Oxegen Festival, Naas, Kildare, Ireland, on the 8th.

After T in the Park, a tour manager booked in Adrian's absence caused problems when refusing to hand over some of the float money to Peter and Mik. Nearly resulting in a brawl back at the hotel they were booked into, the duo grabbed the readies out of his hand and ran off, leaving Adrian's stop-gap to fret about how to settle the bill for their stay.

Shortly after, Adam found Peter and Mik, explaining that some of the money was needed for the band's keep. He was immediately handed a few hundred quid, but his bandmates' disgruntlement at being dictated to saw to it that Babyshambles' latest tour manager lasted just twenty-four hours, leaving Adam and Sally to step in and make arrangements for the next day's Oxegen show.

Drew, meanwhile, had already made his exit, having seen enough to convince him that things could only get worse: "I was outside standing near Zane Low and the guitar player from The Thrills. And a fucking table goes through the window of our dressing room, and the guy from The Thrills almost wet himself. I just remember thinking: what the fuck?, and I grabbed my bag and got on an aeroplane to Oxegen.

"I called Fionn Regan on the way to the airport and said: 'I'm coming to stay with you.' I just left. I knew it was going to get worse, and I said to Adam as well: 'If you want to come with me, I'm going to stay at Fionn's house – it's going to kick off, I can smell it.'

"I think there was more hotel-destroying and the tour manager going through the halls of the hotel looking for Peter – all sorts of fun antics. Whilst I was sat with Fionn Regan, listening to Bob Dylan, drinking red wine in front of the fireplace in Dorking."

Adam — "I felt quite bad for him [the tour manager], 'cos the next day I think he thought they'd wake up and it'd be fine. We had transport taking us to the airport, but there's Peter and Mik going: 'He ain't coming with us, Ad, you've gotta tell him.' It wasn't down to me, so I sat back and put my hood up...

"I saw him come down, all fresh, and you just see someone put his bag back in the hotel as we drove away... It was kinda awkwardly funny."

Mik — "A lot of people who work for us, when they first start working for us they all have the impression: 'Oh, it's Babyshambles, let's have a laugh,' and they've still got a job to do. And you know what? I don't mind people doing that, as long as they can still do their job; why should you mind if they can do their job and do it one hundred per cent, like they would if they were sober? It shouldn't be a problem, and if you know your limits it won't be a problem.

"We won't mention his name, 'cos it's not fair. I spoke to a lot of people about him, and they've all said good things about him. So it must have been the fact that he was with us. But, when all's said and done, we're fucking professional when we play, so it's just a shame that some people think it's all fucking fun and games one hundred per cent of the time, 'cos it's not."

The Oxegen date behind them, Peter prepared for his next stay in rehab, in Harrogate, North Yorkshire, which he walked out of a week before. Beginning on the 23rd, he left four days later with an anti-drugs implant and, on 3rd August, sporting a shock of peroxide blonde hair, played his first gig since treatment.

A hastily organised show at the Scolts Head pub, Dalston, staged in honour of Wolfman's birthday, featured a handful of guest appearances, including Patrick – back in a Babyshambles line-up for the first time in over a year, with a view to joining up for the *Shotters Nation* arena tour – The General, whose new band, The Arc of the Covenants, followed Babyshambles' turn, Alan Wass and the birthday boy himself. The only Shambler not present was Drew, a nasty bout of food poisoning – "I was vomiting out of my arse and shitting out of my mouth" – accounting for his absence.

Adrian Hunter —

"That gig was the archetypal Babyshambles pub show. At short notice, you have to pull together a PA and let everyone know what's happening, and try to assure the landlords all'll be well. The locals in the pub were quite intrigued as to what the hell was going on in the back room of 'their' pub, and started getting shirty when they were asked to pay if they wanted to find out. Bloody hell! The fans were paying, for fuck sake, so why the hell shouldn't they?!

"The usual collection of fans and the usual other motley crew were milling about, and it was actually quite fun. I love meeting the fans at these events, because I never get the chance to at bigger shows, as I simply don't have the time. Some of them have even become pals. Hi Jamil! You're in the book! My other memory of that night is paying The General twenty-seven pence for his worthy contribution to the affair. I think I got a bargain there."

The following week, at West London Magistrates' Court, Hammersmith, Peter pleaded guilty to four counts of drug possession and two driving offences. Bailed on the proviso that he stayed out of London, the case was adjourned until 4th September, District Judge Davinder Lachhar warning that a jail sentence was an option if he didn't clean his act up.

Driven out of the capital by the court order, Peter decamped to Marlborough a few days later. Moving into a cottage sourced by his management, he would, in being situated a couple of hours' drive away from London, stand a better chance of eluding the hangers-on likely to take advantage of his vulnerability, thought Adam: "It was a nice, pokey little house, full of clutter. We recorded some of the "You Talk" video in his house. I think it definitely calmed him down a bit, stopped him running around London. I think it matured him slightly, it helped. But it didn't take long till the paps found where he was, and the same old problems started."

Adrian Hunter —

"The local paper printed a picture of the house, so, in a town this small, it wasn't too difficult to find out where it was. They had threats going up from the BNP on their website and all sorts. I called them, and in very few words asked them what the fuck they thought they were doing? This was not the reason we came to Marlborough. They tried to appease me by offering a feature in their homes and gardens section – 'At Home With Pete Doherty'. Didn't quite work, although I did think about it."

Peter returned a little closer to London for a solo gig at the Tap n' Tin, Chatham, on 12th August, and joined Drew, Adam and Mik at the Parades de Coura Festival, Portugal, the day after, prior to the band's appearance at the V Festival.

Split between Chelmsford and Staffordshire, on Saturday 18th and Sunday 19th respectively, a man was freed from an overturned car en route.

Having stopped off at a service station, Drew, Adam and Mik had only just climbed back into the bus taking them to Chelmsford, when a man hit an island in the middle of the car park, his vehicle somersaulting in the process.

"We pulled him out of the car, checked he was alright," recalls Drew. "First aid and police turned up, and all that stuff, and the next day it was in the papers: 'Pete Doherty saves man in motorway accident.' So, yeah, that was true. Except for the Pete saving him bit."

Peter's name was nonetheless passed to the media as the one responsible for helping the injured party, in order to prevent the issuance of a fine for turning up late at the festival. Contrary to press reports the following day, he had, in fact, made his own way to the festival.

Adrian Hunter — "At times like this, you take your chances. We knew it was press-worthy, so we reported it to the press officer, and it was printed – obviously, with Peter being a lone hero, practically. Actually, it was Mik who spotted it, and Drew, Adam, Hannah and myself followed him down to rescue the guy. Poor cove was quite shaken up.

"After we checked for signs of serious injury, we got him away from the still-smouldering car and into the service station, to wait for the emergency services. Needless to say, we disappeared off into the night like true heroes, before the police got wind of who we were and turned us over for fun. Mystery heroes, indeed."

Michael Deacon of the *Daily Telegraph*, who described V as "the definitive 21st-century festival, all about love, peace and understanding the importance of communicating core brand values", said Babyshambles "genuinely do like a proper band now: they keep time, they don't beat each other up, and you can almost hear some of the words." *The Times'* David Sinclair thought the boys supplied "a welcome frisson of unpredictability", playing "with their usual air of ramshackle defiance."

Late for both shows – so much so at the second show that they were moved to a smaller stage than the one they'd been pencilled in for – Peter was back in custody the day after.

Pulled over by police in the early hours of the morning, he was taken in with co-manager Andy Boyd and girlfriend Irina Lazareanu, inadvertently drawing attention to himself when, sitting in the back of Andy's Jag, he switched the light on. Dressed conspicuously in a top hat, and with a cloak draped over him, he was an easy spot for the rozzers that early morning.

Peter —

"How unlucky was that? I was, like: 'What the fuck are you doing, mate: going down Great Eastern Street? Let's go through the city. Let's cut through the city.'…And he told me to take my hat off and turn the light off in the back. As soon as the Old Bill see the cigarette and the hat, especially round that area…

"I don't mind saying on record, either: [they] can't half be cunts, that lot. Especially when you've been nicked by someone wearing a… it wouldn't have the same significance to you, but I've been nicked by someone wearing a 'Free Pete Doherty' badge – it is not a pleasant irony, man. Very unpleasant thing. I think it's a bit sick, personally."

Held at Bethnal Green police station on suspicion of possessing drugs, Middle England flew into a rage when Peter was released on a technicality, the charges against him dropped due to the failure of the police to present him to a court within twenty-four hours. Prosecutor Anjulika Vatish told District Judge Susan Williams that the court "has no jurisdiction to deal with this matter any more", thus expunging any possibility of his being locked up for breaching bail conditions.

Escaping London again to boost his chances of staying clean, Peter fled to Tintinhull, near Yeovil, Somerset, to stay with his relations, though any hope he had of a sedate recovery were soon shattered when he lashed out at a photographer who snapped him with Irina.

With the police launching an investigation into the incident, and Babyshambles' arena tour only a few months away, the following day, on 23rd August, he checked himself into Clouds House, Salisbury, Wiltshire, to remove the possibility of another stretch inside. Another arrest would almost certainly land him in the clink, and rehab provided a clean, safe environment in which to sort himself out.

Drew, Adam and Mik visited on a couple of occasions, in the first instance seeing how their friend was and offering moral support.

On the second visit, Adam showed up an hour earlier than Drew and Mik. Using that time to engage in a warm but frank exchange, Peter confessed to a number of failings, apologising for any upset caused. Adam, delighted "to be reminded of the real Peter, rather than the demon he can be with those drugs going through his system", explained that, as far as he was concerned, drugs offered users a safe, impenetrable bubble that blotted out the consequences of their actions and the hurt caused to others.

Adam — "He was just apologising, really, for being a bit of an arsehole. So I just backed him up and said: 'Yeah, you have been a bit of an arsehole', and explained that although he's been an arsehole, we know it's to do with the drugs. And that when the drugs aren't around, he's not an arsehole – we see him for the real Peter that he is. The drugs just cloud him – they just bring out the evil in everyone, especially him.

"So we had a good chat about that, and I think he found it a bit uncomfortable for me to put him straight on it: that he had been an arsehole, rather than me being: 'Nah nah, mate, you're fine.' But it was nice to actually clear a bit of the air then…

"He was clear, he was really happy. For the first time, he said he thought he could see a future where he's clean of drugs, so we were all really buzzing about that – thought: maybe this is the time he's gonna get clean; and he's serious about it now, late twenties, it's that pivotal time in most people's lives. Growing up a bit, and he wants to knock the drugs on the head, so that was great."

Adrian Hunter — "The times visiting Peter in Clouds were great. Seeing him clean and happy, you relish those times with Peter. Me, Andy, Peter and a counsellor were sitting on the lawn one day, and the counsellor asked us what differences we could see in Peter. I told him how good it made me feel to see him clean physiologically, and also physically, and how nice it was to be able to speak to him. He seemed quite shocked, but you've got to be honest in these places. I told him that it was the first time in months I could really talk to him and get sensible answers, and the first time in months that he'd had clean hands.

"Another memory of that time is in group with me, Peter and Andy. Peter had once said something quite profound and touching to Andy – something I can't reveal – and to discuss that in group was a very poignant, emotional moment. I don't judge people on what they do – nor do I wish them to judge me – but there is something inherently despicable about a crack and heroin cross-addiction. It turns the loveliest of people into cunts – not cunts all the time, but it'd turn Jesus Christ into someone who'd leave you wondering why you spent time with him (sorry, Him). You wish for the good times to last, but there's always disappointment around the corner, so you enjoy those good times and deal with the bad."

Peter's rehabilitation prevented him from appearing at West London Magistrates' Court on 4th September, a date reconvened until 2nd October, to enable him to continue treatment, his lawyer, Sean Curran, announcing: "I think he's serious – it was his idea to do the residential rehabilitation. He's asked to go in and he's still there, so he's trying his best."

It also meant that Peter was unable to help promote "Delivery", the first release from the impending *Shotters Nation*. Out on 7th September, "Delivery", which entered the UK Singles Chart at number six, was initially aired without the support of live performances.

Deprived of their frontman, Drew, Adam and Mik spent an entire day at EMI conducting international phone interviews, otherwise doing whatever they could to push the track until Peter rejoined them.

The *NME*, which in its 15th September issue gave a vinyl seven inch version of the single away and named it 'track of the week', thought that: "if the music reflects Pete's resignation to his fate, it also signposts a way out of the vortex of self-destruction. The explosive fury of "Fuck Forever" may be gone forever, alas, but as songs they can play on radio go, "Delivery" is still head and shoulders above the rest."

Casper Llewellyn Smith of the *Observer Music Monthly* wrote that "Delivery" was "bushier of tail than it has any right to be," and *The Guardian*'s Carline Sullivan decided that: "This piece of urgent blues-rock proves that he [Peter] is more than just everyone's favourite waster."

By the time Peter left Clouds on 4th October, having completed a six-week course of treatment, he moved back to Marlborough, a fact embraced by Mik; well, for the most part, if not wholly: "It's good for him to be out there, 'cos all the arseholes – all the hangers-on – aren't there taking his money all the time, so that's good. I like it out there; it just gets a bit bleak when the electricity runs out. The house is heated by one of those old Aga cookers, so when the oven runs out, there's no heating. Sometimes there's no heating, no electricity. Cooped up with sixteen cats pissing and shitting everywhere – makes for a little bleak house."

Shotters Nation had already been released on 1st October, the predominantly positive reviews of the record handing it a début at number five in the UK Albums Chart.

In his interview with the *Daily Mirror* on 31st July, Peter said: "I've never been in a position before where, God strike me down for saying this, I've actually made a record I can listen to and get off on. I've always been a bit weird about listening to my own stuff."

Adam —
"The album was getting a lot of good acclaim and, finally, we thought things were starting to turn, with people recognising us for the music, which was really nice, 'cos we don't really have that – it's normally about Peter's drug use and whatever naughtiness various members are getting up to. So it was a welcome change from the press we were getting."

Adrian Hunter —
"I remember getting a finished, mixed, eQ'd, mastered CDr of the album, and driving around in the car with Andy thinking: we've cracked it – this is the album

Babyshambles needed. While nothing is flawless, nor perfect, I really think that we had a fucking great album on our hands. Now what to do with it next… ?"

Drew, while generally happy with the record's sound, thinks that a few too many tracks were shorn of their tougher edge: "There were a couple of things I wasn't happy with: "Unstookie Titled", before Stephen put the extra bits in it. It sounded more like Sonic Youth, "Unstookie Titled" – kind of a gougey punk song, still with melody and beauty in its own way, with the guitars bathed in sort of ghostly piano music. That was really hard and driving, and he smoothed all the hard edges. And there were a few instances on the album like that where it was just too glossy and shiny for my liking."

The Fly awarded the record four out of five stars and called it "an incredibly personal album complete with fascinating confessional lyrics and musical creations bursting at the seams with energy and ideas, all imbued with that bewitching Doherty charm. A long awaited return to form then, and just in the nick of time."

The *NME*, which scored it eight out of ten, said that the album was "very much a team effort – both with the freakishly reliable Drew McConnell, Mik Whitnall and Adam Ficek line-up of Babyshambles, and producer Stephen Street… If you had to give Street just one standing ovation for this record, it would be for turning Pete into one of the most recognisable and idiosyncratic singers around."

A five-star hit with *Uncut*, the magazine said that: "Babyshambles on *Shotters Nation* sound quite frighteningly functional. [Stephen] Street gives them a big, surging sound – supernaturally bright guitars, walloping drums, upfront bass, choruses as big as houses."

"Behind all the tabloid headlines there was a great Pete Doherty album waiting to get out. Now it's here", cried the *Observer Music Monthly*, another five-star applauder; while four-star fan *FHM* opined that: "… suddenly, somehow, from out of nowhere, just when you thought his [Peter's] musical career – and perhaps the man himself – was going to shrivel up and die, he's delivered a contender for album of the year."

The *Evening Standard* declared that: "Genuine music fans can marvel at the fact that Doherty's drug-addled promise has not completely evaporated after all", and *Clash* magazine said: "Babyshambles are now starting to sound more like a band with a purpose."

Among the less enthusiastic were *Q* and *Mojo*. *Q*, despite warming to "UnBiloTitled" – "a moment of true magic, pivoting on a gorgeous chiming guitar figure that could liquefy your heart" – thought that "elsewhere there is something missing from the revamped Babyshambles."

Mojo, while pointing to "flickers of the long-promised genius", thought that "this new effort continues Pete Doherty's could-do-better, must-try harder saga."

And though it praised the "frequent examples of a freshly discovered clout based on the interplay of [Mik] Whitnall and drummer Adam Ficek" and "the dolorous delight" of "UnBiloTitled", ultimately it believed it left "a creeping sense of missed chances, made more painful by the fact that Babyshambles have so obviously raised their game."

The Guardian's Alexis Petridis, another who failed to be fully won over by the record, bemoaned its "half-formed ideas: "French Dog Blues" is a great Motown-ish bassline in search of a decent song", though he was impressed by the strides made by the four-piece, who he deemed "almost unrecognisable" from *Down In Albion's* "murky chaos, with its reek of not-caring… replaced by a sharp, very English-sounding garage rock."

Shotters Nation has been the band's most successful release to date, though some agreed that Peter's negative media coverage helped restrict sales.

Stephen Street — "I think a lot of people just refused to listen to it, dismissed it straight away, because of his tabloid image. I think people who listened to the album noticed how coherent it is – a good pop/rock/indie/whatever you call it, record. It's a good record and, hopefully, should stand the test of time."

Cenzo Townshend — "A lot of bands have suffered from that, but sometimes it may get over-hyped and people might get bored of them, 'cos every time they open a paper, or every time they open something, there's a story of them, something about Peter. There's been a bit of overkill about it. I think there's an enormous amount of pressure on him, which must get in the way of his creativity."

Unable to resist playing, in early October Peter staged an impromptu gig at the Sun Inn, Wiltshire, the quaint, sleepy town he decamped to as part of bail conditions preventing him from returning to London. The following week, he, Drew, Adam and Mik flew to France to help promote *Shotters Nation*, participating in radio and television sessions, and interviews.

The band has a really strong fanbase in the country, and played a number of primetime television shows, including *Taratata*, on which bands were invited to cover a track of their choice, along with a song of their own. But on the journey there, disagreement as to which tune to cover meant that they left themselves with no chance to rehearse it.

Opposite: Drew and Peter backstage at Northumberland Uni during the Pipedown Tour.

Adam —

"All the bands had been working on their cover… [but] as usual we just turn up and bust through it. We end up doing "She Loves You", but cut out a verse and the last chorus. I don't know how we got away with it… Then we got booted out for smoking. Mik sparks up and we get booted out."

Towards the end of their French sojourn, Peter's penchant for cocktails had amassed such an enormous slate that EMI adjusted the capping of its artists' drinks allocation, those late-night piss-ups helping to promote the feel-good factor in the camp at the time.

Mik —

"We had a really good time, it was such fun. That's what it's like in this band – everything's a good laugh, and that's the way it should be; I mean, if you can turn a negative thing into a positive thing. You say to most bands: 'You're going to do a tour, do interviews', it's, like: 'Oh, God no, forget it', but with us it was, like: 'We want to do it again.' I suppose it's about how you spend your time, and trying to have a good time as much as we can."

Any alcohol in the band's rooms was confiscated as a consequence of the drinking frenzy, including Drew's – in spite of his having paid for his stash out of his own pocket.

Drew —

"The first night we were there, Peter bought about nine hundred quid's worth of cosmopolitans. At one point, the table was full of undrunk cosmopolitans, and he was just sat there with a tear in his eye, saying: 'It's the most beautiful thing I've ever seen.' Meanwhile, I'd bought some alcohol myself. I'd bought myself a couple of bottles of wine and a bottle of gin…

"I've lots of friends in Paris, and I had some friends over to stay in my hotel room – we were having a bit of a knees-up. And I'd put the alcohol I bought in the fridge in the hotel room, and the next day I get back from the day's promotional activities and they'd nicked all my alcohol.

"And I went downstairs to where the bear-wrestling was about to kick off, and was, like: 'Some cunt's nicked all my booze – the hotel's out of order.' And Julien from EMI was, like: 'I told them to do that, 'cos we didn't want to have to pay for your booze anymore.' I was, like: 'I bought that and you nicked it, you fuckers!'"

Adrian Hunter —

"This outburst had taken us somewhat by surprise. After the previous evening's cosmopolitan episode, it was, in fact, wise of EMI to curb the bar bill. Of course it was – it was ludicrous… though great fun.

"What had actually happened was that Julien was completely unaware that Drew had purchased any booze of his own – how would he know? – but he'd kindly gone out and bought drinks for the boys, which, as yet, hadn't arrived at the rooms. Drew was not to know this, as he didn't hang out with us downstairs much, and thus kind of lost his rag when he discovered he was boozeless, as it were.

"We were fine for the moment, as we were enjoying the now more limited free drinks at the bar, so we weren't bothered yet. I remember Mik saying, as Drew stormed off from his tirade: 'Fookin' 'ell, mate, you had a nose-full or what?' – which broke the tension nicely."

The aforementioned "bear-wrestling" occurred when, after a performance on Canal +, Peter and Mik rumbled in a high-brow hotel they were staying at, in which Peter left more evidence of his having been there, pissing in a lift. "He's a gentleman", sighs Drew. "What can I say?"

A harmless wrestle escalated into a mammoth brawl that uprooted fixtures and fittings, Adam helping to calm these "breathing-heavily, post-traumatic fighting animals" down towards the end of their tussle by playing jazz chords on a piano; at least that was his intention – as far as Mik was concerned it was: "more like country and western on a honky tonk piano. Um, it was weird. It was ridiculous. I think there's some footage on the web."

Mik —   "When he gets drunk, he always thinks he can beat me up. He just attacks me – he's like a pup. All of a sudden he'll come gambolling out of dark corners and pin you to the floor. It went on for two hours, man. We were at one of the poshest hotels in Paris and the whole place had been smashed, with fucking tables going over and all sorts.

"The management were brilliant. The next morning I apologised, but they were, like: 'It's no problem.' He ripped the shirt off my back with his teeth that night."

Adrian Hunter —   "Peter borrowed my laptop in the lobby that night, and went off to another area to mess about on it. When I say 'mess about'… Peter can mess about with laptops like no-one else. So I went off to rescue it. Not sure quite what happened, but we ended up wrestling. Peter's technique involves a lot of high-pitched screaming and depends a lot on his height. This, however, was no match for my up-close nipping method – 'the sair nip'.

"That's kind of where it all began, and then he foolishly tried to take on Mik – more fool Peter. Mik's specialist move is 'the sweep', and it proved more than a match for 'the tall squeal'. During the bout between Peter and Mik, the head of Alias Promotions arrived to find one of his priority bands for the year murdering each other in the lobby of a very posh hotel, surrounded by pieces of furniture… He loved it!"

Following a gig at the Glasgow Barfly on 21st October, the band left for Munich, and the MTV EMA Awards, staged on 2nd November. Babyshambles played "Delivery" at the event, but, had it not been for Drew, the track would have sounded considerably less explosive.

Drew — "We'd done two soundchecks and a dress rehearsal, and everything was working fine. And it got to the point just before we played, and I just move by instinct before we play – always, I just take the mute pedal off and just make a little noise, just to check the bass is working. And I did that, and it wasn't working. The bass wasn't working. The amp was on, all the leads were connected – it wasn't making a peep.

"I was, like: 'Nooooo!' I had tunnel vision! Seven million people watching on television, we're about to play the biggest televised gig in the middle of the stadium at the MTV Awards, and my bass wasn't working. I just had cold sweat – fuck! And if it fucked up, it was going to be my fault – I was going to be the guy who fucked it up.

"And it was counting down – like, ten seconds before Snoop Dogg introduced us – I just quickly took my bass off, ran down to where all my pedals were, tightened all the leads and one of the pedals. The connection was loose, so I quickly tightened it and ran over to the amp, and checked. And one of the leads seemed loose, so I fixed that and ran back and unmuted it again. And it was working, and then: 'Do do do do do do do doooo' – the song started! Fucking hell, man – imagine if I hadn't checked?! We'd have just gone and played with no bass! Fucking hell, that would have been so embarrassing!"

The Sun's publishing of photos revealing that Peter, who had escaped jail with a suspended sentence on 26th October, for possession of four types of drugs, had fallen off the wagon, briefly threatened the forthcoming arena tour, which had, in some quarters, inspired criticism that, in playing to larger audiences, the band had sold out.

Even among the band opinion was divided, with Drew expressing a preference for smaller shows. Generally, though, it was deemed an opportunity not to be missed – a once-in-a-lifetime chance, maybe – and not for the financial rewards alone.

Certainly, Mik considers the arena tour the realisation of a dream, and a barometer of how far the band have come since their much-maligned beginnings: "We're not the kind of band you'd expect to see on an arena tour. But, as Drew put it, we're seen as the band that could have achieved more than we actually had. But it's two fingers to everyone who thinks we're crap and not capable of doing high-profile stuff.

"We've done an arena tour, and even though the press/some people said it was a failure, it was far from that – it was brilliant. Most venues were three-quarters full, some of them were sold out; no-one does an arena tour, anyway… And for our band – basically a band with a punk ethic – to go round and do an arena tour is a big achievement. No matter what anyone says, we'll always have that. I'm a musician and have been since I was a kid. And if I'd known back then that one day I'd be playing Wembley Arena, I'd never have imagined it."

Peter—

"Oh my word. First of all, to have completed it, in my mind, was an unbelievable success. Something I'm really proud of. Never thought we'd do it. Never thought we'd pull it off, even though we had the capability."

Drew —

"I fully admit it, I didn't want to do it. I didn't want to do it because I just thought it was punching above our weight – not just in terms of selling tickets and so on but, also, prior to the arena tour, we'd never had so much as a backdrop, we'd never had a lighting engineer…

"As a punter, I've seen bands that I like in arenas, and seen bands that I like in smaller venues. And it's not that I'm not ambitious – I am ambitious – but some of the big bands on tour, instead of playing Wembley arena, they'll play four nights in Brixton. Wembley's fourteen thousand, Brixton's five thousand. So if you do three nights at Brixton, that's already more people than Wembley Arena…and it's also much more of an intimate environment, you know?

"Even if you're at the back at Brixton, you're still quite close to the stage, and in Brixton Academy you can stage-dive, you can crowd-surf. If you want to pick your friend up and put her on your shoulders, no-one's going to give you a hard time. It's easier to get to the bar.

"Wembley Arena's such a clinical environment. On the ticket you get told exactly which wing of the building you have to go to, and you're only allowed to go that area, and on the balustrades there's all these people in yellow jackets and flashlights looking for people… I remember watching Tool there, and there's this couple stood beside me, and the guy had his girlfriend on his shoulders, and I didn't think anything of it. And all of a sudden there's all these flashlights in my face, 'cos I was stood beside them, and all these guys in yellow jackets came down and pulled her off his shoulders… Fuck me, man – that's no way to enjoy a gig.

"A few years ago I saw Tool play three nights at Brixton, and it was amazing – so amazing! When I saw them at Wembley, I was quite underwhelmed, you know? I think the size of the venue can dilute the impact of the music – especially for the people who are further away.

"I think I'd prefer to play three nights at Brixton than one night at Wembley. That's just a personal thing. But, you know, Andy and Adam and everyone said: 'Think about it like a benchmark, a goal.' Adam was, like: 'We'll be able to say we headlined Wembley Arena.' 'Ah, okay, fair enough – actually, that's kind of cool.'…

"And then I kind of warmed to the idea, because I started getting more creatively involved, seeing it more of a challenge, getting more excited about the projections, and figured out where we were going to have screens and the whole set – the whole *Oh What A Lovely War!* tour theme, with the drum lines and cigarette packets and that kinda stuff – and got more excited about it… It's fun to do it once. Never say never again, though."

Andy Boyd — "I don't see any good reason why Babyshambles can't play to twelve thousand people on their own… That to me just makes perfect sense, to do that. I think people have got a thing about the word: arena. In reality, they're not that huge, those gigs…

"[Take] Glastonbury – how many people watch you at a festival? That's all right – oh, because it's a festival. It's not all right if you have, like, a tenth of that people at your own gig."

Adrian Hunter — "If they were fans they'd follow the band, and they know where the band plays; they know the band can be found in a local boozer any given night of the week…

"The fact that they're playing larger venues is irrelevant, because they'll play more smaller venues. They could come out of the last gig of the arena tour at the SECC and then end up playing in the Dog and Duck round the corner the following night, so, pardon my fucking language, but selling out? Nah."

Plans were put in place to bring Patrick back into the fold for the tour, to add a bigger sound and recognise his valuable contribution to the Babyshambles cause. But during two days of pre-production work, hopes of a cohesive, carefree tour evaporated.

Based in a huge bunker in Reading, the projections and lights that had been promised failed to materialise and, with Peter absent for most of their rehearsal time, the band began the tour, at the Manchester Evening News Arena, considerably short of practice. To exacerbate matters, Patrick walked out before the show, in part because of a disagreement over the conditions under which he agreed to rejoin.

Adrian Hunter — "I remember that day being one of various disappointments. I arranged transport for me, Drew, Adam, Patrick and a friend of ours, Sol, who was going to audition to add some keyboard parts. Arrangements were made, and the four of us, minus Patrick, rendezvoused at The Lord Stanley, bang on time. Then, throughout the day, it was constant rearranging with Pat about when and where to pick him up, and the hours ticked on, as did the rental of this massive pre-production sound stage in Bray.

"Pat eventually arrived – without even a guitar, I believe – just in time to catch rush hour, which then added even more time onto this journey. I think we four met about midday, and it was pitch dark before we got Pat and got there. When we got there, Peter was only in the mood to play a few more tracks – so there's the rehearsal fucked.

"Drew had a face like a skelped arse, because the bunting hadn't arrived. Adam was complaining that the stage set looked like flat pack – ahem, it is: it gets packed flat in a truck every night – and the lighting/projection team hadn't gotten their shit together, so there was no rehearsal of the back projections. The guy's telling me all sorts of technical gobbledegook about rendering and some such shite, and all I'm thinking is: you've made me look a right cunt! The stress of that day even made me and Andy argue – which NEVER happens – so that'll give you an indication of what a waste of a day it was. I'm trying to keep my chin up in the face of a never-ending series of complaints, disappointments and fuck-ups. Horrible day, fucking horrible."

Patrick — "I was clean, but there were still drugs around, and I was feeling tempted myself… But I was told there wasn't going to be drugs around… I got really angry, walked out… Maybe it was a bad move on my part."

Drew — "He's a recovering addict, and I was worried that being in an environment where there were people taking drugs was going to be bad for him, so, to be honest, how many hours we rehearsed was the least of my worries at that particular moment…

"I think he was freaking out about lots of things, and I think being back in that environment was bringing it all back for him for him – reminding him of what it was like, and I think he was freaking out that he was going to end up using again. And I think he was just snatching at any reason to get upset, so he could leave… It was probably for the best."

On the morning of the show, Patrick rose earlier than the rest of the tour bus. Hungry and broke, he found the nearest supermarket and managed to get some sandwiches. It had been assumed by the band that Patrick realised they would all eat together at the venue, so when he rejoined them, highly charged, at the MEN Arena, where the band were eating breakfast, they were surprised to see him in such a state.

Patrick complained that he should have been given access to money, for food, and resolved to go home. Attempts to persuade him otherwise proved unsuccessful, and so he was given enough to cover his return fare to London.

Adam — "I don't know whether it was the tension or stress, but Pat was really fired up. He came into the catering area and started getting very emotional. We all calmed him down, but he still wanted to leave, after us trying to persuade him to stay. We felt it best for him to get a train home. It was a dark way to start a large tour."

Adrian Hunter — "At the end of the disastrous day in Bray, Peter decided he wanted to go back to Marlborough. Sally was cosily wrapped up in a blanket, reading a novel, and made it clear in not so many words that she wasn't going anywhere. I was damned if I was going to let Peter go off on his own into the night the day before the biggest date of his career so far, though. He then refused to let me go with him, and had a bit of a tantrum.

"Sally still wouldn't be stirred, so me and Peter had to have a bit of an argument, then a bit of a wrestle. I won, so I was allowed to go with him. I plotted up in a B&B and picked him up in the morning. He decided he wanted to go to Clouds before Manchester, so off we went, and it was great. Just me, him and his counsellor. We had a good talk, and many things were said. In the car afterwards, Peter told me that he was really glad I'd come, which was really nice – one of those moments when you actually think you're doing something right for someone.

"Our trip from Manchester to Marlborough was relatively uneventful, other than a stop in Stroud, Gloucestershire. I was despatched to get some essential supplies, while Peter and Justin, our driver, parked up. I got back and, of course, Mowgli's seen a charity shop and ambled off. I got in there to find him serenading the folk in there on a battered old Spanish guitar.

"By this time a crowd was gathering – and not a nice one. I'm sure Stroud's a lovely place if your mum's your auntie, but let's just say the UK's most notorious 'junkie' wasn't going down with the none-too-cosmopolitan gene pool of Stroud. I collared Peter and bundled him into the car, just as someone shouted in the gathering mob: 'It's him! Let's spit on them!' I baled into the car and shouted: 'Drive!' to Justin, just before the collected phlegm of Stroud rained down on us…

"We got to Manchester to find Pat had bolted, using me and Andy as a reason for his having to leave. I understand just how hard it must have been for him to be back in an environment with so many triggers. After the previous day, and eight hours in a car, though, as you may imagine, I was quite peeved.

"Thankfully, everyone knew it was far from our fault, and pretty much understood why he went. Pat, to his credit, phoned me and apologised for what he said. He didn't need to apologise for leaving, as it was always made clear that if it became too much, he MUST go, simply for the good of his health. I like Pat – he's a great guitarist and a good man."

Losing Patrick was a blow, but the band were determined not to let his absence kill the tour. Yes, they'd miss the fuller sound he would have brought, but they would push forward without him and prove that they could work the larger stages.

The *NME*, in a review of the opening night, thought that Babyshambles had "evolved into a tight urch-pop group with a frontman who's more coherent, focussed and in better shape than he's been for years… as a snapshot of where the band are at this very moment in time, tonight's set is telling: this may not be their most natural environment, but Babyshambles are at their most musically focussed for years."

The Guardian's Alexis Petridis, who thought the boys' Brighton Centre gig, on the 25th of November, worthy of a four-out-of-five star rating, wrote that "Babyshambles are far from the lackadaisical live catastrophe they were in the past. Even in such cavernous surroundings, their scratchy, trebly sound seems urgent, rather than malnourished."

Opposite: Drew at the flat with friends.

The *Bournemouth Daily Echo*'s Jeremy Miles decided that, at the band's Bournemouth International Centre show on the 26th: "Babyshambles have been transformed from a ramshackle car wreck of an (sic) cartoon into a meaty, beaty, big and bouncy celebration of the absolute joie de vivre."

The standard frivolity that accompanies life on the road was in evidence again courtesy of Mik, who, on the morning of the Bournemouth show, mistook toothpaste for moisturiser, brushing his teeth with it before the penny dropped, Drew recalling: "We caught Mik brushing his teeth with moisturiser. Just a normal day! Nothing out of the ordinary there – there's probably something equally ludicrous I could tell you about Mik every day of his life, whether he's on tour or not.

"I think he just realised what he was doing. He says: 'This toothpaste tastes right funny. Tell you what – they don't make Colgate like they used to', rubbing toothpaste on his face. Mik, man – get it together, man!"

Mik also employed an old trick to lead some of the crew into thinking they'd wet themselves, a sound engineer among his victims.

Mik —
"He was getting really feisty and drunk, and a couple of nights I thought: I want to put a stop to this. He was on our bus, and he becomes quite annoying when he's pissed. I love him dearly but, bloody hell, he goes on when he's drunk, so I thought I'd better stop it.

"When he was pissed one night, and annoying everyone, as he does, he fell asleep face down. So I got a carton of fruit juice – the ones with the screw-tops, a litre of fruit juice carton – and half-opened it, and laid it down between his legs, near his arse. And about an hour later he woke up, and was, like: 'Oooh, nooo!', picking his underpants off because he thought he'd wet himself.

"And no-one let on, and the whole tour he thought he'd pissed himself. But it did the trick because he didn't get pissed again the whole tour. Which was the main objective of the exercise."

Another year was almost finished. And though the one that followed has hitherto delivered a plethora of controversies not totally dissimilar in nature to their predecessors, the music, finally, at last stands some chance of rivalling the more lurid headlines that punctuate the band's existence.

The uncomfortable truth for their critics is that Babyshambles have never been as in-demand as they are right now.

And, one suspects, that as long as the band remain together, the slow, troublesome shift towards positive exposure – at least as far as what really matters is concerned – will continue.

15

The Future

From near-universally-maligned, so-called shambolic beginnings to a widely-acclaimed second album and arena tour, a transformation achieved on the back of a rollercoaster ride of intense highs and lows.

But while the band's music has grown from a wiry, scrappy nucleus into a tight, muscular sound, the air of unpredictability that has underpinned Babyshambles from the start remains. Turning up for a gig still means not quite knowing what you're going to get, what's going to happen. And, though far less so nowadays, if anything'll happen at all.

Morphing from an interchanging cast of musicians into a solid collective, the songwriting has swung from the Peter/Patrick axis to far more of a shared process. As Drew explains: "The whole approach to knocking a song into shape is more of a forward thing now than it was before, which is great. It makes you feel more accomplished when you're involved in that kind of thing."

Undoubtedly the spearhead of the band, the predominantly negative perception of Peter attracts the wrong kind of attention, the music too frequently lost amid the rubble of gossip-mongering.

It is somewhat ironic that treading the path of a libertine has in so many ways compromised his freedom, his gross, tabloid-generated caricature ensuring that Middle England's brow – and countless others, besides – remain firmly furrowed, ignorant to the unwavering invasion into his personal life and the strength required not to crumble under such gigantic pressure. How often is he portrayed as little more than a human pin cushion whose selfish cravings preclude him from acts of human warmth; which, as those who know him best will vouch, is his greatest attribute?

As Sally Anchassi says: "They never write any of the good stuff that he does. You know, there's been times when he's got a letter from a fan who's in hospital, and he's gone to the hospital to see them, and he's done a little gig in the hospital. But none of that ever gets into the press.

"And, you know, nothing good, nothing positive. If they do a really good show, no-one ever writes: 'Oh my God! Pete Doherty does really amazing show!' They're always looking for the bad angle, something really horrible about him; what's he's done that's really horrible that we can write about, so that we can crucify him even more…

"He's a really easy target for them, so they're not gonna stop picking on him. And, you know, he's newsworthy – he does interesting things. I think the drugs thing they're a little bored of – they're trying to find more sensationalism. Because the thing is, after you print someone injecting themselves, you do a story where someone's kind of said: 'Yeah, you know, I take loads of drugs,' how interesting can it be?"

Peter — "My relationship with the media is a false one, because it involves quite an unpleasant group of people – them – and someone that doesn't exist, which is their portrait of me: a caricature of a cartoon; someone that actually doesn't exist…

"Would I swap fame for anonymity? No, because the nature of what I've done, and the way I've done it, I had no choice. If it was going to succeed – if it was going to be considered genuine and true – I had no choice but to reach as many people as possible. And that involved becoming famous. I knew how to do that. And I knew from the start, that was what I wanted. It's quite sick – you have to be missing something, to be damaged, to desire fame."

But with fame creating more problems than it solved, a simpler way of life makes for a far more pleasant alternative to the crude press interference of present. "Honestly, it's very simple… the trials and tribulations, the ups and downs, relationship problems, fucking tax bills – whatever. On a day-to-day level, like today: take a group of friends for a little walk through the woods, which costs nothing. Stop off in a little pub, which costs nothing, 'cos we got a little tab going, as the fella owes me some money, as I kicked his arse at pool a little while ago. We had something to eat and we had a few drinks, and we had a fucking good laugh. And we listened to some good tunes, and we came back, and I had strum on the guitar. That's what I enjoy. A life, basically.

"That's what I desire – and liberty, above all. Above all, liberty, because there's nothing mildly, remotely romantic or pleasant about sitting in a cell or being told what to do and when to do it, by who… No-one can tell me what to do, right?"

And, yet, it would be naïve to think that the press would turn a blind eye to Peter's more wayward behaviour. And as Iain Gore says: "How does the press treat anyone? They can be really good if they like you; they can be a complete bunch of cunts [if they don't]. If you're in that position of any form of fame, if the press are behind you for whatever reason – I dunno how it works – but it seems that if you're a famous person and the press are into you, they'll be into you and they'll say nice things about you and take your picture. But as soon as they can spin it round and cut you down, they'll be straight in there. Everyone loves a controversy, don't they?

"I think, generally, the press will put you in a position where they say nice things about you, then they can flip it round for a controversy and sell some more papers. It's shallow, isn't it? But everyone loves a bit of tabloid.

"I think he gets unfairly treated, and there are unfair things written about him and a lot of lies, but that goes for any celebrity, really – if you put yourself in that position you've got to know that that will happen. And I think to put yourself in the limelight and have that much fame, and that much press attention, it doesn't just happen because it happens – you've got to drive yourself into that position... I think that people who want fame will get it, and I think that's just part of the shit that comes along with it."

And as Amah-Rose Abrams points out, using the *Mirror*'s exposé of Kate Moss as an example, the tabloid, in printing the story, was taking advantage of an offer put to it by whoever offered it up in the first place: "I reckon it's more down to the person who sells the story than the *Mirror*. If someone gives them a story like that, they're gonna print it – that's what the tabloids do... They went to the length of filming it and selling it to somebody for their own gain. That's where the blame lies."

Which brings us onto those who betray him. Open and welcoming by nature, Peter consistently leaves himself open to abuse. And though the majority of those in his inner circle would never sell him out, the occasional turncoat will gladly surrender their dignity for the price of a story.

Mik — "With his mates, he's very loyal, Pete. And it takes him a long time to sort of admit to himself that some of 'em are absolute tossers and not his mates... They're always giving it, like: 'Yeah, well, you know, I've known Pete years, and years mean a lot.' Years mean fuck all, I tell yer; years mean money to most of them fuckers."

Luca C — "Some of the people around the band haven't helped matters in any way over the years, and they're still around... the usual suspects. That's something I never really understood, and something I will steer clear of, 'cos I can't handle it – there's some people that just take the piss.

"Unfortunately, there's some people who just keeping coming back, causing more and more trouble every time, and that's the one thing I really hope finishes at some point... I mean, how can you consider someone a friend when he stitches you up over and over again over the years and he's dishonest to everyone? They've tried to befriend me at different stages, but I've never given them the time of day, because I hate them."

Peter's drug use is regularly cited as the central factor in his downfall. Like many people of an artistic persuasion, the lack of rigidity in his daily routine can, to an extent, stand in the way of motivation, believes Roger Pomphrey: "I think his main motivation is verse and music, but part of the problem of being an artist and a singer/songwriter or a creator is that artists don't live within the same boundaries that the man in the street does."

"You're allowed to live outside of these boundaries, you are allowed to misbehave. You are allowed to intoxicate yourself, so subsequently wild indiscipline will grow in that scenario, because there's no boss telling you: 'If you're not in tomorrow on time you'll lose your job.' You can do what you want to do, and if it takes you three months to write a song, instead of a week, it doesn't really fucking matter because you'll get there in the end."

But while Peter is routinely slammed for his prodigious drug intake, never would he seek to encourage others to follow in his path. To the contrary, he actively discourages such behaviour, only too aware of the pitfalls inherent in adopting such a lifestyle. As Matt Bates says: "I can honestly say, when I've been around him, and certain kids got on the bus and started talking to him, going: 'Oh go on, Pete, let me try some… I don't want you to stop doing drugs, Pete,' he's turned around and said: 'Don't be a fucking prick. You idiots.' Every time I've been in a situation where a kid's said to him: 'I'm dead impressed with it. I want to be like you, Pete, doing drugs,' Pete's told them: 'No. Do you fuck.'

"You do still worry, with him being hero-worshipped, what effect that will have on somebody… [But] I think there's a lot more factors in your life [that] would turn you to be a drug addict, or to make you do drugs, than just because someone you admire does drugs. I think there's a lot more social factors to take into account than just one person. And I think anyone who ever turns around and blames themselves getting into drugs because Pete Doherty did drugs is a very, very weak person in the first place."

Confessing that a lack of lucidity can impede rather than assist the creative process, Peter has nonetheless managed to churn out a steady flow of material, consistently of a high standard. Which beggars the question – how much better would his work be if straight? Scarborough Steve, now clean himself as he aims to fulfil his solo ambitions, offers an answer: "I think Pete's a brilliant performer. I think he needs to do an album not on drugs, and I think that album will be the best album he's ever done."

"If he records an album straight, they'll be songs about all the experiences he's had, on drugs and off, and with the press… and it'll be a wicked album if he does that. I think he should record an album straight. And then get fucked-up afterwards."

Peter's mounting spells in rehab have hitherto failed to garner the desired results on a consistent basis, yet each time he draws closer to his goal. And as Grant Dobbs reminds us, the drive to change lays in Peter's hands alone: "The thing is, the guy's got so much going on in his mind. The guy's a genius. It'd be like tying down a stallion horse that's just fucking running around being mental. He can't be trapped in a room and being told what to do. He's a free spirit."

Next page: Adam backstage after a gig.

As for the compulsion to create, the entire band, regardless of how long they stay together, will continue to entertain. Patrick Walden in late 2007 launched Big Dave, together with Seb Rochford and Ruth Goller. Adam is already busily working on his side project, Roses, Kings, Castles, whose first album was released in September 2008. Drew continues to work together with a variety of musicians, and to passionately promote the cause of Love Music Hate Racism, a cause close to all of the boys' hearts, and one which Babyshambles has been involved with since 2005, when Peter's arrest meant that the band couldn't perform, as planned, in Trafalgar Square.

Peter has supported the cause since his time in The Libertines, but "as Peter's got more fucked over the years", says Drew, "I've kind of taken over the reins a bit, keeping Babyshambles involved by having something with a political consciousness."

April 2008 marked the 30th anniversary of an event put on by Rock Against Racism and the Anti-Nazi League in 1978 in Victoria Park, with 100,000 people turning up to protest against the BNP and Drew curating the event: "The carnival's a big deal for me... that it's in the history books that Babyshambles were involved in the thirty-year anniversary of what happened in Victoria Park in 1978."

Drew also keeps himself busy with his solo project, Helsinki and Mongrel, a collaboration with Jon 'The Reverend' McClure, Joe Moskow, Matt Helders, Andy Nicholson and rapper, Lowkey, that look set to deliver a début album in the autumn of 2008. Drew also plays double bass and piano with Fionn Reagan. Mik, already with a wealth of experience behind him, and who regularly rehearses with friend Amy Winehouse, would find himself in considerable demand should the Shambles journey come to an end, while Peter will continue to inspire those who see beyond the tabloid caricature so readily taken to be the real thing, while infuriating those who breathe life into it.

And while Peter is undoubtedly the focal point of the band, the contributions made by Drew, Adam and Mik – not forgetting Patrick, Gemma and others before them – mustn't be forgotten.

Roger Pomphrey saw at first hand the dissatisfaction expressed by Patrick as he fought for shared recognition: "He is the main motivation and the artistic driving force to the band, but there was definitely a power struggle going on, in so much as that Patrick very, very, very much wanted the Babyshambles to be seen as a complete entity in its own right, as opposed to Pete Doherty's group... Subsequently, to the point where, rightly or wrongly, Pat was often, not distressed, but was often concerned that the media and the fans saw the Babyshambles as exactly that: as a group of four musicians, all equally contributing to the common good, as opposed to it just being Pete's backing group.

"And I think it caused Patrick concern, and I witnessed that a few times in the recording studio and when we were on tour. Patrick had fits of kind of cantankerousness or argumentativeness, sort of demanding his territory, really – that it was recognised that his input was important as Pete Doherty's. In actual fact, you could argue to some degree that maybe it was, because he co-wrote "Fuck Forever" with Pete, didn't he, which is arguably an absolute killer song – it's an anthem. And there aren't many bands that produce anthems. And that is most definitely an anthem, and so his point of view was valid: that he was contributing very much to the sound and the drive of the kind of music that they make."

Drew, too, has felt marginalised at times, keen that his contribution to the Babyshambles cause receive the attention it merits: "I'm not going to care what the media think or don't think, 'cos they're a bunch of vacuous wankers. And the press that I do care about do seem to care about the rest of the band and the songs, as opposed to anything else.

"When all the efforts to keep things on track, and all the love, blood, sweat and tears that Adam, Mik and I have toiled to keep this band on track are disregarded or not appreciated by Peter, or by someone that you care about, that's when your feelings get hurt."

Danny Newman noticed the strain Peter's public profile placed on his bandmates, while acknowledging that the music is fighting for precedence, up against the focus lavished on Peter and whatever antics he's supposed to be indulging in during any given week.

Says Danny: "I think before a lot of people would turn up to see Pete Doherty, and either adore him [or] throw tomatoes at him… But I think now, as the band's gone on, it's all about the music… These are musicians; it's not just about Pete and the tabloids and all the shit. And I think they're doing it right, you know: it's writing music together – good music, he's a great writer – and it's about doing shows and putting on good, good, good shows, 'cos that's where it's all going: records and sales and all that, they're going downhill."

Clearly, when the group dynamic works, it works well, producing great music, camaraderie and togetherness. Drew attributes this to the spectrum of personalities within the band balancing each other out: "I think the people in the band's various personalities are echoed in the way they play: Adam's quite a stoic, pragmatic, logical kind of guy, and I think that comes across in his playing a lot – you know, very solid. Since Mik's been in the band there's been a new element of kind of ska-flecked [sound]… He's really into Jamaican, reggae-based stuff, and that's been really exciting. Peter's playing is very much like his personality: erratic and unpredictable, and charming.

"And it never really gets boring. Every gig's different… the more we play, we're reaching a benchmark of quality… so, every show there's a level we're not dropping below, which feels good, you know?

"Stylistically, before, with Peter and Patrick, Patrick would take quite a standard pop song that Peter had written and make it wild and punky. Now the roles have kind of been reversed a bit. Mik's very solid: he's quite a classic song writer; the chord progressions, and so on and so forth that he comes up with, are great, but they're quite standard – which isn't a bad thing. Peter now seems to be the one who's taking that element and giving it a punkier edge.

"Mik's guitar playing is very understated. He can wail if he wants to… but, when it comes down to it, he prefers to keep it understated and play what's right for the song, which, I think, is what we need."

Having got this far – a miracle in itself, some might say – the only question remaining now is: what next for Babyshambles?

Given the slim likelihood that Peter will settle into a life of domesticity and, with the band's growing popularity seeing them leave an ever-expanding global footprint in their wake, it seems certain that interesting times lay ahead. Quite what, and for how long, remains a mystery.

Danny Clifford — "You never know whether Babyshambles will be over today or [if] they'll go into the next phase and be around for the next thirty years. You just don't know… It's such a story, which is kind of addictive in itself, and that's why journalists are addicted to it.

"I've not witnessed anything like this, with Babyshambles, since my earlier days in the music industry, back when I started, when there were a few bands around that were real, like this. And this is real. It's not pre-fabricated, corporate shite – this is real."

Danny Newman — "I think it's a day-by-day thing. Sally said that to me once: she said it's great to have a plot and a plan for these things but, you know, it's day-by-day – tackle what's in front of you… I think it's a different scenario now. I think there's room for more of a plan and a plot with it, and something to look forward to."

Stephen Street — "I'd like to see them continue for as long as they wish and desire. I think there's still a lot of great music to come out of Babyshambles, I really do, but it's just Pete's got to be in a good place…

"I think they could be great, I really do. I think *Shotters Nation* proves they can make really good records, and I'd love to get involved on another one with them. I think they're very talented, and in Pete they've got a great songsmith, when he's on good form, and I'd love to see them carry on. I'd hate to see it all disintegrate because of other, outside influences."

Cenzo Townshend — "There aren't many bands like them that have such a strong sound, a strong lyricist and poet, but, having said that, musically they're very good, too.

"Hopefully, they'll write some more songs and we'll hear from them soon. I don't think they're going to go away. I hope they don't go away. But, I mean, I can't see them trying to change their sound enormously and trying to jump on the bandwagon, become the next big thing by changing their sound. I think the band have a very definite sound – that's a great thing."

Sally Anchassi — "Everything's so up and down all the time that I don't think it will change. It will be like that unless Peter makes some serious lifestyle choices.

"I don't know if they'll become the biggest band in the world... but there's no reason why they shouldn't, apart from they're too erratic. Because the talent is there and the ability is there. But I don't know if they really want to anymore, because they're kind of at that point now where they're trying to get through the next day – see what happens next week, or see what happens the week after – whereas normally bands are, like: 'Right, okay, we'll try and do this, we'll try and break America, or we'll try and do this...'

"They can't tour America, they can't tour Japan, and they can't even predict with any certainty if they're still gonna be together in a month's time, and that makes it difficult for them to achieve all that they should. But I really hope they will, because I don't think there's any people who deserve it more."

Carl Barât — "One day, I'd be happy to [play with The Libertines again]. If Pete's happy and sound of mind, and he's not hurting himself or anyone else... [but] I wouldn't want to be making out that it didn't break down for no-reason at all."

Drew — "Obviously, I actually really hope that we just continue making great music, making great albums and playing great shows. You know the bands from the sixties and seventies that survived through the eighties, and started sucking really badly in the nineties – when d'you think that's gonna happen again?

"I have no fear of the band splitting-up; if the band split-up tomorrow, I wouldn't care. I mean, I do care, but I'm not afraid of it, though. I joined this band thinking: this might last a few days, might last a month, might last a year... I've seen drummers come and go, and if it was all to wind-up tomorrow I could carry on making music. I'd be gutted, 'cos I love Babyshambles and I love being in this band, but... there's no point worrying about what's going to happen.

"And I like Carl a lot, I like The Libertines, and if they were to get back together, then good for them – I'd push Peter out the door if there's a chance they'd reunite. And if they did reunite, that doesn't mean that Babyshambles have to stop playing. I think if everyone just relaxed and did stuff with other music, and stop acting like jealous girlfriends, there'd be more good music and less paranoia.

"And, at the end of the day, that's all that's going to be left when we're dead and gone, is records. And I think we should try – we owe it to ourselves and everyone else – to make as many of them as possible."

Peter —   "I think it probably winds Adam – in fact I know it winds Adam and Drew up – when you get the old 'Pete! Pete! Pete!' chant, and that's one of the only things that really, I think, drags Babyshambles down. Because if I was anonymous, if there'd been no success with The Libertines [and] we'd jacked it in all those years ago, and I'd just come through with Babyshambles… I think we'd probably be the biggest band in the country by now, purely for the music's sake…

"I dunno yet – time will tell – but to be remembered for being in a great band, and being a great songwriter, would be the ultimate… I still get up in the morning feeling the same thing, dreaming the same dream."

Whatever the future holds, one thing is certain: Babyshambles can rightly count themselves among the greatest bands of their generation.

Seen through the prism of the gutter press, Peter Doherty is a shambolic junkie worthy of contempt, though, increasingly, the music that he and his bandmates create garners accolades that have been far too long in the making.

Perhaps the winds of optimism haven't blown regularly enough, but they are gaining momentum. And while it would be foolish to expect Babyshambles to steer clear of controversy, "when the dust all settles, the music will still be there, and there'll be four people that have made it," as Adrian Hunter puts it.

"I want to create a band that people will be sorry to miss, and obliged to adore," Peter wrote in his diaries, prior to the rise of The Libertines. And while Babyshambles have yet to become a band that obliges widespread adoration, the world would be considerably poorer were it shorn of their colourful presence.

In another passage, Peter wrote how he wanted to create "something very English – imagine having melody; range, emotion, something to say and wear that attracts attention and informs even instructs those who buy your records and mouth your words."

Perhaps, in that regard, he has moved a little closer to his ambition, aided by a cluster of friends along the way.